American Capitalism at a Crossroads!

Truth will ultimately prevail
Where there is pains taken
To bring it to light.

George Washington

AMERICAN CAPITALISM AT A CROSSROADS!

Where Do We Go from Here?

A Chronicle of How Three U.S. Presidents Missed Sound Economic Advice to Resolve the Problems of Inflation, Unemployment, Poverty and Deficits in the Balance of Payments

Dr. Anghel N. Rugina

Professor of Economics and Finance
Northeastern University, Boston, Massachusetts

An Exposition-University Book

Exposition Press   Hicksville, New York

FIRST EDITION

Library of Congress Catalog Card Number: 75-46176

ISBN 0-682-48485-7 (hardcover)
ISBN 0-682-48486-5 (paperback)

Printed in the United States of America

In memory of Walter Eucken (1891-1950), Freiburg, i.Br., West Germany, a master of economic and monetary analysis, with whom I had the privilege to work. Eucken, a prominent member of the Freiburger Universität to which once Max Weber belonged, was the one who taught those who engineered the "economic miracle" in West Germany in the 1950's under the political leadership of Konrad Adenauer and Ludwig Erhard.

The heritage of the Freiburger School, as refined in this book to its final conclusion, has application for the United States in the 1970's too!

Contents

Dedication

This book is dedicated to the American youth of today and in particular to my former students at three universities (Portland University, Oregon; Niagara University, New York; and Northeastern University, in Boston, Massachusetts) where I have taught between 1950 and 1975. They were the first to receive the new message that there is also an "Economics of Stable Equilibrium," i.e., the "Economics of Full Employment and Price Stability," which is quite different from the prevailing Keynesian "Economics of Disequilibrium." It is also different from the old Classical Economics taught in American schools prior to World War II, which stressed and praised the free enterprise type of business society without the awareness that this system—in order to be stable—requires a special monetary, banking and financial framework which did not exist at the time.

To all my former students I owe a word of gratitude for their patience in listening to new ideas and for their intelligent questions that helped their teacher to sharpen his tools for the greatest argument of the century: *Does money need to be covered by a certain commodity like gold, silver or other suitable goods, or can we dispense with this requirement?* Very few people realize that on this issue will depend the favorable prospects of a rebirth, or the dismal likelihood of an inevitable decline of American, and in general, Western society, civilization and culture. My students have admirably understood the drama and the dilemma of our time, and I hope the American public, too, will grasp the significance of the issue after reading this book.

Preface

Modern capitalism in the United States and elsewhere is beleaguered by insurmountable problems: inflation, unemployment, social inequities in the distribution of national income, undue concentration of economic and financial power in business or in government, and chronic deficits in the private and public budget and balance of payments. Continuing this confused and confusing state of affairs indefinitely means flirting with the danger of being unexpectedly engulfed by a catastrophe reminiscent of 1929 with no hope of help from other nations. At the same time, we are exposed to the prospects of a radical change in our social and political structure sneaking in through the back door as a *fait accompli.*

Let us take a look at the facts surrounding us every day. Whenever the U.S. government studiously attempts to resolve the problem of inflation by using traditional monetary and fiscal policies, it soon becomes clear that by following this Keynesian road, recommended by the greatest economist of this century, the problem of unemployment is aggravated. This is what the Ford Administration experienced in 1974.

On the other hand, when the government attempts to fight unemployment by applying these same policies, the specter of a more violent inflation emerges, with even larger deficits in the private and public budget and the balance of payments. This is actually what the Ford Administration can expect in 1975-1976. In signing the tax-cut bill passed in 1975 by Congress, the President announced a possible budgetary deficit of $100 billion in 1976, the biggest deficit not only in American history but in any country in modern times. And still there is no firm assurance that such large deficits will resolve the problems of unemployment, rising national debt, poverty and the balance of payments.

Obviously there is a pernicious problem here, and no matter what our government does or will do under the status-quo monetary and financial framework the end result is that millions of innocent Americans will be subjected to suffering the ill effects either of an inflation or of unemployment. Professional economists call this perverse state of affairs the *Phillips-curve effect.* In reality, a better term for this situation that confronts modern capitalism in America and elsewhere would be the "Paradox of Despair."

This book reveals the story of how three consecutive Presidents of the United States have failed to consider or ignored the advice of sound economic policies and long-overdue reforms on how to overcome the "Paradox of Despair." Back in 1965 when President Lyndon B. Johnson asked Congress, and insisted through the Democratic majority, to repeal the 25% gold requirement for *bank deposits* created by the Federal Reserve System, this author and many others knew that we were taking the wrong road and that our mixed free enterprise system would be weakened and exposed to even more difficulties in years to come.

Armed with three papers on the stabilization of the American dollar and finances, the author requested in January of 1965 the opportunity to testify before the U.S. Senate Banking and Currency Committee, and this was granted. On February 9, 1965 I warned the members of the Committee that *"the repeal of the 25% gold requirement, in part or entirely, sooner or later will create more difficulties than we have now. In other words, neither the domestic economy will recover completely nor will the deficit in the balance of payments disappear."* My prediction became reality exactly as I had foretold. I repeated my warning in separate letters to President Johnson in 1965, 1966, 1967 and 1968, when the last section of the 25% gold requirement for bank notes was abolished. The country then went to 100% paper money and monetized bank credit, and the dikes were split open to permit an uncontrollable inflation.

I renewed my warnings to the Nixon Administration, first in a long letter to the President-elect on November 29, 1968, and then in two Memoranda, *"On the Serious Situation of the American Economy and Finances,"* one dated February 25, 1970 and the other March 25, 1972. In a special *"Memorandum on Some New Thinking with Adequate Policies for a Definite Solution to the Crisis of the American Dollar"* (January 19, 1972), this author brought these problems also to the attention of then Secretary of the Treasury, John B. Connally. Finally I wrote an open letter to President Nixon dated December 31, 1973, but to no avail.

Seeing that my analysis and predictions since 1965 have been correct all along, I presented the case to the Ford Administration, first in a letter of August 15, 1974 with *"A Brief Exposition of the Problem of Inflation and a Determinate Solution Through a Program of Consistent Reforms,"* and then in a letter of December 4, 1974 with two long Memoranda, but these did not receive the proper attention either.

Finally the author decided to publish all these papers and letters addressed to our last three Presidents, hoping to stir up public debate and make those in responsible positions aware of the gravity of this fundamental issue upon which the livelihood of more than 200 million Americans depends. We are now privileged to have a President who is willing to listen, but unfortunately, the kind of new sound economic advice needed to resolve current problems does not seem to reach him or key members in Congress.

Although not simple, the issue is nevertheless not insoluble. The President as well as key members in Congress receive ambiguous and often contradictory advice from available experts. We should remember that in the United States an entire generation of economists has been trained only in Keynesian economics promoting a government-managed currency and economy. Consequently, these economists are more or less apprehensive, if not directly antagonistic, to a different, better alternative. The Keynesian school of thought in America is, however, divided into two streams—one liberal and the other conservative.

The *liberal Keynesians* do their thinking within the framework of the "Phillips-curve," with the result that they persistently recommend more government deficit spending and price and wage controls. This, however, further weakens the American system and prepares the terrain for a completely government-controlled economy. Conversely, *conservative Keynesians* are afraid of more deficit spending because they instinctively sense inevitable failure along these lines. Thus they withdraw into a sort of blurred image of the old laissez-faire capitalism. Their advice is to do little or nothing, trusting in the universal law of supply and demand which never produced any miracle in a system of paper money and monetized bank credit. Strangely enough, conservative Keynesians by their inaction also contribute to the same gradual process of erosion of the strength and benefits of American capitalism.

In brief, the solution to the impending real problem of how to purify the existing system of all harmful and inconsistent elements and practices and put it under conditions of stable equilibrium remains elusive through the liberal-conservative argument. At present the most difficult task is how to free ourselves of two false notions inherited from the past. One is the *blind belief* in the law of supply and demand which, without an adequate stable monetary and financial framework, inevitably leads to the same old problems of instability and social inequities so well known under the earlier system of laissez-faire. The other is the *blind acceptance* of prevailing Keynesian Economics which in practice perpetuates the "Paradox of Despair" by inducing conditions of even more instability and more social inequities than existed in the old system. The proof for this is attested to every day by mounting negative and ambiguous news about the American economy and its finances, including the precarious position of the U.S. dollar in internationl markets.

At a historic moment when the American people will soon celebrate 200 years of independence of the most powerful and prosperous free republic in modern times, this book heralds a unique message. It shows *first* that there is a better alternative to the present deplorable state of affairs—specifically it indicates how to overcome successfully existing difficulties. *Secondly,* it presents the opportunity of uniting the entire nation (liberals, conservatives and other groups of the left or right, including the uncommitted) so that finally, through appropriate reforms enforced by the democratic process, we may achieve the American dream of a new, better society and economy based on freedom, social equity in the distribution of income and stability from within, with a minimum need for government intervention.

* * *

For the realization of this book, I owe special thanks to several persons. First to my wife Irene-Aurelia, who patiently typed and retyped this material. Second, to my colleague and good friend, Dr. Edward R. Willett, former Chairman of the Department of Finance and Insurance in the College of Business Administration at Northeastern University in Boston, who for many years followed the development of this book and helped in many ways to see the day of its publication. I am also very grateful to my colleagues at the same institution, Dr. Dean S. Ammer, Dr. Charles J. Collazzo, Dr. Robert J. Hehre, Dr. Paul Gross and Dr. Philip McDonald, who, on short notice, kindly consented to read parts of this work and help to improve its style and content. However, the author assumes full responsibility for whatever mistakes or errors in judgment it may contain.

Finally, a word of special thanks is due to the publisher, Mr. Edward Uhlan, President of Exposition Press, Inc., Hicksville, New York, who sensed the urgency of the new message for the American public expressed in this book and helped to bring it to the market of ideas in record time.

Boston, Massachusetts
November 1975

Anghel N. Rugina

Introduction: Toward a New American Dream!

In many respects, this is a book like no other printed in this century on the subject of money, banking, finance and economics. It raises new questions regarding the explanation of the prevalent state of disequilibrium in a modern economy and its finances. It provides a set of new answers on how to reach and maintain conditions of stable equilibrium consistent with full employment, price stability and the maximization of social equity in the distribution of national income. It shows how a balanced budget and a balance of payments in order can be achieved with minimum government intervention once the monetary and financial framework has been restructured according to standards of inner stability.

The book has a special message for both theoreticians and practitioners, for those who are in government and those who are not. It is addressed also to the large masses of people who pay taxes, underwrite government policies (irrespective of whether they are good or bad), and who very often do not receive, directly or indirectly, the full value of the public services they deserve. The problems are presented in a simple, straightforward manner, without the need for mathematical formulas, so that not only the trained professional but also the layman can understand what the main argument is all about and where the correct solutions can be found.

The content is related to a number of memoranda and papers addressed to three consecutive Presidents of the United States between 1965 and 1975, with strongly-worded warnings that Keynesian monetary and fiscal policies, including wage and price controls, do not and cannot work successfully in a free democratic society. Such controls expose a free country to unnecessary dangers with far-reaching consequences for future generations. Among the great American Presidents, Abraham Lincoln sternly warned that if ever the United States were defeated, this would happen *not* at the hands of external enemies but rather from internal weaknesses, contradictions and moral decay. We are already witnessing visible signs that the day of reckoning for past and present mistakes is not too far distant. Indeed, the future of our cherished freedoms will be in jeopardy if we do not soon come up with new, bold and effective solutions to reverse the trend, that is, to change the course of history in the right direction.

What is the basic problem? American capitalism, like modern capitalism in other democratic countries, is passing through a *crisis of structure* due to inherent instability in the monetary, banking and financial framework. It is the financial sector which is responsible for the present crisis and where the roots of an inevitable disequilibrium are planted. This built-in financial disequilibrium constantly disturbs the economy and, unfortunately, cannot be corrected by direct or indirect government policies, as will be shown later in the text. The institutional framework of our financial system is inherently unstable going back to the Federal Reserve Act of 1913 and even prior thereto.

The prevailing thinking in both *liberal* and *conservative* circles in America today is dominated by the Keynesian heritage of the 1930's, namely, the *presumption* that a modern government with sufficient powers and financial means can manage a paper-money system, including monetized bank credit and the economy, in such a way as to reach and maintain full employment, price stability and a balance of payments in equilibrium. This is the monetary and economic philosophy which has been applied in the United States since the 1930's by both Democratic and Republican administrations, differing at times in degree but not in nature.

It is fair to mention that recently the advice given by Keynesian economists in government and elsewhere has been questioned. At the 1974 annual meeting of the American Economic Association in San Francisco, the outgoing President, Professor Walter W. Heller, declared publicly: "He who comes to praise economics risks being buried in the barrage of indictments that economists have brought against themselves and their brethren."

Moreover, in recent times we find in newspapers across the country articles pointing out that "the credibility of economists has declined sharply"; that "economic thought which has dominated the profession—and the nation—for decades is in serious question"; and that at Harvard University, the birthplace of Keynesian economics in America, "a shake-up is under way." (See: Economists in Demand Though Credibility Down" by Saul Friedman, Knight Newspapers writer, in the *Boston Sunday Globe* of March 23, 1975).

There is no doubt that a crisis exists in the American School of Economics as far as application is concerned. But a clear diagnosis of its causes and proportions is not yet available. While Professor Paul A. Samuelson, a Nobel-prize winner from Massachusetts Institute of Technology, has diagnosed the situation as a kind of professional-psychological "identity crisis," another colleague of his in the Nobel-prize community,

Professor Friedrich A. Hayek, bluntly declared in London, "The responsibility for current world-wide inflation, I am sorry to say, rests wholly and squarely with the economists, or at least with that great majority of my fellow economists who have embraced the teachings of Lord Keynes." (See: *New York Times*, Op-Ed page, November 15, 1974.)

To understand fully the dilemma of our time, it is of paramount importance to recall and reexamine the basic structure of Keynes' system of thought and reasoning, which can be expressed in five fundamental tenets:

1. The theorem that money does not need to be covered, supposedly because it can be managed.
2. The multiplier effect, which assumes that if the government, during hard times of unemployment, injects into the economy a certain dose of deficit spending, this will then automatically produce a multiple increase in national income and employment.
3. The presumption that a more active type of government with advice from professional economists can manage the supply of paper money and monetized bank credit in such a way that the national economy will provide full employment, an acceptable degree of price stability and a balance of payments balanced.
4. A new economic philosophy recommending that people would be better off if they spent all their income immediately and saved nothing; otherwise, according to Keynes, they are exposed to the danger of mass unemployment due to the "Paradox of Thrift," as exemplified in the famous "bananas story," where happy, free people were condemned to starvation and other social evils once they were induced by a successful advertising campaign to save on a large scale.
5. The use of a special technique of thinking in reverse, or *ex post* analysis, characterized by the fact that the economic process appears somehow lopsided or inverted in the natural sequence of events. For instance, the natural statement "output determines income and expenditures," is reversed in Keynes and becomes "expenditures determine output and income."

Keynes' system of thought fascinated his contemporaries, perhaps because they did not understand the inverted type of analysis and conclusions. In any case, it has produced a revolution in economic thinking, and this is the basis of what is today called *New Economics*. Keynes definitely has dominated not only British but also American economics and politics from 1934 to 1974. It is also true that U.S. monetary, financial and economic institutions and practices have been changed significantly during the same period to fit the new economic doctrine.

What are the results of the application of Keynesian policies in the United States during the last four decades? If we look at the record of the American economy between 1934 and 1974 we can see unquestionably that none of the promised goals were achieved. In fact, a conflict developed among the major goals during the same period. In addition, the national debt increased by 31 times from $16 billion in the early 1930's to $500 billion at the end of 1974, whereas the Gross National Product over the same period increased from $104 billion to $1,428 billion, almost 14 times.

Should the multiplier theorem be valid in practice, then in the long run both the public and the private debt should decline. A sort of economic miracle in the form of a multiplier effect as a result of relatively little additional government deficit-spending should create additional income to more than offset initial debt. Unfortunately, U.S. financial history of recent decades contradicts the existence of such a miraculous and beneficial multiplier effect. Instead we find evidence of continuous inflation, chronic deficits in the budget and a cumulative expansion of private and public debt. Why is this necessarily a bad thing? The answer is simple: if an individual, a community or a nation spends continuously more than the current stream of real income, that individual, community or nation inevitably gets deeper into debt until bankruptcy becomes unavoidable. The 1975 financial crisis in New York City is a good example.

As if this is not bad enough, the picture of American Capitalism under Keynesian policies appears even more grim when we consider the fact that the United States in the 1930's was a creditor nation, and four decades later it has become the biggest debtor country in the world, with a staggering external debt of dollars in foreign hands which in all probability now surpasses $200 billion. This cannot be called a success by any standard!

Based on the historical record, we can therefore conclude that:

1. The Keynesian theorem that money does not need to be covered is not valid in practice, certainly not in a free enterprise system.
2. The much-heralded multiplier effect appears to be a well-guarded myth that did not prove to be effective in practice; otherwise, we should not have been exposed to an ever-rising public and private debt.
3. A democratic government cannot successfully manage the supply of paper money and monetized bank credit in such a way as to have full employment, price stability and a balance of payments in order, because a financial system based on this type of money has inherent instability, not curable by government intervention.
4. The new economic philosophy of Keynes against private savings did not bring about any benefits but more social harm by weakening the

natural capital formation in the economy, thus undermining the economic independence of free people.

5. Finally, although thinking in reverse may be fascinating in theory, in practice it easily leads to grave errors of judgment in the forging and selection of workable economic policies.

To avoid any misunderstanding, I do not dispute that Keynesian policies have their own merit as a possible, though not the best, solution for disengaging a national economy from a depression, but only in the stage where a drastic deflation or the introduction of a multiple currency unit has drained off the inflation of the previous boom. I said "not the best solution" because Keynes believed in good faith that a modern government could successfully manage the monetary and economic affairs of a country. Therefore, he was *not* concerned with another, even more important, problem—that is, how to construct a *stable* monetary, banking and financial framework so that booms or depressions may not recur in the foreseeable future. On the other hand, Keynesian policies and philosophy are useless and even harmful when applied to a country like the United States, which in 1975 is faced with conditions of simultaneous inflation, unemployment and a large deficit in the balance of payments.

To this end, this book is a direct challenge to the prevailing Keynesian approach and method of thinking. Yet, it is not anti-Keynes since it recognizes the merit and genius of Keynes, who also tried, during a historical moment of confrontation with visible contradictions of modern capitalism in the 1930's, to provide a pragmatic solution. His recommendations of government deficit spending, the manipulation of the rate of interest, the regulation of the supply of paper money and of government budget, we now know did not work satisfactorily in practice. The problem of mass unemployment of the 1930's was resolved not through the miracle of the multiplier effect but rather by war mobilization during the early 1940's.

If traditional Keynesian policies do not and cannot work, especially not under present-day conditions, what then is the alternative? This book is skeptical of both socialism and national planning as a possible alternative to modern capitalism in its present welfare-state version. This negative position is not influenced by ideology, but is based on the fact that we do not have the necessary *mathematical formula to calculate and maintain continuously in a dynamic economy under a free democratic society the equilibrium supply of paper money and monetized bank credit consistent with full employment, price stability, maximum of social equity in the distribution of national income and a balance of payments balanced.* Without such a formula and the suitable means to apply it, the application of monetary and fiscal policies, socialization of the means of production or the use of the French Indicative Planning becomes an exercise in futility with incalculable negative effects, confusion and unnecessary suffering by innocent masses of people.

The framework of the present U.S. monetary, banking and financial system lacks a strong *natural parameter* in the form of *Numeraire* (100 per cent covered currency) needed for general stable equilibrium, as scientifically proved by Leon Walras one hundred years ago. The Numeraire's major function is to hold a system of free markets together. Thus the status-quo order has inherent instability which, as mentioned earlier, cannot be corrected by any reasonable government policies. This interpretation is fully confirmed by the United States economic and financial history of the last four decades.

The primary cause for our problems today does not reside principally in the nature of the free enterprise system as such, nor in the behavior of big business or big organized labor (even though the existence of problems in these areas is not denied). The basic reason for our troubles lies in the *unstable framework* of our monetary, banking and financial system, which does not provide the proper (equilibrium) supply of money to satisfy the function of *liquidity* needed for the smooth distribution of goods and services for current consumption and the function of new *investment* and *capital formation* necessary for the improvement of future supply of goods and services.

There is no sense beating around the bush by recommending a massive injection of funds in the economy through a tax cut, a huge deficit in the budget and easy-money policies in order to cut down unemployment, as now recommended by many voices in Congress and by the present administration. The reason is obvious: Under the status-quo financial framework, a large portion of the extra supply of money will go purely for speculative purposes in both the securities and commodities markets. Thus the economy will be deprived of conditions of stable equilibrium with full employment. In addition, we will have to struggle in the future with an even greater degree of inflation (of not only two, but possibly three digits) and even higher deficits in the balance of payments. This road leads to a potential danger of a financial collapse, *first* of the external value of the American dollar in international markets when a large number of countries may refuse to accept it any longer and then a potential collapse in our internal financial markets, starting with payment defaults by large cities, large states, and large corporations. The 1975 financial difficulties of New York City and the failure of the Franklin National Bank in 1974 are ominous examples of what might happen in the future if a drastic but competent cleaning of our financial house is not undertaken.

Beating around the bush, too, are those who strongly advocate that together with a massive injection of funds, wage and price controls—or even central economic planning—must be introduced. In this case one important fact is forgotten. Under the status-quo financial framework, immediately thereafter a hidden inflation will develop, which will bring with it shortages, black markets and other more serious distortions in the economy. That was the result of the British experiment after World War II and of the Nixon Administration's adventure in playing the game with price and wage controls.

We should also be aware of the lesson presented by the vast experience of all socialist countries in Eastern Europe where governments are faced, in the second half of their five-year plans, with the perennial problem of significant gaps between the promises of the national plan and the actual results. If a national plan cannot be successful in a socialist-communist country where the government has unlimited powers, how can we expect it to succeed in a country like the United States, where the government has limited powers and people are accustomed to a good life and freedom?

Other than encouraging the perpetuation of vested interests and wishful thinking, more government intervention does not provide anything new or better. Socialism and national economic planning and controls must therefore be rejected, not on ideological grounds, but for a number of practical and scientific reasons:

1. The American way of life based on freedom is in direct conflict with the concept and application of national economic planning and controls. Indeed, this concept requires social coercion, which in turn demands an arbitrary limitation of freedom, incentives and aspirations, irrespective of whether the means of production are socialized or not.
2. Socialism and national planning as known in this century have been plagued by problems of hidden inflation, unproductive employment, hidden unemployment and social inequities, sometimes on a much greater scale than under capitalism. Of course, it is possible to have a socialist economy under conditions of stable equilibrium but only under three basic conditions: (a) The supply of money must be composed only of Numeraire; (b) domestic trade must be under open markets with flexible prices; and (c) there must be convertible currency and free movement of commodities and capital in international markets. Such a socialist system did not and does not exist now. It could be called "*Liberal Socialism*" or what Dubcek wanted to achieve in Czechoslovakia under the banner of "Socialism with a Human Face," even though at the time no mention was made about the Numeraire requirement. The Yugoslav experiment was going in the same direction but could not ultimately succeed because of the same deficiency: a lack of understanding of the first requirement; namely, that a socialist economy too cannot reach conditions of stable equilibrium

without the natural parameter of Numeraire, or what Marx assumes in Volume I of his *Capital* as gold-money and the simple circulation of commodities [$C_1 \times M_{Nu} \times C_2$].

3. So far socialism and national economic planning as applied in this century have not further provided conditions for a balance of payments in equilibrium, neither within the community of socialist countries nor with the rest of the world.

It is true, nonetheless, that both socialism and national planning appear attractive at first glance, especially when offered on a democratic basis, or whenever modern capitalism displays visible contradictions. But, as a thorough scientific examination unmistakably shows, neither offers a better alternative to the existing mixed and unstable capitalist system.

This book presents a better alternative to both socialism and national planning by offering the best possible improvement of the existing capitalist system, in America and elsewhere. It explicitly shows practical ways and adequate reasoning *why* and *how* to shift from the present mixed, unstable system to a stable framework capable of guaranteeing the realization and the maintenance of full employment, price stability, maximum of social equity in the distribution of national income and a balance of payments in equilibrium within a period of six months, without additional difficulties.

There are a number of issues vitally important for the understanding of the real nature of today's problems and tribulations which have not been revealed to the American people. Below is a list of the most important truths of which the public is not aware:

1. That paper money in a free, democratic country is public enemy No. 1 because it is unmanageable in the sense that it creates instability and social inequities and cannot be controlled and regulated in such a way as to reach equilibrium conditions.
2. That free monetization of private and public debt or credit through our private banking system [with the help of the Federal Reserve System] is public enemy No. 2 because it is the biggest source of inflation, unemployment, social inequity in the distribution of national income and chronic deficits in the balance of payments.
3. That the mixed character of our monetary and financial system introduced through the Federal Reserve Act of 1913 and the suspension of the convertibility of the dollar inside the country in 1933 are the initial causes of our financial instability today. The subsequent changes of the Federal Reserve Act in 1945, 1965 and 1968 have weakened, not strengthened, the system.

4. That the suspension of the convertibility of the dollar in international markets in August 1971 (when a better alternative was offered by this author to the Nixon Administration) unleashed an international financial crisis, resulting in a sudden and continuous depreciation of the American dollar which, in turn, among other things, brought about the oil crisis.
5. That big government with ever-increasing powers to control people's income and activity is not a social necessity in an advanced industrial society but rather an inevitable consequence of a financial system based on paper money and monetized bank credit which produce continuous disequilibrium, that in turn requires permanent government intervention and props.
6. That the existence of an abnormally high level of unemployment is due not to inexorable economic laws in a free enterprise system or to highly sophisticated technology which requires only highly skilled people, but rather to our financial system where the money-market function is mingled with the capital-market function, and an enormous amount of funds is retained for the purpose of speculating in securities and commodity markets instead of being used for productive purposes to create more jobs and more real income in the economy.
7. That an ever larger portion of the national debt is now maturing and our government cannot repay all of this accumulated debt; consequently, a huge demand for funds merely to postpone maturities is leading to conditions of inevitably higher and higher interest rates in the long run. This in turn hampers the realization of full employment and stability in the economy.
8. That minimal payments or the guarantee of minimum income by a negative tax or other devices through the welfare-state agencies do not and cannot resolve the problem of poverty. On the contrary, all these government deficit-spending schemes, while giving aid with one hand, take away with the other through inflation a good portion of this supposed help, thus perpetuating poverty. It is not sufficiently stressed that the problem of poverty can be resolved only through a reasonable social reform and the introduction of stable equilibrium conditions whereby every person capable of working can earn a decent living without being robbed through inflation or demoralized by unemployment.
9. That undue and unnecessary concentration of economic and financial power is directly related to our banking system. Through monetization of relatively cheap credit, our banking system encourages and supports many corporations to use part of their resources and managerial skills to control other businesses instead of concentrating

on productive activities in serving the public at a normal (equilibrium) rate of return. The higher echelon of government apparently does not realize that the best solution of the problem of monopolies and the potential conflict of interest between business and society lies in the adoption of a *Code of Ethics in Business* in the form of a *Law for Social and Economic Justice* requiring that any transaction (regardless of the size of the firm or the amount involved) be concluded at an equilibrium price where only the real costs and a normal rate of profit have been included.

10. That the Federal revenue-sharing program that grants a few billion dollars to the states annually far from resolves the real problem of an equitable distribution of the public income among the three levels of government. The time has come to forge objective standards for devising a proper line between the basic functions of each form of government and to provide each one with an adequate source of public income without creating a political "dependence effect."
11. That in order to achieve financial and economic stability with full employment and price stability for the entire country, it is necessary to have conditions where not only the public sector but also the aggregate budget of the private sector (consumers and business) is balanced. However, this goal can be reached only when the volume of credit used in the economy for private and public purposes is limited to the volume of real income, that is to say, under conditions where credit has real backing and is not monetized.
12. That the public budget cannot be balanced and national debt cannot stop rising as long as we maintain a financial system based on paper money and monetized bank credit.
13. That it is impossible to have a balance of payments in equilibrium unless the dollar is fully covered and freely convertible both at home and in international markets.
14. That the public at large should be informed that there is a better but not debated alternative to the present dreadful state of affairs.

All those who seek the highest positions in government including members of Congress should be questioned thoroughly and asked for an explicit public statement on each of the given points above so that the American people know whom they elect and what to expect from them.

In capsule form, here is what this book proposes.

The *first step* is the introduction of a new, higher value dollar ($25 old for one new dollar) as the only method left to completely drain the existing double inflation of dollars at home and in international markets. Nobody will lose or profit through this operation, since on D-day all prices, incomes, debts (domestic and foreign), savings and checking accounts, taxes, foreign exchange rates and all other claims or obligations (private and public) will be reduced in the same 25:1 proportion. The great advantage of this first step is that once the financial house has been cleaned of the longstanding stagnant inflation, and other provisions of this plan implemented, the U.S. dollar at home and in international markets will stop depreciating and instead will become stable at a much higher value than today.

The *second step* is the revaluation of the gold stock at Fort Knox to a realistic price of between $150.00 and $160.00 per ounce. This revaluation will allow us to pay foreign creditors who desire gold and to restore the free convertibility of the dollar at home and abroad at a new parity. Once the international markets are rid of the plethora of depreciated American dollars, the turbulent oil crisis could also be settled in a reasonable manner, as shown in Chapter I.

The *third step* is the long overdue reforms needed to create a stable framework for our monetary, banking and financial system so that inflation, unemployment, social inequities and chronic deficits in the budget and balance of payments may not recur in the future. A reasonable and limited social reform is recommended to accompany the change of old dollars into new for the purpose of strengthening the social fiber of our society and rendering future social unrest and upheavals unthinkable.

This book fully documents this unique program of reforms to make American capitalism stable and much more equitable than any other system in the modern world while preserving and strengthening traditional American freedoms. The proposals were submitted in different versions to the Johnson, Nixon and Ford Administrations.

We must remember that American capitalism, no matter how imperfect, has virtues as well as evils. Although its virtues are recognized, they are not adequately explained and emphasized in schools and in publications. It may be useful to repeat them. American capitalism has best preserved human freedoms; it is the most productive and efficient system ever created, given favorable conditions; its relatively free markets are abundant and thus provide affluence, even though this abundance is not shared by the people as a whole in a perfectly equitable manner. Being an open type of society, it can be improved at any time if we so choose by selecting the right methods.

All the good features notwithstanding, it may also be useful to repeat the social and economic evils of our system. It does not offer assured financial and economic stability. Thus we have recurrent inflation and unemployment. It does not provide enough social justice in the distribution of national income and wealth. Thus we have poverty and social unrest in the midst of affluence. It is conducive to undue concentration of economic and financial power through the monetization of credit by modern banks. This favors those who are already economically and financially strong, thus furthering social unrest. Because the human desire for maximum profit is not tempered by a code of ethics in business requiring equilibrium prices, the system allows accumulation of wealth based on illegitimate profits, over and above normal, earned profits deserved as the return for the management function. The existence of such illegitimate profit also leads to the abusive use of available human and natural resources. The ultimate purpose of this book is to demonstrate how all these social evils can be terminated within a short period of time without creating other problems.

Few books (if any) published in this century have indicated explicitly that by preserving and further improving conditions of freedom we can eliminate all the accumulated social evils under modern capitalism without losing our freedoms and destroying modern society and civilization. It is a challenge to realize analytically that such a vast cleaning operation in a modern capitalist society is possible by peaceful means when most views on this issue in recent decades either ignore the need for reforms or suggest that such reforms are not possible without political dictatorship.

Unlike other books on economics which use statistics extensively, these will be referred to only when strictly necessary. A flood of statistics may confuse an issue by diverting the reader's attention from the real nature of the problem. At times, statistics have been known to be manipulated to serve a particular purpose. Admittedly, reliable and detailed statistics are needed and most valuable in two instances: (1) to show the magnitude of a given problem, and (2) to measure the effects of certain policies applied over a period of time. Statistics, however, no matter how well organized, can never precisely pinpoint the real causes of a respective problem. Thus, statistics cannot be considered or accepted as the sole basis of policies. In this respect, both the public and the experts too often fail to distinguish between (1) problems of adjustment within the existing system, or status quo, which usually are quantitative in nature, and (2) problems of the quality of the institutional framework of a given system, which have nothing to do with quantities.

Our policy makers have concentrated too long on thinking of these problems in terms of quantitative adjustments, or what they refer to as compensatory policies, whereas the real problems are hidden in the poor quality and inconsistency of our institutional framework, especially in the monetary, banking and financial area. Mathematical economics, including econometrics to which so much attention has been given for the past few decades, cannot help us resolve effectively and efficiently the kind of major problems with which we are struggling and which—as stated—are of the framework and *not* within the system. What policy makers are currently doing when they rely solely on quantitative analysis and models is nothing more than taking the bull by the tail instead of by the horns! It is no surprise that in recent decades none of the fundamental problems in the United States or other democratic countries has been effectively resolved.

This book firmly asserts that our government is not using the *right method of analysis* in forging economic and financial policies relating to both domestic matters and international transactions. Our *real* problems cannot be expressed quantitatively. Again it is necessary to stress by repetition that mathematical models and reasoning, no matter how sophisticated, cannot assist us to find the right solution to our present ailments. *Our major problems derive from the poor quality of the worn-out institutional framework of our financial and economic system ridden with inconsistencies and contradictions, some inherited from the past and others added by unwise changes in recent decades.* The existing institutional framework of modern capitalism in America and elsewhere, through the application of Keynesian policies and reforms, has deteriorated to a point where inherent instability seems to lead to the inevitable conclusion that there is no salvation other than sooner or later accepting a government-planned and -controlled economy.

This work raises the biggest argument of the century. Contrary to the prevailing Keynesian stream of thought, it shows that there is salvation through a much better solution than a government-planned and -controlled economy. We need not abandon the free enterprise system; we need to improve and strengthen it by rationally overhauling the monetary and banking system wherein lies the inherent instability. The specific method is the rigorous application of the newest, but in a way the oldest, *Economics of Stable Equilibrium,* with stability coming from within the system. The economic function of the government in this case is restricted to introducing necessary reforms for a new system of stable equilibrium and seeing that the rules of the game are respected by all concerned. This better alternative is called "*Social Liberalism*"—a system of full employment, price stability, maximum of social equity in the distribution of national income, balanced budgets and a balance of payments balanced, all at the same time.

The road toward Social Liberalism is not an easy one, considering the substantial reforms that have to be completed in a single day. But there is no other, more secure, road to prevent a repetition of the 1929 debacle or the imposition of a government-controlled economy and society. The complete success of such reforms as proposed here in a maximum of six months will serve as an outstanding example to the rest of the world that the cause of human freedoms, social justice and stability, in the short as well as the long run, is not lost nor a matter of the past but rather a great challenge of the present. Further, the American message of this book is that any nation can attain this goal, each in its own way and according to its own history and aspirations.

Others in the profession, journalists, television and radio commentators, all bristling for new ideas, members of the present Administration and Congress, as well as the American public, must seriously take up the challenge presented in this book. The text of the letters to three of our past Presidents which accompanied the memoranda sent to them is included as part of the record to prove that besides official pronouncements, there was available a better alternative which, for some reason or no reason at all, was not considered. The gravity of the situation in 1975 when American capitalism is placed on trial requires such a disclosure. For the rest, only history can and will pass the final judgment.

In his book *Breach of Faith: The Fall of Richard Nixon* (New York: Atheneum Publishers, 1975), Theodore H. White states (pp. 182-183): "It would be entirely unfair to blame Richard Nixon for the disaster which was now about to happen to the American money system in the next year, or the crisis of confidence in all values which was about to take place in the next two years. *If anyone could have given him the right advice, he would have taken it*—for bread and butter, as he knew, moved politics. But his economists were reaching the margin of their own understanding of the world, as were all economists."* (Italics added.)

The truth is that President Nixon *did* receive the "right advice" from this author as far back as 1968. In a letter to the President-Elect dated November 29, 1968, I warned him: "I am taking the liberty of writing to you since, to my knowledge, *none* of your announced economic experts (with due respect to their recognized authority in the field) has a workable and consistent solution to this basic monetary and banking problem, and I would not like to see your Administration begin under constant pressure of a financial crisis, whose intensity in our type of society nobody can measure in advance." The warning was repeated in 1970 in a long "Memorandum on the Serious Situation of the American Economy and Finance," and again in 1972 in a Second Memorandum, and finally in "An Open Letter to the President of the United States" dated December 31, 1973. This material is now included in Chapter II. But Nixon never listened to the "right advice"! That is the historical record.

In concluding, it is worthwhile to remember the optimistic view of George Washington: *"Truth will ultimately prevail where there is pains taken to bring it to light."* Let us hope that the new message of this book will confirm Washington's optimism for the good of this country and its people.

*Theodore H. White, *Breach of Faith: The Fall of Richard Nixon* (New York: Atheneum Publishers, 1975. Copyright © 1975 by Theodore H. White), pp. 182-183.

Part One: Applied Economics
Matters of Policy

A Methodological Glossary

For the professional reader, a few basic methodological relationships are given below as a guide to better understanding of the material presented in this book:

1. The concept of economic, social, political and other human freedoms is considered to be indivisible in theory and practice in a free, democratic country.
2. The rule of the separation of government business and finance from the private sector of the economy and finance is required by the law of general equilibrium.
3. The natural limits of individual (personal) freedoms in economic matters are determined by the other two great human ideals: social equity in the distribution of income and social harmony or peace.
4. Free competition alone, as an expression of economic freedom, cannot create conditions of stable equilibrium. This was a great weakness in the old classical economics. Competition is actually an invisible social force, which in practice may lead to equilibrium or disequilibrium, depending on whether it is acting in an environment governed by a carefully constructed institutional framework consistent with conditions of stable equilibrium or in an environment lacking such conditions.
5. The economic justice of an equitable distribution of income and wealth can no longer be neglected in the second half of the twentieth century. Economic freedom and economic justice have to be treated by the same standards of scientific objectivity and given the same consideration.
6. Concerning social inequities inherited from the past, a one-time reasonable and limited social reform is preferable to the hodgepodge measures offered by the welfare state, which in reality perpetuate poverty.
7. For a better future in terms of social equity and preserving human freedoms, we need a carefully constructed institutional framework where goods and services are produced and sold at equilibrium prices. The equilibrium prices should be composed of the real cost

of production or acquisition (taxes included) and a normal rate of profit equal to the opportunity cost of management. This in turn would make possible an equilibrium distribution of national income with no conflict of interest between producers and consumers, between business and society, between individual and government. The problem is how to achieve this goal in real life, and this is the subject of this book.

8. For an equilibrium distribution of income, proof must be provided that all major sources of income in the economy—rent, wages, interest, profit and taxes—are determined by one and the same principle or set of rules.

   Under the system considered in this book, there are, with specification, not three, as commonly assumed, but rather five indispensable factors of production: Land, Labor, Capital, Management, and Government. The income for all five factors is determined by the same principle of marginal productivity (in regard to returns) and the principle of marginal utility (in regard to values).

9. General stable equilibrium is characterized in principle by a unique set of conditions whereby the major forces in the economy, be it from consumers or from producers, from the private sector or from the public sector, from the domestic economy or from the balance of payments, in the final analysis, all converge toward one and the same position of stability from within.

10. Leon Walras (1834-1910) was the first economist who attempted and succeeded in scientifically establishing the requirements and the conditions of a system of general (stable) equilibrium.

11. Walras formulated his law of general equilibrium based on two requirements:

    a. A system of free markets where monopoly forces are assumed to be reduced to zero at the limit, or what he called pure and perfect competition; and

    b. All prices for consumer and capital goods, factors of production and foreign exchange are to be expressed in "Numeraire," or 100 per cent covered money. Numeraire in reality serves as a *Natural Parameter* for a free and stable economy and society.

    Government was excluded, and management was not considered an independent factor. Other economists, like M. Pantaleoni and E. Lindahl, later attempted to prove that in a really democratic country, government income, i.e., taxes, is determined (under certain conditions) by the same principle of marginal utility and productivity. This book accepts this conclusion, and in addition it raises entrepreneurship or management to the rank of an independent factor whose income is and must be determined in the same way as the other factors.

Walras did not establish a third requirement: (3) that all major institutions in the economy (banking, securities market and the public sector) should be in their nature and functioning consistent with the natural parameter of the "Numeraire." This is vitally important not only for practical application but also for a complete analysis of a system of general stable equilibrium.

12. A clear distinction should be made between (1) stability from within and (2) stability from without.

Stability from within is natural and self-generating in the sense that it is based upon a set of self-regulating mechanisms associated with normal behavior of the people, all converging toward a position of equilibrium. This is synonymous with general stable equilibrium.

Stability from without refers to any sort of artificial equilibrium associated with a more or less arbitrarily determined distribution of national income maintained by social coercion. The most common form of present social coercion today is government-imposed and -controlled economy. Such a system initially was in disequilibrium, but later, instead of being geared toward stable equilibrium, certain social and political forces were successful in introducing government controls and regulations supposedly to counterbalance disequilibrium elements in the economy. This is, however, a precarious sort of stability, which under the best conditions will be a compound of 50:50 stable versus unstable elements and forces. Since under such conditions no change is possible at the limit, this appears as shaky stability that may be called unstable equilibrium.

The national program for reform and stabilization advanced in this book is based on the concept of stability from within, or general stable equilibrium.

13. The conditions which characterize a system of general stable equilibrium, some from Walras and some developed by this author, are:

(1) Effective demand = available supply for finished goods, capital goods, factors of production, public goods and foreign exchange.

(2) Prices of goods and services = the least average total cost per unit of output or ATC = marginal cost = marginal revenue = average revenue.

(3) Prices paid or imputed for the factors of production:

Rent = marginal productivity of land
Wages = marginal productivity of labor

Interest = marginal productivity of capital
Profit = marginal productivity of management or entrepreneurship
Taxes = marginal productivity of public services.

(4) New investments = voluntary savings.
(5) Credit used in the system = real income in the economy.
(6) No monetization of debt or bank credit in the economy.
(7) The basic rule of finance: first income and then spending, applied to both private and public sector.
(8) Money incomes (rent, wages, and so forth) = real incomes.
(9) Capital formation based only on voluntary savings.
(10) Public budget as well as private budgets are balanced from current income.
(11) Internal value of the currency = its external value.
(12) Foreign exchange rates = official parity.

14. A new theorem of the Natural Parameter of the "Numeraire" and an institutional framework structured according to stability from within, are innovations presented in this book. As explained in the text, no system in the physical or in the social universe can reach and maintain a position of stable equilibrium or close to it unless it has a strong natural parameter in the form of a central axis (a constant magnitude) which holds the parts of the system together.

For a national economy the natural parameter is the "Numeraire," without which no position close to stable equilibrium can be reached. Indeed, the Numeraire is a constant magnitude (the monetary unit = a fixed quantity of a selected commodity like gold or silver), and all other magnitudes in the economy are variables.

Figure 1 is a composite picture of a national economy in a system of general equilibrium with a 100 percent Numeraire. The diagram shows a double circular flow of real income and employment which are in continuous contact: one is in the monetary sector (I) and the other is the non-monetary sector (II). This double circular flow secures constant full employment without government intervention.

15. The practical significance of the natural parameter of Numeraire is illustrated by the following:

(1) The 1929 financial collapse occurred because the Federal Reserve Act of 1913 provided a rather weak natural parameter in the form of 40 percent gold-backed official money, which as used in the entire monetary system (monetized credit by private banks included), became even further diluted to the incredible proportion of about 10 per cent Numeraire and 90 per cent anti-Numeraire (disequilibrium money).

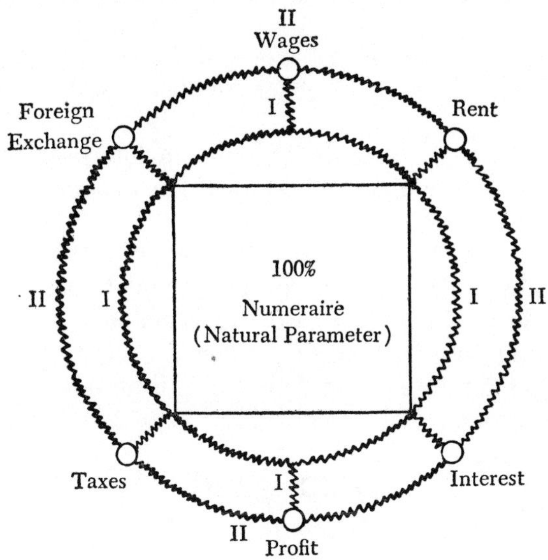

FIGURE 1

I–the circular flow of real income and employment in the monetary sector
II–the circular flow of real income and employment in the nonmonetary sector

(2) The first wave of inflationary pressures after World War II emerged not only because of the huge government expenses during the war financed through paper money, but also because the natural parameter of the Numeraire to support official money in 1945 was reduced to 25 per cent gold backing.
(3) The deluge of inflation after 1965 can also be explained by means of the same parameter. Between 1965 and 1968 the already weakened natural parameter of the Numeraire was reduced to zero—in fact, was legally repealed.
(4) In 1971 the U.S. Government suspended the convertibility of the American dollar in international markets, where it was functioning as a Numeraire, even though somewhat crippled.

Conclusion: Without a strong natural parameter in the form of a Numeraire, there is no chance for price stability, full employment or a balance of payments in equilibrium. This is the lesson we should have learned from the U.S. economic and financial history of recent decades.

16. The significance of general stable equilibrium for a national economy, identified in the book as "Social Liberalism," is that it should provide concurrently:
    (1) Full employment without government intervention;
    (2) Price stability without the traditional monetary and fiscal policies;
    (3) Maximum equity in the distribution of national income without any welfare-state type of accommodations;
    (4) Balanced public and private budgets; and
    (5) An equilibrium balance of payments.
17. Figure 2 is a diagram of a single business firm in a system of general stable equilibrium:

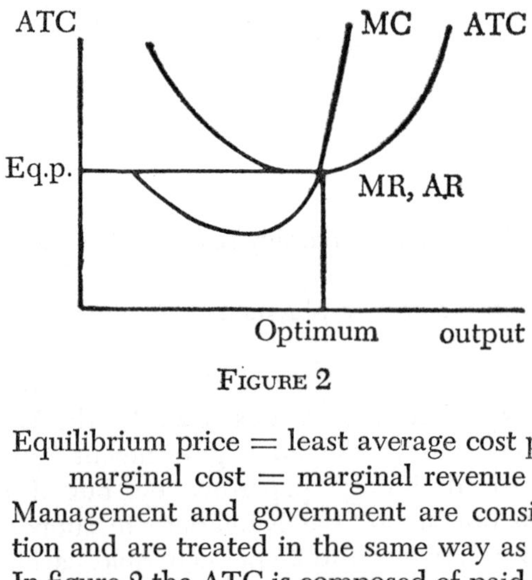

Eq.p.—equilibrium price
ATC—average total cost per unit of output
MC—marginal cost
MR—marginal revenue
AR—average revenue

FIGURE 2

Equilibrium price = least average cost per unit of output (ATC) = marginal cost = marginal revenue = average revenue.

Management and government are considered as factors of production and are treated in the same way as the other traditional factors. In figure 2 the ATC is composed of paid and/or imputed rent, wages, interest, taxes and equilibrium profits calculated per unit of output.

18. A clear distinction should also be made between (1) the law of supply and demand under conditions of stable equilibrium, and (2) the law of supply and demand under conditions of disequilibrium where an anti-Numeraire is used on a large scale.

The law of supply and demand under stable equilibrium conditions, with 100 per cent Numeraire, is the one explained in all text-books on Economics and is represented by figure 3.

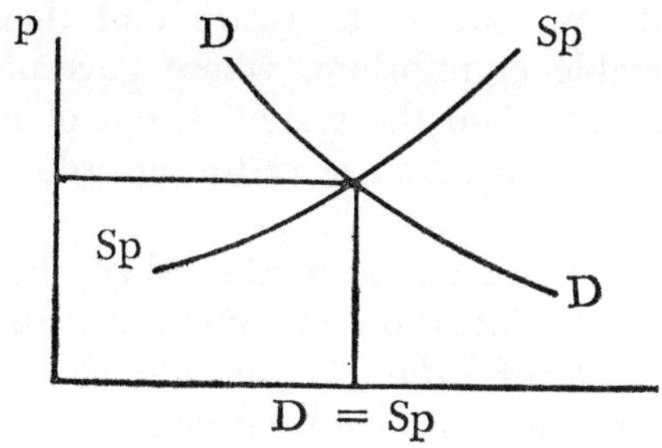

Sp = supply
D = demand
p = price
Eq.p = equilibrium price

FIGURE 3

These are called normal or Marshallian supply and demand curves and are based on normal behavior of the people. Nowhere is it mentioned, however, that such behavior and curves exist only when a 100 per cent Numeraire is assumed.

The law of supply and demand under conditions of disequilibrium. What happens when anti-Numeraire in the form of paper money and monetized bank credit is used on a large scale? Then we have strong inflations or deflations, forcing people to change their behavior. At one time they are induced to buy more at higher prices (inflation), and at another time to buy less at lower prices (deflation). This rather abnormal behavior radically changes the slope of the curves, and we are then dealing with *inverted* or *abnormal* supply-and-demand curves. Such inverted supply-and-demand curves characterize the present conditions of disequilibrium, but this is never clearly explained.

Figure 4 portrays the law of supply and demand under conditions of disequilibrium with a 100 per cent anti-Numeraire:

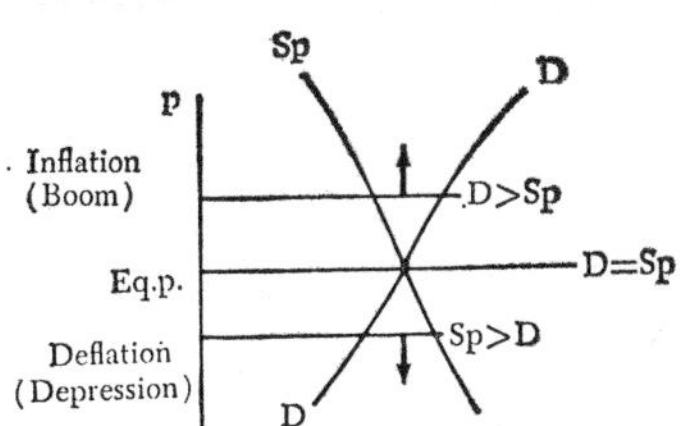

D>Sp↑ = a continuous rise of prices (sign of a major disequilibrium)
Sp>D↓ = a continuous fall of prices (sign of a major disequilibrium)

FIGURE 4

The distinction between the *economics of stable equilibrium* and the *economics of disequilibrium* is fundamental. Yet, because it is not included in textbooks, students acquire only half-truths based on a model of instability where government intervention appears or becomes a necessity. Students are not made aware that there is another alternative, that of stable equilibrium, where government intervention is not needed except when the system is out of order and then only with the specific qualification of restoring order, and not to perpetuate controls.

19. After conditions of stable equilibrium have been established, thereby reducing risk and uncertainty in business to a minimum, it is understandable why a permanent *Code of Ethics in Business* should be introduced for the purpose of social equity and harmony in society. This Code should require that all business transactions, without exception, should be concluded at equilibrium prices as previously defined.

    Such a reform would strengthen the free enterprise system in America and elsewhere by making that system consistent, not only with the ideal of freedom but also of social justice and peace. After all, business and the economy exist to serve man and society, and not vice versa.

20. Economic ethics, freed from individual, strictly personal value judgments and based on adequate economic theory where the requirement of social equity has been included, has the major task of determining reliable targets and adequate goals for economic policy based on conditions of stable equilibrium. In turn, economic policies, defined in this way would reach a new dimension of scientific stature in developing practical measures and institutions adequate and efficient enough to realize equilibrium targets and goals without creating other problems. In this way economic theory, economic ethics and economic policy would finally come under the same roof.

    The concept of economic science is thus enlarged and appears as a composite body with five different, yet interrelated, branches:

    (1) Economic History
    (2) Economic Theory
    (3) Economic Ethics
    (4) Economic Policy
    (5) History of Economic Thought

21. An attentive reader can envision by this time that the method of analysis used in this book is a dual one, namely, that of equilibrium versus disequilibrium types, forces and behavior. Consequently we are faced in theory and practice with two different categories of concepts and realities:

The Equilibrium type of:	*The Disequilibrium type of:*
–Money, banking and securities market;	–Money, banking and securities market;
–Rent, wages, interest, profit, taxes and foreign exchange.	–Rent, wages, interest, profit, taxes and foreign exchange.

22. A last but not least important (for some perhaps the most important!) clarification in understanding the message of this book is the distinction between:
    (1) *Natural or objective philosophy of thought* based on the application of Classical Logic, which was concerned with both the form of expression and the content of a statement and
    (2) *Nominal or subjective philosophy of thought* based on the application of Contemporary or Modern Logic as initiated by Bertrand Russell and Ludwig Wittgenstein, which is concerned only with the form of expression of a statement, considering its content secondary.

This book was conceived and is presented in terms of the natural or objective philosophy of thinking, which seems to be more adequate for the study in question.

Chapter I

The Ford Administration (1974-)

"In vain I pleaded with the members of the Senate Banking and Currency Committee before which I testified on February 9, 1965: 'I have sufficient reasons to expect that the repeal of the 25 per cent gold requirement, in part or entirely, sooner or later will create more difficulties than we have now.' (Ref. Gold Reserve Requirements. Hearings 89th Congress, First Session, February 1965, p. 198)

"What happened thereafter was exactly as I had foreseen, which in itself was not a matter of prophecy but rather a clear, scientific sequence of events."

From a letter to President Ford of August 15, 1974

"Mr. President, we cannot afford to wait for miracles in an environment where business, government and the people in general do not possess a *reliable monetary standard* to make appropriate decisions which in the aggregate determine the position of the economy. Right now we are at a crucial moment in our financial history, and we already have paid dearly for past honest errors and false actions. The initiative is still in your hands before Congress convenes in January 1975, and there is little evidence that your package presented in October will find a favorable vote."

From a second letter to President Ford of December 4, 1974

1. LETTER TO THE PRESIDENT

August 15, 1974

The Honorable Gerald Rudolph Ford
President of the United States
Washington, D.C.

Dear Mr. President:

First I would like to join the many millions of Americans throughout the country who wholeheartedly want to congratulate you and your family on this great occasion in your life of becoming the President of this free Republic and to wish you and your Administration full success in every respect.

In your address to the joint Congress, among other issues you rightly focused attention on "Inflation . . . our domestic public enemy No. 1." It is true that a long and chronic inflation, associated with other social, economic and even political consequences, can erode day by day the foundation of this country and weaken its moral fiber.

As Chairman of the Board of Economic Advisors to the Governor of Massachusetts between 1965-1970, I had the privilege of visiting you in Washington in 1965 and 1967 and asking for your support in a lonely battle with the Johnson Administration with reference to the very same problem of inflation which now torments the entire nation.

In vain I pleaded with the members of the Senate Banking and Currency Committee before which I testified on February 9, 1965: "I have sufficient reasons to expect that the repeal of the 25 per cent gold requirement, in part or entirely, sooner or later will create more difficulties than we have now." (Ref. Gold Reserve Requirements. Hearings 89th Congress. First Session, Feb. 1965, p. 198). What happened thereafter was exactly as I had foreseen, which in itself was not a matter of prophecy but rather a clear, scientific sequence of events.

By 1970 a "stagnant inflation" had already pervaded the American economy and its finances. With the new Nixon Administration I hoped that this time I would have more luck to be heard. Through the good auspices of Secretary of Transportation John A. Volpe and Elliot L. Richardson, Secretary of H.E.W. with whom I previously worked, I sent to the White House three long Memoranda (copies attached, dated Feb. 25, 1970; March 25, 1972; and December 31, 1973), but there was no reaction.

In view of my previous negative experience with the White House, may I say, Mr. President, that I was highly pleased with two other excellent points you made in the same address to the joint Congress: (1) The White House will be open to those who have something relevant to say on a given issue; and (2) you personally want to preside over "a domestic summit meeting to devise a bipartisan action for stability and growth in the American economy." Especially was I impressed by the ingenuity and the immense importance for the future of your proposal that the President will chair a dialogue among legislators, the President's economic consultants and some of the best economic brains from labor, industry and agriculture—not behind closed doors and tight security, as in the past, but "in the full view of the American Public."

This may become the greatest innovation of your Administration, which may be followed and remembered long thereafter: great decisions on difficult issues should first be debated in a public forum where representatives of the Executive Branch, of Congress and of professional people have a chance to express and test the strength of various views and possible alternatives before the President makes a final decision. I wholeheartedly support such a move, and I hope that with your approval I may be permitted to participate in the coming domestic summit meeting to which I feel I can contribute constructively.

With this in mind I have prepared "A Brief Exposition on the Problem of Inflation and a Determinate Solution Through a Program of Consistent Reforms," enclosed here, and which I would like to present for your consideration. As a point of further information, may I attach also three other reprints pertaining to inflation.

Respectfully yours,
Anghel N. Rugina

Enclosures: 6

August 15, 1974

To:

The Honorable Gerald Rudolph Ford
President of the United States
The White House
Washington, D.C.

2. A BRIEF EXPOSITION OF THE PROBLEM OF INFLATION IN THE UNITED STATES AND A DETERMINATE SOLUTION THROUGH A PROGRAM OF CONSISTENT REFORMS

I. *The Whole Program of Consistent Reforms in Capsule Form*

1. The immediate introduction of a new, heavier U.S. dollar to drain off the existing inflation to its bottom over a weekend, both at home and in international markets. There is no other method to deal successfully with the given problem.

2. The effective use of our gold stock at Fort Knox in conjunction with a few consistent reforms in the monetary, banking and financial system which will support an immediate convertibility of the American dollar without any conditions, both at home and abroad. This is an indispensable condition for any hope in establishing a sound, equilibrium framework for stability and a normal growth of the American economy.

3. The immediate introduction by law of a *Code of Ethics in Business* requiring, in the name of social justice, that any commercial transaction, regardless of the size of business or the amount involved, shall be concluded at a fair, equilibrium price, calculated in good faith to correspond

to the real cost of production or acquisition, to which a normal rate of profit (equal to the opportunity cost of managerial services and the rate of interest for personal capital invested) and nothing else, shall be added. This will finally resolve the old problem of monopoly.

The attachment of a reasonable and limited social reform with the occasion of exchanging old, inflated dollars for new, stable dollars. Much of the unproductive bureaucracy of the welfare state will become obsolete once people at the lower level of the social scale have something tangible to start with and can earn a decent income, not eroded by inflation.

The next question is: Why do we need such a program, and how can we implement it without creating other difficulties? The answer comes from the text that follows.

II. *The Present Dilemma: Monetary, Fiscal and Incomes Policies Are Based on an Unrealistic Assumption and Thus They Cannot Work Satisfactorily*

Since the 1930's and according to the canons of Keynes' "New Economics," our government has conceived and executed monetary and fiscal policies based on a dubious assumption that government, with advice from professional economists, is able to manage the supply of money in circulation (paper money in form of notes and deposits issued by the FRS and bank credit monetized by private banks) and indirectly to control the aggregate volume of demand and investment. In addition, it has been maintained that there is no other solution but active and continuous government intervention in order to preserve the benefits and virtues of a free society.

By now we have enough evidence to see beyond any doubt that our government is not able to perform satisfactorily such a vast and intricate task. These negative results are not interpretations but historical facts, recognized even by the man in the street. There is truly much sense in the words of President Ford when he said before the Joint Congress: "The American wage earner and the American housewife are a lot better economists than most economists care to admit." The naked truth is that the "New Economics" as applied between 1934 and 1974 has not helped this country to resolve effectively and efficiently the basic problems of price stability, full employment, maximum social justice in the distribution of national income and a balance of payments in order. This failure strongly suggests that there must be something fundamentally wrong in the approach used so far in the study of the problem of inflation.

Not only the President and every member of Congress, but every responsible citizen of this country would and should be interested in knowing exact reasons for this failure of our government policies over a period of 40 years. The answer follows: The truth of the matter is that there is absolutely *no mathematical formula* for calculating at a given time, and *no practical means* for reinforcing the equilibrium supply of paper money and monetized bank credit, consistent with the realization of our four major goals: price stability, full employment, maximum social justice in the distribution of national income, and a balance of payments in order. Thus the belief that a modern government can manage the economy and its finances so as to attain equilibrium with price stability and full employment is in fact a myth and not scientific truth tested by reality. This creates a serious dilemma for the credibility of success of our government policies of today.

III. *A Solution to the Present Dilemma*

A. Diagnosis

The United States is suffering the ill effects of a double inflation, one within the country and the other in international markets—and both are mutually interrelated.

The problem of inflation can be located in the following places:

1. The first (simple) layer of inflation due to an overissue of paper money (notes and deposits of the FRS);
2. The second (cumulative or multiple) layer of inflation due to an overissue of monetized credit through the private banking system;
3. The third (simple) layer of inflation due to any arbitrary manipulation of prices by monopolistic business practices (regardless of size) or arbitrary distortion of wages by powerful labor unions;
4. U.S. government deficit-spending, as well as business deficit-investment (pure speculations) provide fuel to the inflationary mill under the existing system; and
5. The U.S. Congress, too, becomes a party to the same inflationary forces whenever it approves additional expenditures which bring about a deficit, or it allows budget deficits to be covered simply through a rise in the ceiling of the national debt.

Any reasonable and effective program to eliminate inflation and secure a sound framework for stability and growth of the American economy has to cope systematically with these five sources.

B. Immediate Steps and Measures to Drain Off the Existing Inflation

Unless this now stagnant inflation has been drained off to its bottom, no government policy can work successfully. The task is difficult because we must clean out not only an internal inflation but simultaneously an external inflation of paper dollars in international markets. Nevertheless, this problem can be solved in the following manner:

1. The introduction of a new, heavier U.S. dollar on a given D-day to replace the old, inflated dollars.
2. The revaluation of our gold stock at Fort Knox at the real price of today (around $150.00 per ounce) and its active use in backing the new, heavier dollar to be declared convertible again, this time at home and abroad.
3. A good ratio for exchanging old dollars for new, convertible dollars could be 20:1 or 25:1.
4. By using a ratio of 25:1 we have enough gold to cover the new dollar 100 percent on D-day and will have absolutely no difficulties in reinstating its free convertibility. In addition, we shall have a substantial gold reserve for future needs.
5. In order to avoid other serious difficulties on the same D-day, all current prices, incomes, banking accounts, debts and all other sorts of claims (domestic or foreign), including taxes, must be reduced in the same proportion of 25:1.
6. Right after D-day the price used the previous day to revaluate gold reserves, i.e., the $150.00, shall be expressed in new, heavier dollars, specifically in the same proportion of 25:1. That will establish the new parity: The official price of gold shall be six new, heavier dollars per ounce.
7. The government should use all appropriate means of communication to explain to the American people that this operation of cleaning the financial house of inflation through a new, heavier dollar is purely technical and is conducted in the most equitable way so that nobody will lose or gain anything. Indeed, the real incomes, assets and liabilities of the people are absolutely the same as before the reform, with the nominal difference that they are now expressed in smaller figures but in a higher and stable monetary standard.

C. A Monetary, Banking and Financial Reform Consistent with Price Stability, Full Employment and a Balance of Payments in Equilibrium

The most important thing is what will happen after D-day once the old inflation has been wiped out through the new, heavier dollar. There will be a new system which is constructed in accordance with conditions of stable equilibrium.

Any system composed of many parts—in the physical as well as in the social universe—in order to reach and maintain a position of stable equilibrium, requires a natural (concrete) parameter which holds the component parts together. The natural parameter can be defined in terms of a consistent framework, where a central force acts and coordinates all other possible actions and reactions within definite limits. In the physical universe the natural parameter is given, whereas in human societies we have to discover it first and then reinforce it by adequate laws and institutions.

As far as a national economy and its finances are concerned, Leon Walras was the first economist who clearly saw the need of a natural parameter in the form of "Numeraire" (or 100%-backed currency) and the force of free competition to hold a system of free markets together. Walras, the originator of the concept and law of general equilibrium, insisted that in order to have equilibrium prices, we must organize a system of free markets, where monopoly forces are reduced to zero at the limit and thus competition reaches its maximum, plus a monetary and financial system where all prices (for consumer goods as well as for capital goods) and implicitly all sources of income, including capital formation, are expressed only in terms of Numeraire.

The natural parameter of Numeraire requires further a number of other conditions which makes the new system consistent with stable equilibrium at the domestic level and in international transactions:

1. Independence of the Federal Reserve System from both the public budget, including national debt, and the financial interests of the private banking system.
2. Any new issue of official money shall be Numeraire.
3. A reform of the private banking system whereby monetization of credit be declared illegal as being inflationary.
4. A reform of the public budget and finances, whereby monetization of public credit through the central bank or the private banks be declared illegal as being inflationary.
5. In order to dissipate completely the fear shared by many contemporary economists that eventually there may not be enough gold to support a normal, balanced economic development and also to give to the new system of Numeraire even more flexibility, it is recommended that the Federal Reserve System study immediately how to offer the American public the opportunity to monetize and demonetize a certain durable commodity selected in each of the 12 districts. Upon delivery of such standardized commodities in certain public warehouses in each district, the FRS shall issue an equal amount (minus a small discount) in banknotes called "Commercial Commodity Dollars." These "Commercial Commodity Dollars" shall be freely convertible in their original backing.
6. Under a 100 percent Numeraire-currency system and with a stable

structure in banking and finance (private and public) the United States will have no problem with the balance of international payments.

D. A Code of Ethics in Business

The millions of Americans who suffered irreparable damage during this and other inflations are crying for social justice which they deserve. This plan recommends the adoption of a constitutional law in the form of a permanent *Code of Ethics in Business* requiring: All business transactions of any nature and regardless of the amount or size of the firm involved, shall be concluded at fair or equilibrium prices. The equilibrium price in turn shall be calculated in good faith, respecting the letter and the spirit of the law, to make up for the cost of production and acquisition to which a normal rate of profit was added. Sharp penalties should be applied to those breaking this law.

E. A Reasonable and Limited Social Reform

If it is desirable, this plan recommends a limited social reform to be attached to the operation of exchanging old, inflated dollars for new, stable dollars. This means that a certain portion, f.i., on a graduated scale of 5 to 20 per cent of any sum in excess of a certain *minimum* level of cash and savings (measured by the average standard of living), will be temporarily blocked in a special "Fund for Social Peace and Reform." Meanwhile, during the process of exchange of old money, statistical information will be available for determining (on an individual basis as well as in the aggregate) the exact number of those who are really poor (below the above specified minimum). Financial help should be granted to these disadvantaged people only once from the above special fund.

To reinforce the constructive character of this social reform, two things may be added. First, some definite requirements may be specified whereby the recipients of such financial aid must use it only for productive purposes. Second, after this reform is completed, no welfare payments in any form should be given to persons capable of working. In this way the immense bureaucracy of the welfare state developed in recent years can be curtailed legitimately.

Respectfully submitted,
Anghel N. Rugina
Professor of Economics and Finance
Northeastern University, Boston

3. A SECOND LETTER TO THE PRESIDENT

December 4, 1974

The Honorable Gerald R. Ford
President of the United States
The White House
Washington, D.C.

Dear Mr. President:

First, I would like to thank you respectfully for your kind letter of September 12, 1974 in regard to a previous Memorandum, "A Brief Exposition on the Problem of Inflation," which I sent to you with my letter of August 15, 1974.

In your News Conference on December 2, 1974 you correctly stated: "We are currently facing three serious challenges, all at the same time, inflation, recession and energy." It is also true, as you stressed further, that our economy is healthy and strong, probably still the strongest in the world. Unfortunately, we cannot say the same thing about our monetary and financial system, which after the change in 1965 and 1968, is based solely on paper money and monetized bank credit.

Our Federal Government has now exhausted the use of the traditional monetary, fiscal and even incomes policies after 1968, and the results are far from being satisfactory. The basic reason for this failure lies not in the lack of cooperation on the part of the FRS or Congress, nor the lack of wisdom on the part of the Council of Economic Advisors to the President or the Secretary of the Treasury, but rather in the fact that our monetary and financial system after 1965-68 has no trace of a natural parameter in the form of Numeraire-currency. According to the Walrasian theorem of general equilibrium, Numeraire constitutes an indispensable element for stability from within.

Mr. President, we cannot afford to wait for miracles in an environment where business, government and the people in general do not possess a *reliable monetary standard* to make appropriate decisions which in the aggregate determines the position of the economy. Right now we are at a crucial moment in our financial history, and we already have paid dearly for past honest errors and false actions. The initiative is still in your hands before Congress convenes in January, and there is little evidence that your package presented in October will find a favorable vote.

Under these circumstances I am taking the liberty of sending for your consideration the two enclosed papers listed:

1) THE PROBLEM OF INFLATION HAS A DETERMINATE SOLUTION!

This is the final version of my earlier "Brief Exposition" of August 15. I would like to say, as strongly as I can, that the problem of inflation and recession *can be resolved over a weekend* by the introduction of a new, heavier dollar and absolutely without any harm to our citizens or to the economy as a whole. This part of the surgical operation can be performed by Executive Order, it being an emergency case. The more difficult part refers to the changes in the Federal Reserve Act and other previous legislation in order to render impossible the return of inflation or deflation in the future.

2) A MEMORANDUM ON THE INTERNATIONAL OIL CRISIS AND A REORGANIZATION PLAN OF THE IMF TO AVOID SUCH CRISES IN THE FUTURE,

which deals with the energy crisis.

Above all, we need as soon as possible the passage of a law of social and economic justice requiring all businesses (regardless of size) to calculate in their transactions only equilibrium prices where a normal rate of profit is included and nothing more. Such a Code of Ethics in Business is urgently needed, both at the national and international levels. If you can move Congress—and I see no reason why you could not succeed!—to pass such a law, then your name will be remembered in our history as "President Ford, the Just."

I realize that my proposals are a contingency plan. Should you conclude that there is some merit in my proposals, I would appreciate an appointment to see you at your convenience.

Respectfully yours,
Anghel N. Rugina
Professor of Economics and Finance
Northeastern University
Boston, Mass.

Enclosures: 4

4. THE PROBLEM OF INFLATION HAS A DETERMINATE SOLUTION! A BLUEPRINT FOR A U.S. MONETARY, FINANCIAL AND ECONOMIC STABILIZATION ACT, BASED ON CONDITIONS OF STABLE EQUILIBRIUM

> An "Economic Miracle in America" is still possible! . . . If we are prepared to undertake the necessary and adequate reforms before we reach the point of no return.

I. Introduction: Diagnosis

1. What Are the Problems?

The American economy is faced in 1974 with a number of problems which are not new, except in their unfettered acceleration toward a point of no return. More and more evidence is accumulating every day to prove that these problems cannot be resolved effectively by manipulating traditional policies within the status-quo framework. As a point of information these problems are: (1) a double inflation of paper dollars and monetized bank credit, one at home and the other in international markets; (2) a rather high rate of chronic unemployment; (3) monopolistic positions and practices which keep certain prices and wages above their equilibrium level; (4) growing social and economic inequities; (5) a sagging stock market dominated by pure speculation; and (6) a balance of payments exposed to cumulative chronic deficits.

Inflation is now considered to be the No. 1 problem in the nation, as President Ford has stressed in announcing the Economic Summit Conference scheduled for September 27-28, 1974. The Nixon, Johnson, Kennedy and Eisenhower Administrations have also tried, at one time or another, to slow down the inflationary expansion, but without much success, considering what we have inherited from the past. What then is the lesson that we should learn from the economic and financial history of recent decades?

2. Neither the Old "Laissez-Faire" Medicine nor "Fine Tuning" and/or Wage and Price Controls Seem to Work

As long as the status quo of our rather volatile financial system, i.e., the existing inflationary mill of paper dollars and monetized bank credit, remains in action, there is absolutely no chance for price stability, full employment and a balance of payments in equilibrium.

Under the present set of institutional arrangements, the application of what is now called the old economic religion of "laissez-faire," or the conservative proposal to cut the federal budget and keep money tight, leaving other things as they are, leads inevitably to an open deflation and more unemployment, as we very well know from past experience. This is not, therefore, an effective solution to the problem of inflation.

The new economic religion of the 1930's crystallized in the method of "fine tuning" (i.e., maneuvering with monetary and fiscal policies but leaving the institutional framework full of inconsistencies) did not have much success either. In fact, the bad situation we have now is the result of the blind belief in the myth that fine tuning can work. At least by 1974 we should have been able to detect the economic truth that, during a stagnant inflation with high unemployment, neither a tax cut, nor large budgetary deficits to finance public works projects, nor easier money policies to encourage more private investments can operate efficiently, since all these measures intensify the existing inflation and make the economic situation of tomorrow worse. Consequently, fine tuning also must be discarded as an effective solution to our No. 1 problem.

Finally, members of a more independent and radical wing of "New Economics," frustrated by the fact that fine tuning alone really cannot do the job, advance what they consider the inevitable: wage and price controls in a new format of guideposts. This may be called the "new, new economic religion." Fortunately or unfortunately, from the experience during the Nixon Administration, and more conclusively from the British experiment, we know that on this road we are exposed to the danger of "hidden inflation" with serious distortions in economic decisions and unwarranted shortages which ultimately nurture black markets. In view of past and present failure, not only in capitalist but also in socialist countries, mandatory wage and price controls do not seem to offer an equitable and effective solution to the problem of inflation either.

Is there any alternative to this apparently hopeless situation? Yes, indeed! There is an alternative which will be presented in this plan, but it is not an easy one. And it is difficult not because its attainment requires great sacrifices on the part of the people, already mercilessly plundered by the ongoing inflation, but rather because it necessitates certain institutional reforms which run counter to a number of vested interests in the financial community and even the political body. In addition, it implies that we free ourselves from a certain mode of economic and financial thinking inherited from the 1930's and which for some time has been enjoying a monopolistic position in the market of ideas.

Let us take a look first at what is not possible and should be avoided, and secondly, at what is possible and what we should strive for.

3. The Impossibility Theorem, or What Is Undesirable and Not Possible

Theorem 1: If we think about the issues in question in terms of status quo, i.e., preserving the existing framework of paper money and monetized bank credit as institutionalized especially by the last changes of 1965, 1968 and 1971, then there is no determinate solution to the problem of inflation, and consequently no rational monetary, fiscal or income policies exist which can be applied successfully.

Explanation: Our monetary and financial system after 1965-1968 (at home) and 1971 (abroad) has no trace of a natural parameter; its framework is inherently unstable, and consequently it is exposed to cumulative fluctuations in all directions. A financial system of inherent instability in turn directly affects the economic system with which it is organically interrelated. Considering this relationship, inflation and the other troubles in our economy are not due to unreasonable behavior of our people, nor to lack of good statistics or unwise decisions by our government, Federal Reserve System and Congress, but rather to a vicious circle of unpredictable effects and reactions derived from the present monetary and financial system lacking a natural parameter.

Our government practices in vain the strategy of full employment and price stability by using the method of fine tuning, since the final result is condemned to be the same—an open or a hidden inflation or deflation. The lesson from history is therefore clear: Paper money and monetized bank credit are associated with an inherently unstable framework which cannot be managed to support conditions of stable equilibrium. In fact, there is no mathematical formula or practical means to calculate and reinforce in real economic life the equilibrium supply of paper money and monetized bank credit consistent with price stability, full employment, maximum of social justice in the distribution of national income and a balance of payments in good standing.

This is what is not possible and what we cannot afford to continue in 1974 and thereafter. The validity of Theorem No. 1 has been confirmed not only by realities but also at the first meeting of the 21 most prominent economists in the country invited to the White House Conference on September 5, 1974 to discuss the problem of inflation. None of them could offer any definite solution for a speedy cure of the inflationary nightmare, as if economics as a science never existed! The sad truth is, there is no determinate solution as long as we maintain the status quo of our present monetary and financial system. But the latter part of the statement was never mentioned during this conference.

It is perhaps useful to recall that Lord Keynes, the master of economic thinking for our time, in his *Treatise on Money* (1930) warned that if the framework of a system was inherently unstable, then there is no chance for developing equilibrium solutions to the given problems. Unfortunately, neither Keynes nor his followers have seen so far that an economic and financial system based on paper money and monetized bank credit has no natural parameter, and consequently embodies an inherently unstable framework. And that is where the confusion starts. We are led to believe that the government and the Federal Reserve System could maneuver within the existing framework and reach a position of acceptable equilibrium, when the economic and financial history of recent decades negates such a possibility.

4. The Possibility Theorem, or What Is Possible and Desirable

Theorem 2: If we think about our present economic and financial problems in terms of a system of general equilibrium based on stable, 100%-covered currency called "Numeraire" and a regime of non-monetized credit limited to the volume of real income in the economy, then the problem of inflation has a determinate solution.

Explanation: Any system of stable equilibrium—in the physical universe as well as in human societies—requires a natural parameter, namely, a constant magnitude associated with a force of attraction which under certain conditions within an adequate framework holds the parts of the system together. In our physical universe the sun is the natural parameter and gravitation is the force.

In a national economy the natural parameter is "Numeraire" and the force is fair competition, expressed in the law of supply and demand. Exactly one hundred years ago, in 1874, Leon Walras, a French economist at the University of Lausanne in Switzerland, explicitly formulated the law of general equilibrium. According to this law, stable equilibrium is possible *only* when (1) we have organized a system of free markets where monopoly forces are reduced to zero at the limit, leaving pure competition at its optimum efficiency; (2) the prices for both consumer and capital goods are expressed exclusively in terms of Numeraire. Walras stressed only two conditions: (1) The currency used must be 100 per cent Numeraire, and (2) competition must be pure in the sense that monopoly forces should be reduced to zero at the limit. From the context, however, the law of general equilibrium cannot be expected to be fully efficient unless (3) all other major institutions and practices in the economy are consistent with the natural parameter.

The Walrasian law of general equilibrium needs to be extended further to include not only the private sector (as in the original formulation) but also the public sector (government budget and finances) and the balance of payments.

In a system of general equilibrium there is only one constant magnitude in the economy—the Numeraire—and all other variables in form of prices (foreign exchange included), incomes, expenditures or employment are flexible, free to fluctuate but only within very definite limits in a perpetual adjustment process guided by the natural parameter and always striving toward a position of stable equilibrium. And a position of stable equilibrium means the realization of five major goals: price stability, full employment, maximum of social justice in the distribution of national income and a budget and balance of payments in order, without any conflict among themselves.

This is what is possible as well as desirable. The following of Theorem 2 in practice will provide the proof that "economic miracles" are still possible and certainly on a more permanent basis than those experiments in West Germany and Japan after World War II, which seemed to be temporary in nature and vulnerable to instability. None of those experiments satisfied the requirement of a natural parameter of Numeraire, and therefore it is not surprising that they could not endure the storms of the time.

What can and should be done for the introduction of a system of general equilibrium in the United States to cope efficiently with problem No. 1 (inflation) and the other five issues indicated at the outset?

II. A Blueprint for a U.S. Monetary, Financial and Economic Stabilization Act

PART ONE: SHORT-RUN STEPS AND MEASURES

OPERATION NO. 1:

1. *Target:* To drain off simultaneously both the internal and external inflation.
2. *Means:* The introduction of a Moratorium U.S. dollar (hereinafter called MO-dollar) equal to 25 old, inflated dollars on a given day, preferably over a weekend. The *MO-dollar* receives its name from the fact that the suspension of the convertibility of the U.S. dollar in August 1971 in reality represented a moratorium on all *external* liabilities derived from the possession of American dollars by foreigners. For domestic holders of dollars, the suspension of convertibility in 1933 in practice meant a similar form of moratorium for *internal* liabilities. Thus the MO-dollar has a factual and legal justification.
3. *Additional Measures:*
   a. Reduce all prices, incomes, bank accounts and any kind of claim, including taxes, on D-day by the same ratio of 25:1.
   b. Reduce all foreign claims of any nature upon the U.S. Government and its citizens, i.e., American dollars in international markets, on on the same D-day, by the same 25:1 ratio.
   c. Introduce a monetary subdivision of the present penny or cent to be called "mini-cent" (1 current penny = 10, 50 or 100 mini-cents) to resolve the problem of adjustment of those current prices which are below 25 cents.
4. *Communication to the People:* Our Federal Government should use all appropriate means of communication to explain to the American people and to the rest of the world that this operation of cleaning our financial house of a stagnant inflation through a multiple U.S. dollar is purely technical in nature and is conducted in the most equitable way so that no one will lose or gain anything. Indeed, the real value of incomes, prices, banking account—in one word, assets and liabilities of the holders of dollars (domestic and foreign)—will be absolutely the same as prior to the reform, with the nominal difference that values will now be expressed in smaller figures.

   It should also be stressed that this is the quickest and the most equitable way to stop completely today's prevailing inflationary psychology.

5. *Results:* The total supply of money in the broadest sense of the term (M_3 in the Federal Reserve Bulletin) is estimated here at close to $1,000 billion. By the introduction of the multiple dollar, the total supply of money (M_3) will be reduced to about 40 billion MO-dollars.

OPERATION NO. 2:

1. *Target:* To liquidate the heritage of domestic and foreign claims resulting from the past inflation.
2. *Means:*
   a. To make a revaluation of our gold stock at Fort Knox using the more realistic market price of today as an average over the last 12 months, here assumed at $150.00 per ounce. Our present gold stock of $11.65 billion in June 1974 (at $42.22) recalculated at $150.00 per ounce will give us a total value of $41.35 billion.
   b. To set aside from the available gold stock exactly $40 billion for a "Gold Liquidation Equalization Fund" to match the 40 billion MO-dollars in circulation on D-day resulting from Operation No. 1.
   c. To declare all MO-dollars convertible at the emergency rate of 1 MO-dollar for 1 revalued gold dollar, or 150 MO-dollars for 1 ounce of gold, for both domestic and foreign holders.
   d. This emergency convertibility will be decreed only once in regard to claims resulting from the old, inflated dollars reduced to MO-dollars, which now are declared convertible at a *special liquidation rate* for those who prefer to have gold. This liquidation rate does not refer to the issue of *new money after D-day,* and therefore the Federal Reserve System would not be required to accept 1 ounce of gold and issue 150 MO-dollars. The MO-dollars would be issued only once, for the purpose of replacing the old inflated dollars. The rate of 150 MO-dollars for 1 ounce of gold is used only for the complete liquidation of the inflation of American dollars and for no other purpose.
3. *Official Parity:* The new official parity of the U.S. dollar after D-day will be 6 New Dollars for 1 ounce of gold. This means that the old price of $150.00 will be adjusted by the same ratio of 25:1 for obvious reasons of equity and stability. But it must be made crystal-clear that the new official parity refers only to New Dollars issued by the Federal Reserve System after D-day.
4. *Explanation:* This is the most difficult part of the plan and requires precise answers to specific questions.

a. Does this plan not use two official parities at the same time? The answer is no! Today the official parity is $45.22. The special convertibility of 150 MO-dollars per ounce of gold refers only to the liquidation of claims concluded in inflated dollars issued before D-day. The new official parity for new money created after D-day is 6 New Dollars per 1 ounce of gold.

b. Would foreign creditors not object that this plan was infringing upon their rights, since their claims in terms of gold would appear to be drastically undervalued? Although they might protest, their complaints will not be legitimate in terms of equity. We must compare what they have today with what this plan offers. Their claims are presently expressed in paper, inconvertible dollars exposed to perpetual depreciation through inflation, which one day may even reach zero value. This plan gives them a choice between accepting a conversion of their claims in simple MO-dollars, without any loss whatsoever, or the liquidation of their claims in gold at an emergency rate. Granted, under this plan the convertibility of MO-dollars into gold is not profitable, but no one is forced to accept this solution, since they have the option to avail themselves of the alternative of settling the same claim by accepting simple MO-dollars.

c. Would gold-producing countries have any unjustified profit if this plan were put into action? The answer is absolutely no! After D-day the Federal Reserve System may accept gold at the new official parity of 6 New Dollars per ounce of gold, minus the mint charges, and issue gold certificates. There is no illegitimate profit in this kind of transaction. It could create extra profits if the Federal Reserve System were to issue new money at the emergency rate of 150 MO-dollars per ounce of gold, but that would be illegal on D-day and thereafter.

d. Would the oil-producing countries reap any unjustified benefits through this plan, since they presently hold a very large amount of dollars? Again the answer is no. Their claims in old dollars will be reduced by the ratio 25:1, and if they want gold they have to accept the liquidation parity. Under the new conditions created by this plan, the oil prices inevitably will go down to adjust to an equilibrium level, whereby the comparative advantage will be shared equitably by both exporting and importing countries.

e. What would happen to the state of international liquidity and the International Monetary Fund? The international liquidity will increase once the United States has decided to revalue its gold stock at a more realistic price of $150.00 per ounce. Most certainly other member countries of the I.M.F. will follow suit. Italy recently has received a credit of $2 billion from West Germany with a collateral in gold valued at 80 percent of the market price and not the official price of $42.22.

The present concern of the international banking community with liquidity problems will receive a boost with this plan, even though this issue requires special analysis. The International Monetary Fund will be faced only with technical problems of recalculation of the U.S. quota in terms of the new official parity.

f. The only issue open for further scrutiny will be the relationship between MO-dollars issued to liquidate the past inflation and New Dollars issued after D-day.

Part Two: Needed Long-Run Reforms

In Part One it was shown how to drain off and liquidate the existing inflation. On D-day the American economy and the banking system will be 100 per cent liquid, and there will be no trace of inflation or deflation nor any immediate danger of a financial crisis. The U.S. balance of payments on that day will also be in equilibrium, with no pressures of accumulated dollars in foreign hands.

The major problem at this point is what to do so that the specter of inflation and deflation may not recur in the foreseeable future. The French experiment of 1959 with the introduction of a new multiple franc (equal to 100 old, inflated francs) was relatively successful in the short run, but it definitely failed in the long run. It is true that the financial situation of France at that time was worse than that of the United States is now. Nevertheless, the ultimate failure of the French experiment consisted in a lack of supporting reforms in the long run.[1]

In order to render a return of the current inflation impossible and also to solve the other problems mentioned in the Introduction, our government must be prepared to undertake a number of reforms required by a monetary, banking, financial and economic framework consistent with the realization of our five major goals: price stability, full employment, maximum of social justice in the distribution of national income and a budget and a balance of payments in equilibrium.

1. *The Independence of the Federal Reserve System*

(1) A New monetary Act should clearly state that the Federal Reserve System is an independent public institution, entrusted to issue official money but separated both from the administration of the public

budget, including national debt, and from the interference of the private banking system.

(2) The Federal Reserve System in point of administration shall be divided into two different sections. One department should be concerned only with the issue of official money and be called Department A, or *Issuance Department of the Federal Reserve System.* The second department shall deal in usual banking business with other banks or governments but only up to the limit of the capital provided by the free portion of the old gold stock resulting from revaluation, that is, $1.35 billion converted into New Dollars (see Operation No. 2). This should be called Department B, or *Banking Department of the Federal Reserve System.* This appears to be similar to the Robert Peel Act of 1844 in England, and it is, with one significant difference: The Federal Reserve System through this plan will not assume any part of the national debt. This innovation corrects one major weakness of the Peel Monetary Stabilization Act.

(3) Department A of the Federal Reserve System shall be in charge of issuing official money in form of Numeraire and commercial dollars.

2. *The Natural Parameter of Numeraire*

The cardinal condition for the realization and maintenance of stable equilibrium prices (as demonstrated by Walras) lies in a natural parameter of Numeraire-currency (for which there is no substitute) embedded in a system of free markets where monopoly forces are reduced to zero at the limit. Numeraire means that the monetary unit is equal to a certain quantity of a special commodity (like gold or silver, or any other suitable commodity), which is selected to serve as material for the monetary standard. Numeraire is a *constant magnitude,* which, together with the force of competition, freed of monopoly pressures, helps a system of free markets to develop and maintain equilibrium prices. How the free markets will be relieved of monopoly forces is shown below under point 5, "A Code of Ethics in Business."

Why do we need Numeraire in the first place? As mentioned earlier, any system expected to generate stability requires a natural parameter like Numeraire-currency. In addition, it has inherent value, i.e., a common denominator between money and all other commodities and services, a quality needed for any reliable and objective monetary standard used to measure exchange values, current incomes, including assets and liabilities of any sort.

After D-day Department A of the Federal Reserve System will issue new official money in form of Numeraire, according to the new official parity.

3. *Free Convertibility of the U.S. Dollar at Home and in International Markets*

The MO-dollars will not constitute a problem for the F.R.S. because their quantity is limited, in fact fixed, to the amount existing on D-day and cannot be increased thereafter. Their value, consequently, will not depreciate with the passing of time; on the contrary, it may increase as a result of better economic conditions. And this is true for both domestic and foreign holders. In addition, those who want to convert them into gold may do so at the special liquidating rate mentioned under Operation 2. No difficulties are expected since the MO-dollars will be 100 per cent covered and freely convertible. The New Dollars issued after D-day will be fully covered and also convertible at the new official parity.

4. *The Mechanism to Monetize Other Regional Commodities in Form of "Commercial Commodity Dollars"*

In order to dissipate completely the fear shared by many contemporary economists that eventually there may not be enough gold to support a normal balanced economic development, but also to grant even more flexibility to the new system of Numeraire-currency, this plan recommends that the Federal Reserve System organize as soon as possible the necessary facilities so that American citizens can enjoy the opportunity to monetize or demonetize at their discretion, and under certain conditions, a durable commodity representative of a particular district.

A small discount shall be charged in such transactions by Department A of the Federal Reserve System in order to defray warehousing and administrative costs. For any delivery of the standardized commodity in the respective region, the Federal Reserve District Bank will issue bank notes in the same amount (minus the small discount), which are called here "Commercial Commodity Dollars." The prices for these regional commodities will not be fixed but expressed in Numeraire. Since Commercial Commodity Dollars would be backed 100 per cent at all times, this represents stable money and should be declared freely convertible in their respective commodity.

This novel institution will be of great help to the American people. Indeed, whenever the prices in a given district seem to be depressed, the people of that area will have a chance to monetize a part or all of the production of the special regional commodity. Besides increasing the supply of money and reversing the trend on the markets, the issue of new commercial dollars would represent, at the same time, an expansion of real capital formation in the district. On the other hand, when prices seem to be rising, people will have the opportunity to convert bank notes denominated in commercial dollars into the respective commodity and sell it at a profit. The volume of money in the district will shrink and the supply of goods will increase. The final result will again be a reversal of the trend.

In addition to producing more real income and employment through any issue of commercial dollars, the privilege of monetizing and demonetizing a regional commodity may exert a favorable impact on the stabilization of prices and incomes in the area. In a recent study by the New York Stock Exchange it was pointed out that the American economy between 1974 and 1985 may be faced with a gap in capital formation of as much as $650 billion. (See: *New York Times,* September 10, 1974). The introduction of monetization of regional commodities can resolve such a gap without any difficulties for our government or banking system.

One problem for the Federal Reserve System will be to manage skillfully the discount charges at the public warehouses of monetized commodities so that the commercial dollar will remain at par or close to the official parity of Numeraire. This task is manageable so long as the convertibility of the two forms of money (both 100 per cent covered) is preserved, of course each restricted to its own backing.

All in all, free monetization and demonetization of regional commodities, rather than posing any difficult problems, will support a balanced economic development throughout the country without the danger of inflation or deflation.

5. *A Permanent Code of Ethics in Business, Labor Organizations and Government, in Regard to Price Formation*

In order to satisfy the other basic requirements in the Walrasian law of general equilibrium—namely (1) the necessity that monopoly forces be reduced to zero at the limit, and (2) that all prices in Numeraire equal the real cost of the factors used, including the cost of management —there is need for a permanent *Code of Ethics in Business.* Among other things, this code should require that all business transactions of any nature and regardless of amount or the size of the firm involved be concluded at equilibrium prices. The latter, in turn, shall be calculated in good faith, respecting the spirit and the letter of the law, to make up the cost of production or acquisition to which a normal rate of profit (representing the opportunity cost for managerial services) is added. More specifically, equilibrium prices shall be calculated in such a way as to include the real payments made (or imputed) for the factors of production (labor, land, capital and management) actually used, plus government taxes in any form, but nothing else. Research and development will be financed from the voluntary savings of the people attracted to industry and trade business then more than ever. The source of funds for this same purpose will derive from the interest on their own capital invested in business, which, under the new conditions, becomes an imputed element of the cost of production.

The existing rules in regard to labor-management relations shall be revised to correspond to the new Code of Ethics in Business. Recently a number of economists, and even the Assistant Attorney General in charge of the Antitrust Division, complained before the Joint Economic Committee that "in many ways regulatory agencies help maintain artificially higher prices." The new Code of Ethics in Business will resolve this problem because the law of formation of equilibrium prices will have application to any trade transactions, regardless whether the firm is private or public, domestic or foreign, whether or not it receives subsidies and whether or not it is under any government control. In one word, the new Code of Ethics in Business will mark the end of monopoly in America.

6. *The Money Market Must Be Completely Separated from the Capital Markets*

The extended law of general equilibrium further requires that the money market and capital markets be separated and not mixed as they are today. The basic reason for this requirement lies in the fact that the two markets are of entirely different natures. The money market is concerned with the *liquidity function* in the economy, that is, with the demand and supply of immediately available funds necessary for a smooth distribution and reproduction of consumer goods and services during a given period of time. On the other hand, capital markets deal with the *function of investment,* that is, with the demand and supply of savings or long-term committed funds. In order to have general stability, we need an equilibrium rate of interest in the money market and another equilibrium rate of interest in the capital markets. There is no other way to reach the two sets of equilibrium rates of interest except when the two markets are really and completely independent of one another.

In view of this rule of separating the money market from the capital markets, some significant changes will be necessary in the banking system and in the organized commodity and securities markets, as shown below.

7. *Legal Prohibition of Monetization of Bank Credit for Private or Public Purposes*

The natural parameter of Numeraire-currency as a cornerstone of a stable financial system implies legal prohibition of monetization of bank credit in any form, regardless whether for private or public purposes. The basic reason is that monetized bank credit through the Central Bank and/or private banks in reality represents "anti-Numeraire," i.e., a disequilibrium or an inflationary-deflationary type of money. The second basic weakness in the Peel British Monetary Act of 1844, and which made that famous stabilization reform unworkable in the long run, was the lack of this prohibition. The first weakness already mentioned was the taking over of a portion of the national debt by the Bank of England. By now we should have learned the right lesson from that nineteenth-century British legislation, because it dealt with the same economic and financial instability problem of inflation.

On the other hand, we should not confuse the terms *credit* and *monetized bank credit,* which are totally different. Credit as such is a useful institution for human societies and a national economy, provided it is covered and limited to the volume of real income in the economy available for this purpose. This is simple, real, or covered credit in business or personal relations which does not change the supply of money in circulation. Thus real credit is neither inflationary nor deflationary. Monetized bank credit is a horse of a different color, if not a different animal altogether. In this special case, credit or debt through the mechanism of modern banking is monetized, and therefore the supply of money is directly affected, without any link to the real income produced in the economy. This is why monetized bank credit is inflationary and represents anti-Numeraire or a disequilibrium type of money.

If credit cards were issued only by private corporations granting the consumer the privilege of credit up to a certain amount, no problems would be encountered because the credit in question would be real and limited. Unfortunately, in practice the credit involved in the credit-card business is monetized by banks and thus has become a major source of inflation. Hundreds of billions of dollars are monetized and demonetized each year in this way, and yet the Federal Reserve System has never taken any action nor protested against this inflationary practice by private institutions.

During the nineteenth century, monetization of credit in form of bank notes issued by private banks was prohibited by the U.S. National Banking Act of 1863-65 for the same basic reason that it was inflationary. In 1974 in the United States we badly need to complete the reform of the last century and ban by law monetization of credit in form of pure bank deposits, or in any other fashion, issued by private banks, the Central Bank or any other institution, if we want economic and financial stability. Beyond this the use of simple, real credit in business or otherwise should remain free of any arbitrary interference on the part of the Federal Reserve System or the Federal Government.

8. *A Banking Reform Consistent with Economic and Financial Stability*

A new banking law should explicitly point out that (1) the money market transactions shall be kept separate from the capital market transactions, and (2) that the monetization of credit in form of pure bank deposits or any other mode is legally prohibited. Pure bank deposits are those created by private banks during the process of lending on the basis of a small fractional reserve, and should not be confused with real bank deposits resulting from official money deposited with a bank for private or public accounts.

According to this new law, banks (domestic and foreign) should be required to divide their activity into two different sections: Department DD and Departments S&I.

Department DD shall include all transactions dealing in liquid funds which appear in form of demand deposits or any sort of open accounts, subject to the privilege of being used without notice by drawing a check or drafting a payment order. These are transactions belonging by definition to the money market. Since the funds involved must be kept immediately available on call, banks should be required by law to keep all demand deposits or open accounts 100 per cent covered in official money at all times. The banks should continue to be entitled to an equitable charge for the cost of maintaining such accounts.

Department S&I shall encompass all transactions dealing with savings or time deposits and loans and investments. The new banking law must specifically indicate that a bank may not grant a loan or engage in an investment proposition unless the bank possesses the whole amount involved in the respective transaction.

This is the image of a stable private banking system which will provide banking services to the public and business without creating inflation or deflation. In addition, under the new system, no run on the banks can ever lead to a financial or economic crisis because all banks will be 100 per cent liquid. The economy also will be liquid at all times, regardless of whether the respective liquid funds are kept in a bank or are handled directly by the public.

9. *A Reform of the Organized Commodity and Securities Markets Consistent with Economic and Financial Stability*

On the organized commodity and securities markets two different kinds of transactions are conducted at the same time: (1) *real* or *natural transactions* composed of outright buying and selling of commodities and securities, where real capital (equated to savings derived from real income in the economy) is used; and (2) *nominal* or *artificial transactions* composed of betting that the price of the commodities and securities involved in the foreseeable future will eventually either go up (use purchase-options to buy) or go down (use short-sales to sell) and financed mostly through monetized bank credit. The latter type of transactions consists of *pure speculations,* as distinguished from the first, regular type of business activity.

The science of economics and finance does not yet provide a precise analysis to be able to prove that the first kind of transactions leads to equilibrium and the second to disequilibrium. But the fact of the matter remains that outright buying and selling of commodities and securities are governed by the rule of normal demand-and-supply curves, as Alfred Marshall correctly observed. He pointed out further that pure speculations are an exception to this rule. Unfortunately, Marshall did not stress emphatically and explicitly enough that pure speculation tends to initiate and often to intensify a given disequilibrium.

The distinction between real investments and pure speculations is therefore a fundamental one. Yet, in our present mixed capitalist system, the line between the two is blurred beyond recognition, and this important distinction has lost its significance. The fact is, however, that pure speculations are governed by what may be called the rule of *inverted demand-and-supply curves,* or anti-Marshallian curves, which create or aggravate a disequilibrium position.

For these reasons a reform of the organized commodity and securities markets is absolutely necessary if we want economic and financial stability. Specifically, a new law should prohibit under heavy penalties any sort of pure speculation on the organized commodity and securities markets. The New York Stock Exchange and the mercantile market, as well as other exchanges in the country, should be open only to real, natural transactions, with a definite assurance that disguised pure speculation is not taking place.

To realize the importance of such a reform, we should note the sagging stock market in recent years, which is the result of pure speculations and is eroding the healthy background of our economy. We should also consider the immense amount of funds which are tied up in pure speculations instead of being used to finance productive activities and to create new jobs and more real income in the economy at a time when we desperately need to increase real investments and not pure speculations. It staggers the imagination to read that during the hearings of a Senate bill to pass a new Federal Regulation of Commodity Futures Trading, it was disclosed that "the volume of commodities futures trading rose last year to $520 billion, substantially exceeding the value of securities transactions on various United States stock exchanges." (See: *New York Times,* September 10, 1974.) How much more employment and real income would have been induced in the American economy if these $520 billion were used for productive purposes!

10. A Reform of the Public Budget and Finances Consistent with Economic and Financial Stability

(1) The new monetary and financial law must include a provision which should explicitly indicate that the administration of the public budget and finances is to be separated from the issue of official money from now on.

(2) A reminder to the present and any future U.S. Secretary of the Treasury should be added in the same law, that monetization of credit through the Federal Reserve System or private banks in order to cover deficits in the budget or any other public expenditures is illegal and therefore prohibited as being harmful to the national economy because it causes inflation and other social inequities.

(3) The basic financial rule to conduct government business shall be first income (from its own resources or from borrowing), and then spending. This rule is derived from the concept of stable equilibrium and in application will support stability, unifying the whole body of private and public finance.

(4) Under the new financial system safe from inflationary and deflationary pressures, it will be possible, in fact mandatory, for our Federal Government, as well as for State and local governments, to conduct a fiscal policy of balanced budgets. The many forms of subsidies to agriculture, industry or other segments of the economy not justified by national interest must be discontinued after this plan is put into action, simply as being unnecessary and harmful for the nation as a whole.

(5) It is recommended that in the new system the public budget be programmed and voted upon every four years, i.e., for an entire legislative period. Thus, government activity can be planned and conducted more rationally, thereby increasing the efficiency and social productivity of the taxpayers' money.

11. The Stable Equilibrium Mechanism of the Balance of Payments

On D-day, as mentioned above, through Operations No. 1 and No. 2 the U.S. balance of payments will be cleansed of past deficits and will start with a position of equilibrium.

(1) Under a 100 per cent Numeraire-currency system and a stable structure of the banking system, including private and public finances, our government will have no problems with the balance of international payments. The mechanism of the gold-points and the flexible foreign exchange rates will constitute the first line of defense in securing a balance of payments in equilibrium, leaving the possibility of only simple, temporary fluctuations and natural adjustments.

(2) Since no internal inflation or deflation will be possible in the new regime, the second line of defense will be composed of the additional price-income-specie mechanism together with a flexible interest-rate system. This too will provide normal conditions for a fast and, in most cases, mild adjustment process so that the internal value of the dollar will be equal or close to its external value. And this is the true sign that the balance of payments of a given country is in stable equilibrium. As for the self-regulating mechanisms involved in the two lines of defense, they are well known. What is forgotten is that these mechanisms do not and cannot function normally unless the institutional framework of the internal financial system is based on 100 per cent Numeraire and the other implied conditions.

12. A Reasonable and Limited Social Reform

The United States, like other capitalist and like socialist countries, has inherited from the past social inequities which have been perpetuated from one generation to another. Similar conditions in the present continue to add new inequities or to increase existing ones.

We are aware of the economic, social and political conditions which foster social inequities. Here reference is made only to those social inequities which are associated with a reduction in the real income of a large number of people who already happen to have a low level of income. Inflation with paper money and monetized bank credit automatically reduces the real income of the many. The same effect is brought about by monopoly prices of land and other factors of production, including business, by overtaxation (direct or indirect) and every arbitrary manipulation of prices, wages and other income by the government or other institutions.

The ultimate solution to the social problem as defined above can be divided into two parts: *first,* to find a way to compensate the really poor people, in a reasonable and peaceful manner, for some of the inherited social inequities which now constitute a heavy burden upon the present generation, and, *second,* to take necessary measures so that the main causes, just mentioned, for social inequities be eradicated as soon as possible, with no chance of repetition in the future.

As far as the past is concerned, of course there is no way to correct every vestige of social inequities accumulated over many years, for the obvious reason that it is impossible to calculate such inequities for each living person. What can be done, and if successful could become a social landmark of human progress in modern times, involves a limited social reform of reasonable proportions which can be attached to Operation No. 1 of exchanging old inflated dollars for MO-dollars.

For this purpose, a certain fraction, f.i., on a graduated scale of 5 to 15 or 20 per cent of any sum in excess of a certain *minimum* level of cash and savings (measured by the average standard of living), from the amount of old dollars presented for exchange (business corporations being included in the same program) shall be temporarily blocked in a special "Fund for Social Peace and Reform." Meanwhile, during the process of exchange of old money, statistical information will be gathered to ascertain on an individual basis the exact number of those who are really poor, that is, below the above specified minim. A one-time financial aid should be granted to these disadvantaged people from the Fund for Social Peace and Reform. Of course, this social reform could be conducted on an even larger basis by adding a unique special tax on real estate above a certain level.

To consolidate the constructive and productive character of this limited social reform, two things can be added in the law:

First, the recipients of such financial aid may use it only for productive purposes, that is, for buying a home or an additional piece of land, with more or better capital equipment for those living on farms; or establishing any sort of lucrative business or workshops or buying a home for those living in urban areas. Expenses involved in sending children to professional schools should also be included in the same program.

Second, after this reform has been completed, no welfare payments in any form should be granted to persons of either sex capable of working. Thus a good portion of the giant bureaucratic apparatus of the welfare state developed in recent decades, which has not resolved but merely perpetuated the poverty problem, can be legitimately dismantled.

As far as the future of social and economic justice for the many is concerned, this plan recommends, as previously mentioned, a permanent Code of Ethics in Business, Government and Labor Organizations that will guarantee the calculation of equilibrium or fair prices in all economic and financial transactions within the country and in relation to other nations. The time of the aphorism "dog eat dog" will then be over. The temptation of executives of large multinational corporations to bribe foreign officials in order to enjoy special treatment will also come to an end.

It must be stressed that the Code of Ethics in Business should not be interpreted in any way as a new method of arbitrary government interference reminiscent of past controls and regulations. In the new system, business will be free to develop according to the needs of the people but under the basic condition of fairness to all parties concerned, that is, to avoid producing social problems. In a free and stable society and economy of tomorrow as envisioned in this plan, the institution of free enterprise is recognized as an indispensable instrument of economic progress for the nation as a whole, as long as and insofar as it satisfied the law of general equilibrium of prices, as stated earlier.

In the final analysis, a permanent Code of Ethics in Business requiring by law that all transactions be concluded at equilibrium prices, supports the realization and maintenance of general equilibrium, and thus it becomes a legitimate and necessary institution in any free, just and stable society and economy of tomorrow.

* * *

III. Final Remarks: What Are the Choices? A New Message!

We are living in a time of confusion and frustration, not only in the United States but almost everywhere in the world, with rare exceptions. As a result of substantial progress in technology based on applied science on a large scale, people, especially in America, have enjoyed the harvest of many material things which make life more comfortable. But in human affairs we have not progressed very far, and now we have reached a critical point: modern civilization and culture are at a crossroad!

The whole free world is financially drifting in diverse directions, with the danger of inevitable collisions among different national interests. Problems of internal inflations are now superimposed by an international financial crisis as an aftermath of the suspension of the convertibility of the American dollar in August 1971. Before that date the relatively freely convertible dollar performed the function of a natural parameter as Numeraire in international transactions. Having once eased this parameter out of both national economies and international markets, the dikes of inflation were broken everywhere, with no self-regulating mechanism at work.

At the international level, a committee of 20 International Monetary Fund member countries has been discussing for more than two years a possible solution to the existing crisis but without any positive results, mostly because of the stubborn opposition of economic experts used by the U.S. Government, who are notoriously against the use of gold as Numeraire. This is an incomprehensible position, in some ways a mysterious paradox of our time. If there is indeed a country in the world which benefited greatly in this century from the use of gold for monetary purposes, it is the United States.

Let us briefly examine the choices which are recommended by experts in the field to resolve the problem of inflation in the United States. As mentioned in the Introduction, the discussions at this moment are concentrated especially on three proposals which, in a way, are related to each other.

1. First, it is proposed to cut the Federal budget by about $5 billion or more and to maintain a relatively moderate but still tight money policy, with the hope that the inflationary psychology may subside in about two years. In principle, this is the point of view of the Council of Economic Advisors to the President as expressed by its Chairman, Dr. Alan Greenspan, at the opening of the White House Conference on inflation on September 5, 1974 in Washington, D.C.
2. Second, it is recommended that the Federal budget be kept at its present level but that the monetary policy of the Federal Reserve System should make "a very quick, modest move toward ease—even beyond the modest move" in recent weeks. The hope here, too, is that in "a year or two the economy would be back to some kind of normal." This is the proposal made at the White House conference by Professor Otto Eckstein of Harvard University.
3. Third, the view is that monetary and fiscal policies under the given circumstances would not work, and therefore mandatory wage and price controls are inevitable. This is an old recommendation by Professor John Kenneth Galbraith, renewed at the same conference. Recently Professor James Tobin of Yale University, in an article published in the *New York Times* (September 6, 1974), adopted the same proposal.

These three proposals have their own supporters in the economic profession in government and in business circles. But can they work rapidly, effectively and efficiently to resolve the problem of inflation and unemployment at home and the international financial crisis? There are serious doubts that by following any of the three proposals, individually or in a package, we may be able to resolve the problems in question.

None of the three proposals can work effectively under the existing framework of our financial system, because the system lacks, among other things, the natural parameter of Numeraire. The first two proposals do not offer any firm guarantee, but only a vague hope that the inflation psychology may disappear in about two years. The economic body of the nation is already under such strong inflationary and unemployment pressures that a waiting period of two years may be fatal.

The third proposal of wage and price controls seems to offer some immediate but superficial relief, since we would be more or less shooting in the dark—as no firm assurance is given that the inflation will not become a "hidden one" and that the American economy will not be faced with unwarranted shortages of certain raw materials and commodities and run the danger of black markets. Previous experience with this recommendation confirms such dark expectations.

Finally, none of the three proposals touches the problem of inevitable pressures from the second inflation of American dollars in international markets, which is now creating difficulties, not only for the American economy but also for those friendly nations which had confidence in the U.S. dollar. Consequently, we need to consider other proposals of a more comprehensive nature.

This plan offers rational solutions: first, how to clean and liquidate the present inflation at the national as well as at the international level, and, second, how to introduce a stable framework of general equilibrium. It is a contingency plan for the time when our Federal Government and members of Congress and the Federal Reserve System will become convinced that *existing policies cannot work until the existing volatile and unstable framework of our financial system has been corrected.* If there are doubts of the success of this plan in practice, the best thing to do is to conduct a controlled experiment in a small area, like the state of Rhode Island or Delaware, which is possible at any time and does not require an exorbitant amount of money. In fact, some of our large foundations, which do not pay taxes, could easily finance such a vitally important experiment for the entire nation.

The message of this plan is that "economic miracles" are still attainable—if we are prepared to undertake the necessary adequate reforms before we reach the point of no return. The realization of a new, better society based on individual freedoms, social justice, full employment, price stability and a balance of payments in order is feasible sooner than many of us may believe. It is the complete manifestation of the old American dream of a better system, here called "Social Liberalism," which leaves behind both old capitalism and new socialism as being inadequate and insufficient to resolve the major problems of our time.

The whole free world, now at an impasse, is impatiently expecting to see somewhere on the globe a concrete example of how to reach prosperity and stability without losing human freedoms and without being exposed to flagrant social inequities. This plan illuminates the way toward such a result. Will the American leaders grasp this opportunity to open the gates of a new era? We should hope so. The rest of the world can then turn to the United States for the new economic light and successful example of how to regain confidence in the virtues and blessings of a free and stable society and economy, a confidence which has wavered and in certain places has even been lost during recent decades.

Boston, Massachusetts
September 1974

Appendix

1. The Natural Law of the Equilibrium Supply of Numeraire and Price Stability

After the double inflation has been drained and a new stable financial framework has been established in the United States, a legitimate question might be raised: How does the new system work to resolve permanently the most urgent and controversial problems of price stability and full employment? The answer to the first question of price stability is: *The Natural Law of the Equilibrium Supply of Numeraire.*

The concept of natural law as used in this context is not exactly the same as the concept formulated by the classical economists. They thought an immutable order exists in human societies in the same way as does the given order in the physical universe. There is no need to review this old contention that has been disproved by history. However, the classical conception cannot be contested that in reality a *natural order* in human societies is possible but is not given. Natural order refers to *stability from within* (stable equilibrium) resulting from a specific and unique mode of arranging human institutions according to a consistent and adequate framework. This framework must first be discovered, then ingeniously designed, and finally, with proper craftsmanship, applied in practice. Classical economists have done only the first part of the job and were far from delivering a finished product.

Here natural law means a rule of general applicability derived from the structure and functioning of a *system of natural order,* designed to have stability from within. Such a system, compared with the disequilibrium of the state of affairs of today, appears plausible and desirable since it offers numerous advantages at minimum social and economic cost. Its realization requires a strong natural parameter and other basic conditions. Within this framework the course of events can be predicted by a high degree of probability, 90 per cent or above.

In an economic system of general equilibrium as presented in this plan, Numeraire is the natural parameter which is related to all other variables (prices and incomes) that may fluctuate. The possible fluctuations, however, are simple and finite, being kept under orderly control by the unique force of competition, freed from monopoly pressures through a permanent Code of Ethics in Business. There is in action here a sort of invisible law of gravitation in economic and financial affairs which leads to stability from within, or natural order.

Let us take a look at how this invisible law will work in practice under the new system. On D-day the American economy and its finances will be 100 per cent liquid. The supply of new money in circulation will be determined by the real needs of the economy, guided by the natural parameter of Numeraire, in conjunction with the other consistent elements and forces in the system.

Suppose now that after a while a significant number of Americans feel that there is too much money in circulation (official Numeraire and commercial dollars). This is a common phenomenon during a period of relatively higher prices. What can people do under such circumstances? First, they can reduce the volume of commercial dollars by demonetizing them, i.e., by converting them into the respective commodities and thus increase the supply of goods. This automatically will slow down the uptrend of the market. If that is not sufficient, the people can reduce the supply of official Numeraire by importing more foreign goods, which then appear less expensive, and paying for them in Numeraire. This will work in the same direction, i.e., not allowing a rise in prices to develop into a real inflation. The system is capable of preserving and, whenever disturbed, restoring price stability.

We should remember that at the same time that the supply of money is decreasing, it is profitable to invest new or old capital in the production of other commodities and services. In this way the self-regulating mechanism of Numeraire will be strengthened, with an end result of relative price stability without inflation and without any kind of government intervention.

At another time, these same American citizens may feel that they are more than satisfied with the current supply of consumer goods and services but that the supply of money may seem to be insufficient since prices indicate a downtrend. Then the invisible law of general equilibrium under Numeraire can resolve this unstable situation without any government intervention. In this case, the people have an option to invest new and old capital in the exploitation of gold or to produce more goods and services for export in exchange for more gold. The supply of official

Numeraire will increase automatically and the monetary downtrend in prices cannot lead to a recession, deflation or depression. At the same time the output of the standard regional commodity may be increased and monetized in form of commercial dollars. This again will work in the same direction to render the emergence of a deflation or recession impossible and thus preserve relative price stability.

The end result is that in a system of general equilibrium, the increase or decrease in the supply of money follows the real needs of the economy but without allowing the development of inflations or deflations. This is then the essence of the Natural Law of the Equilibrium Supply of Numeraire, which supports a normal functioning of a system of free markets and helps to fulfill the goal of price stability. The function of the government remains to establish such a system, to supervise it at all times in making sure that its functioning is proper according to the specified rules, and to repair the system whenever it is out of order.

2. *The Natural Law of Full Employment*

The production of the standard commodity selected to serve as official Numeraire, in our case gold, requires the cooperation of the factors of production (human and natural resources) in the same manner as during the process of manufacturing any other economic goods and services. The acquisition of the regional commodity which in the new system can be monetized in every Federal Reserve District also implies the use of an equal amount of factors of production. If so, then the *aggregate volume of employment and real income in an economy under a system of general equilibrium can never shrink* but rather will either increase or remain at the same level, depending upon the existing conditions and the wishes of the people. Under such a system, there is a complete circular flow of real income and employment between the monetary and the non-monetary sector of the economy.

Let us suppose, for instance, that for some reason there is not enough employment in the non-monetary sector of the economy, probably during a period of lower prices. Under such conditions, it is more profitable to invest new or old capital in the production of more gold (if the country has gold mines, and the United States has mines), or in the production of those commodities or services which can be exported against gold or convertible foreign exchange. Accordingly, more employment will be generated and more real income will be pumped into the economy. We should not forget also that under similar conditions it is profitable to produce more of the regional standard commodity, which in the new system can be monetized at the discretion of the people. This again will generate more employment and more real income. In the end, the harmful phenomenon of mass "involuntary unemployment"—as defined by Lord Keynes—becomes impossible in the new order of stable equilibrium.

Should conditions develop at any other time where there appears to be too much employment or real income in either of the two sectors, the new system has the flexibility and the self-regulating mechanism to allow shifting of employment and income from one sector to another without additional problems. Indeed, as mentioned above, the aggregate volume of employment and real income in an economy of this type never shrinks but always either rises or remains at the same level.

In conclusion, the natural parameter of Numeraire embedded in a system of free markets, together with an adequate framework for private and public finances, can create natural conditions for full employment and price stability in the short and long run. Full employment is there attainable and can be preserved without any direct government intervention.

Briefly, this is the *Natural Law of Full Employment* for which Lord Keynes was looking in the 1930's but could not find, since his system of thinking lacked the natural parameter of Numeraire. What he developed instead was an inverted concept of full employment based on the unrealistic assumption that a modern government can manage the supply of paper money and monetized bank credit and manipulate the public budget and taxation in such a way as to attain price stability and full employment. The U.S. experiment with Keynesian policies between 1934 and 1974, as well as the British experience over the same span of time, proves conclusively that this is not possible. The lesson from recent history is that our future policies should be directed in accordance with a better model of thinking and analysis like that of the Natural Law of Full Employment and the Equilibrium Supply of Numeraire and Price Stability.

Boston, Massachusetts,
September 1974

NOTE

1. A. Rugina, "Un Plan de Stabilisation Économique, Fiancière et Sociale de la France. Liberalisme Social," *Revue d'Économie Politique*, Paris, No. 2, Mars-Avril 1959, and "Stabilization Through Monetary Reforms," *InterEconomics*, Hamburg, No. 8, August, 1970.

5. MEMORANDUM ON THE INTERNATIONAL OIL CRISIS AND A REORGANIZATION PLAN FOR THE I.M.F. TO AVOID SUCH CRISES IN THE FUTURE

I. Introduction

1. The Nature and Causes of the Problem

The fourfold increase in oil prices over a one-year period by the international OPEC cartel has now become history. Whether this price manipulation will continue will depend upon many factors which cannot be fully assessed at this moment. Certainly this exraordinary event has caught the Western world by surprise, or as Professor Eugene Rostow of Yale put it in a recent article, at a time of "Western non-policy on oil and the Middle East." (See: Op-Ed page, *New York Times*, October 21, 1974.) The developments have shaken almost every expert in the West, not, of course, without sufficient reason when we consider that during a period of only one year an estimated $65 billion in real wealth from the United States and other oil-importing countries will be transferred to the oil-exporting cartel.

From one point of view, the OPEC policies could be envisioned as open economic piracy of the twentieth century! And a much bigger risk for the free world rests upon the possibility that if the present oil cartel strategy proves successful, then appetites may be whetted to develop international cartels for other commodities. The recent sky-rocketing in the price of sugar confirms the potentiality of such a danger. In fact, the news from Mexico City is that "20 Latin American nations, including Cuba, have agreed on establishing a cartel to set the price of sugar on the world market," as reported in the *New York Times* of November 29, 1974.

Concerning the magnitude of the problem for the United States alone, Professor Rostow, in the same article, voiced a strongly worded warning: "We are transferring wealth on a scale that is nearly unimaginable in order to buy our current requirements of petroleum for business and pleasure. In a few years, unless present trends are reversed, we shall have given over wealth equal to the total value of all securities on the New York Stock Exchange before its recent collapse—that value, that is, of the total capital accumulated in 150 years of American industrial growth. . . . Prevailing opinion, even among serious financial experts, is that we can do business as usual if only the petro-dollars generated by our balance of payments deficits are 'recycled' . . . deposited in New York,

London or Frankfurt. It is hard to believe that such nonsense can find any takers. But it does."

Many analysts have attempted to prove that this economic crisis has roots in the political environment of the Middle East. It is my contention that the Arab-Israeli conflict is not a cause of this economic crisis, but only an aggravating and coincidentally simultaneous event. If this is true, then measures aimed at political appeasement will not bring with them economic solutions.

It is rather strange that up to the moment when this memorandum is written, no serious thought has been given to the plain fact that the fourfold rise in oil prices actually matches exactly the fourfold depreciation of the American dollar in international markets, as registered in the market price of gold. This is not a simple coincidence but rather a hard economic and financial reality which must be considered in the total picture of the problem. Indeed, the official price of gold used by the member countries of the Fund is $42.20 per ounce, but the free-market price has passed $180.00 in 1974.

Reversing the coin, the decision of the OPEC countries to raise the price for oil four times was a clever action—even though embodied as an illegitimate cartel strategy!—to protect themselves against the ill effects of a new flood of depreciated U.S. paper, inconvertible dollars. The latest news on this subject is that an Economic Commission of the OPEC cartel met in Vienna and recommended that a new oil-pricing system should tie the cost of petroleum to world inflation. (See: *New York Times,* November 29, 1974). This memorandum leads to the conclusion that the international oil crisis is linked to two major factors: (1) an inflation of U.S. dollars in international markets, and (2) an illegitimate use of international cartel strategy.

2. *The Steady Depreciation of the U.S. Dollar in International Markets After August 15, 1971*

The suspension of the convertibility of the American dollar on August 15, 1971 triggered an international financial crisis which now plagues the entire free world. This event brought the I.M.F. and its member countries to inevitable difficulties. Up to that time, the U.S. dollar performed the function of a natural parameter in form of Numeraire, which helped to determine prices and claims at the international level by serving as a common denominator against which all other currencies were valued.

It was the existence of Numeraire, or freely convertible dollars, and not the Fund as such which contributed to the preservation of a relative price stability in international markets after World War II. The technical term "Numeraire" was used by Leon Walras in formulating the theorem of general equilibrium. It means that a monetary unit in order to serve successfully as a reliable and objective standard for measuring prices, incomes and claims, must be represented by a certain, constant quantity of a special commodity like gold or any other suitable product. The major point in the Walrasian theorem is that without Numeraire and a system of free markets without monopolies, it is impossible to achieve and maintain in real life a position of stable equilibrium, or one close to it.

As long as the American dollar was freely convertible at a constant rate of exchange, it held together the system of both economic and financial markets at the international level. It was not a perfect stability since the dollar was weak at home, specifically because of a growing gap between its internal and its external value. But suddenly, on that fatal day of August 15, 1971, the almighty dollar became paper money overnight, with no official backing. In other words, without any warning the U.S. dollar was converted into an "anti-Numeraire" type of currency. It is not so difficult to understand further that if only Numeraire—according to the Walrasian theorem of general equilibrium—can produce and maintain price and income stability, then any form of "anti-Numeraire," by its nature and functioning, will nurture and perpetuate conditions of disequilibrium translated into price, income and employment instability.

There is no doubt that on that dark day in August 1971 the U.S. balance of payments was in serious trouble, and the American government was facing a dilemma of two choices: (1) to clean its financial house and find a way to drain off the inflation of dollars in foreign hands and stabilize the dollar, as proposed by this author in a "Memorandum on the Serious Situation of the American Economy and Finances" of February 25, 1970, addressed to President Nixon (see Chapter II); or (2) to suspend the convertibility and temporarily freeze prices and wages in the hope that the balance of payments would improve substantially over the short run. The U.S. government took the latter, easier but uncertain road, and the expected improvements never fully materialized. Hence, today's economic problems.

In view of this analysis, it is clear that the suspension of the convertibility of the U.S. dollar in August 1971 represented a heavy blow to the Fund, which overnight was left without a natural parameter as an objective guide in international transactions. The inflation of American dollars in international markets after that date has had practically no limits, because the system was deprived of any reliable mechanism of self-control.

It is at this point that we should draw in the issue of the "oil crisis" because to a large extent it is an aftermath of the suspension of the convertibility of the U.S. dollar in August 1971.

II. Proposals Made So Far Do Not Offer a Complete and Equitable Solution to the Oil Crisis

1. National Energy Conservation Plans Are Useful but Not Sufficient

There are a number of proposals in the making to develop national programs designed to reduce the demand for oil in the consumer countries. Some of these programs are based on voluntary compliance, like the earlier American approach, and others stress the necessity of mandatory controls, like the French plan.

In addition, a new "International Energy Agency" came into existence in Paris with the purpose of insuring that, during any future crisis, available supplies of oil will be collectively administered in a pool whereby every member may receive an equitable share.

In the United States there was considerable discussion of a project called Energy Independence. The proposal was to invest $50 billion to $100 billion to make this country self-sufficient by 1985 and independent of imports from other countries. In addition to creating new inflationary pressures, such a program would mean a shift toward "economic isolationism," which negates liberalization policies fostered by the U.S. government after World War II.

All these proposals and programs on a national or international basis are useful and serve the important purpose of applying a more rational usage system to a relatively scarce raw material like oil. But they are not, and cannot be, sufficient since they do not touch the roots of the problem at hand: first, the lack of a freely convertible or Numeraire-type currency; and second, manipulation of the free-market system by the international oil cartel. Neither of these causes has much to do with the real demand for oil.

2. The Existing I.M.F. Oil Facility Useful but Not Sufficient

At the initiative of its Managing Director, the International Monetary Fund established in 1974 a Special Oil Facility Arrangement to help member countries which may have problems with their balance of payments as a result of the oil crisis. According to this arrangement, the Fund shall borrow from the oil-exporting countries (OPEC) around $3.4 billion and then lend these funds to needy countries at an annual rate of 7 per cent interest payable within a period of 3 to 7 years.

No doubt such an arrangement is useful in the sense that it can temporarily mitigate financial difficulties of a country. But, again, this arrangement does not touch the roots of the problem, and therefore cannot be considered a long-run solution.

3. *The Kissinger Plan Most Comprehensive but Still Inadequate*

On November 14, 1974, U.S. Secretary of State Henry Kissinger in a speech in Chicago outlined the most comprehensive plan to date dealing with the oil crisis. The plan had two ultimate goals: (1) to bring about lower oil prices, and (2) to protect the vitality of the national economies of the countries concerned.

The plan contains five important points, as reported in the *New York Times* of November 15, 1974:

1. To reduce oil imports by industrial nations to about 13 per cent below their current needs;
2. To develop new energy sources through coal technology, use of solar rays and uranium enrichment;
3. To stabilize the financial system by extending support to banks which are already under pressure from the impact of petroleum dollars. For this purpose a "Common Loan and Guarantee Facility" was recommended to distribute up to $25 billion in 1975 and $50 billion in 1976.
4. To create a separate "Trust Fund" attached to the International Monetary Fund for granting easy-term loans to developing countries.
5. Once this organizational setup has been completed and a strong position has been reached, a dialogue should start with the OPEC countries to reduce oil prices.

Conceptually, the Kissinger plan is not oriented toward conditions of stable equilibrium when the major forces in the system are converging toward one and the same point. Instead, its framework is a system of unstable equilibrium, where two opposing forces of equal intensity dominate. At the first disturbance the two forces will diverge from each other, and inevitaby disequilibrium will result. By the cooperative effort of the oil-consuming countries and following the spirit and the letter of the Kissinger plan, the end result, if successful, could not be more than another international cartel, or the Organization of Petroleum Importing Countries (OPIC) organized to bargain with the Organization of Petroleum Exporting Countries (OPEC). This method will not equitably settle the issue but rather sidetrack it into a bilateral monopoly where the lack of agreement through bargaining may lead to the use of political power and thus endanger the peace of the world.

In addition, the Kissinger plan, especially the application of points 3 and 4, will inevitably lead to more indebtedness of those debtor nations that are already under the heavy strain of inflation and unemployment. Under the given conditions, any further rise in external debts of debtor nations means more financial troubles in the future and thus the weakening of an already ailing international monetary system.

Finally, the Kissinger plan is not addressing itself to the problem of inflation of U.S. dollars in international markets or to the need of a restructuring of the International Monetary Fund to avoid such crises in the future. In brief, we still need to seek another alternative, free of any dismal picture of the future. The following plan attempts to offer such an alternative. It is concentrated on two specific tasks:

1. How to neutralize and, in the end, eradicate monopolistic market strategy as used by the OPEC cartel or any other similar organization, including multinational corporations; and
2. How to restructure the International Monetary Fund to be consistent with conditions of stable equilibrium with Numeraire, since this is the only reliable method to avoid similar financial crises in the future.

III. Short-Run Policies: The Revaluation of the I.M.F. Gold Stock of Member Countries at the Market Price

1. The Impact upon International Liquidity Reserves in the Short Run

This plan recommends that the gold stock of member countries of the I.M.F. be revalued immediately at a more realistic price, close to the more recent quotations in the free market, for instance—$165.00 or $170.00.

This measure will automatically increase international liquidity by approximately four times, since it is certain that almost all nations will follow the same step. Thus the financial position of the free world vis-à-vis the OPEC cartel will recapture its strength. In addition, the problem of "recycling petro-dollars" will be limited only to those nations poor in gold reserves, a situation which could be resolved more easily.

By adopting this provision, the Kissinger plan could drop points 3 and 4 and thus become more acceptable, even though still not completely adequate from the point of view of general (stable) equilibrium.

2. Does This Revaluation Not Represent a De Facto Devaluation of the American Dollar, with All the Other Known Consequences?

This is a rather complex question, but nevertheless it can be answered in principle in the negative. The U.S. dollar is already depreciated in the same proportion as the increase in the price of gold. This is only a technical operation designed to adjust the existing official figures of a nominal nature to the prevailing realities as shown in the price of gold and the uptrend of prices of other international commodities. Usually an official devaluation creates for the moment (not in the long run) some advantages for the country which devaluates its currency but only insofar as other nations do not immediately follow the same procedure. Since in this case the revaluation occurs at the same time and in the same proportion for all member countries of the I.M.F., the measure will not become a cause of harm to any nation. No legal problems are envisioned, because the U.S. dollar is not convertible anyway for the time being. On the other hand, of course, the question of stabilization of the U.S. dollar remains an issue in itself, which will be touched upon later in Part V.

3. *The Problem of "Recycling Petro-Dollars" Limited*

Once the revaluation of the existing gold stock of member countries has been accomplished, the problem of recycling petro-dollars would automatically be restricted to the developing countries which do not possess adequate gold reserves or U.S. dollars. For the short run, the existing Special Oil Facility of the I.M.F., mentioned earlier, will be sufficient to take care of this rather limited need.

As for the long run, this plan recommends in Part V that in addition to gold, other suitable international commodities be monetized under the supervision of the Fund. In this way, poorer and less-developed nations would have a chance to create their own international liquidity reserves and thus become financially independent of richer and more developed countries.

IV. *Long-Run Policies A.: The Creation of an International Code of Ethics in Business Combined with an International Court of Economic Justice*

1. *The Use of Compensatory "Economic Sanctions" Against Cartel Manipulations of Prices in International Markets*

The existence of the international OPEC cartel and the experience we have gone through indicate that it is possible in the future to encounter more arbitrary and disrupting manipulations of prices of products traded in international markets at a time when the contemporary world forces are becoming more and more interdependent.

Suppose that after the revaluation of the gold stock reserves the OPEC cartel repeats the same stratagem of raising the price of oil to compensate for their relatively weakened position. Other countries which produce certain important raw materials may follow the OPEC example when they see that it is profitable and without any risk of retribution, as is the case today.

The best and most effective solution against such disruptive maneuverings is to introduce in the I.M.F. Articles of Agreement a new provision, specifically, the application of compensatory economic sanctions against countries which make use of arbitrary manipulation of prices, regardless whether they are members or not. The economic sanctions can appear simply in form of a price surcharge for all products and services sold to the culprit countries, calculated in such a way as to compensate for the losses in the importing countries due to such arbitrary manipulations. These economic sanctions shall be applied by the members of the I.M.F. until the countries in question will give up their cartel practices.

2. *The Necessity of an International Code of Ethics in Business*

The application of compensatory economic sanctions demands further legal machinery at the international level to determine objective rules and standards on how to calculate equilibrium prices expressed in Numeraire or stable currency. An "International Code of Ethics in Business" should explicitly require that commercial transactions at the international level must be executed at equilibrium prices composed of paid or imputed wages, rent, interest (for owned or borrowed capital), taxes and a normal rate of profit equal to the opportunity cost of management and a small percentage of incentive return for innovations or improvements. There is no other reliable means of determining unfair economic practices except through such a code. This requirement of equilibrium prices would refer to both developed and developing countries, and thus the gap between rich and poor countries would be narrowed.

Certainly, the prices in international markets shall remain free and flexible in order to secure an equilibrium between effective demand and available supplies but within the limits of an equilibrium framework with Numeraire. Real problems are created only whenever the basic rule of equilibrium prices has been broken. This could happen when a country is selling a product at an artificially lower price (meaning lower than the equilibrium price), which is called "economic dumping," a practice declared illegal in many countries and punishable by anti-dumping tariffs. The recent experience with the OPEC cartel is an example of the other possible case of countries forcing upon the consuming or importing nations an artificially higher price (meaning again higher than the equilibrium price). This cartel strategy could be called "predatory pricing" or "economic plundering" in international markets.

An International Code of Ethics in Business recognized as an international law should specifically prohibit the manipulation of prices through such practices as "economic dumping" and "economic plundering" under heavy penalties applied by the rest of the concerned nations. The strict application of this code to all nations, regardless of their social system, would create a better international atmosphere nurtured by more confidence and more reliance on justice under law rather than sheer economic power as in the past. This in turn would also serve the cause of peace, which often in history has been disturbed by insoluble economic conflicts of interest.

3. *The Establishment of an International Court of Economic Justice*

In order to have a legal mechanism at the international level equipped with necessary expertise and prerogatives to decide when the Code of Ethics in International Business has been broken and what kind of penalties shall be applied, there is need for an International Court of Economic Justice. This issue has to be decided by the United Nations General Assembly in a special session called for this purpose. The proposed institution could be set up as an independent section of the International Court of Justice in The Hague, concerned with political disputes.

The OPEC manipulation of prices for oil shall be the first case tried before the new International Court of Economic Justice if the practice is repeated after the revaluation of the I.M.F. gold stock at the current price. The decision of the Court shall be binding for the parties involved. The International Monetary Fund would be a proper authority to present the case before the Court. Matters of legal procedures remain to be studied as a separate issue.

4. *The Multinational Corporations of Any Sort to Be Brought Under the Jurisdiction of the Same International Court Of Economic Justice*

It would be unfair and unrealistic to single out the monopolistic policy of the OPEC organization and leave untouched many existing multinational corporations which at one time or another have engaged in similar strategy games of economic dumping or economic plundering, depending on their own interests. It may be true that so far the multinational corporations have not applied their strategy in as extravagant a form as has the OPEC cartel. But this does not change the fact that multinational corporations and other similar international combinations able to manipulate the prices of certain products, under the disguise of "price stabilization," have the power to practice such strategy games at the expense of consumer nations.

In a world of increasing interdependence, we cannot be safe from open conflicts of interest among nations unless we have an appropriate International Code of Ethics in Business which legally prohibits price manipulations. The countries exporting oil, other raw materials or industrial products deserve no more or no less than equilibrium prices where a normal rate of return for each factor is included, if we want to have equity, freedom of trade and stability.

5. *A Reexamination of the Issue of Pure Speculation in Futures Trading of International Commodities*

So far, contemporary economists in general have accepted the view that pure speculation in futures trading is harmless and in the end helps to realize a more nearly perfect determination of stable prices in international markets. This view, however, does not seem to be consistent with perennial complaints from undeveloped countries where the commodities in question originate. The complaints are that the primary producers are cheated by artificially lower prices (below equilibrium level) determined in distantly located financial centers, like London, Paris, New York or Chicago, where they have no voice and are at the mercy of profit-oriented speculators.

Much publicity was given recently to a letter from the President of Venezuela to the President of the United States (see: *New York Times*, September 25, 1974), which complained that industrial countries have plundered the undeveloped nations by receiving raw materials at artificially lower prices over a long period and that the time has come to compensate for past economic injustices by accepting higher prices for oil. There was no hint in this letter that the injustices in question may be associated with the practice of pure speculating in futures trading. Nevertheless, if some objective merit is to be granted to such complaints, then that can be justified by reconsidering the issue of pure speculation in futures trading. Economists at the new International Court of Economic Justice would have a good issue to look into! But whatever injustice may come from pure speculation, it has nothing to do with the President of the United States. In any case, only an International Code of Ethics in Business combined with an International Court of Economic Justice as a law-enforcing agency can resolve this problem.

The letter in question could have raised another case of inequity in international trade by touching upon another subject that deserves more attention, and that is the possible injustice in the terms of trade between undeveloped and developed nations, an issue clearly observed by Friedrich List more than 100 years ago, even though his explanation may not have been sufficiently supported by adequate analysis. Economic history of the last 200 years can prove beyond a shadow of a doubt that a developing country with a soft, depreciated currency, in trading with a developed economy with hard, more stable currency, is liable to suffer the effects of relatively inequitable terms of trade. Here again the undeveloped nations may have a strong case of international inequity. The culprit, however, is not the government of the United States or any other industrial country, but rather their own weak governments which did not see in the past, and even now do not see, that it is in the interest of their own countries to have a hard, convertible currency of the Numeraire-type, both for domestic and external transactions. Hard, convertible-currency systems in both developed and developing countries can help to bring about conditions of equity, freedom of trade and stability in international markets.

V. *Long-Run Policies B.: The Reorganization of the International Monetary Fund According to Conditions of Stable Equilibrium*

1. *A Stable Framework for an International Monetary System Requires a Natural Parameter in the Form of 100% Numeraire-Currency*

Any system—in the physical universe or in human societies—in order to reach and maintain a position close to stable equilibrium must have a natural parameter, that is, a unique framework with a constant axis. The major forces in such a system, through self-regulating mechanisms, coordinate from within the motion of the subsystems or parts in such a way that possible fluctuations will be simple and finite. The adjustment process in this case takes the form of a convergence toward one and the same position of equilibrium based on stability from within.

In our physical universe, at the macro-level the sun is the natural parameter, and gravitation and electromagnetism are the forces which hold the planets and the rest of the system together in an orderly manner. In human societies, the natural parameter is not given, so in order to reach and maintain stability from within, we need to discover an adequate parameter and reinforce it through proper institutional machinery.

Exactly 100 years ago Leon Walras, in his classical standard work *Elements of Pure Economics* (first French edition, 1874), formulated the theorem of general equilibrium, which can be applied to a national economy. This theorem requires that, in order to have general equilibrium, we need (1) a system of free markets, where only pure competition is acting (monopoly being reduced to zero at the limit), and (2) the prices for both consumer and capital goods to be expressed only in terms of Numeraire-currency. Numeraire was defined as a constant quantity of a selected commodity chosen to serve as an objective monetary standard. Walras did not use the term "natural parameter," but evidently "Numeraire" in a system of stable equilibrium performs the major function of a *constant axis,* which, in conjunction with the force of competition and human desire for improvements and innovations, holds a system of free markets together. Indeed, Walras provided the proof that, given Numeraire and pure competition, possible fluctuations in prices and implicitly in incomes are reduced to simple and finite adjustments.

In all fairness, it should also be mentioned that Walras formulated the theorem of general equilibrium somehow in an incomplete fashion, since he missed pointing out explicitly that the same theorem requires that all basic elements in the economy, such as banking, financial markets and public budget and the balance of payments, be consistent with the natural parameter of Numeraire. This is not a permanent deficiency, however, since all we need to do is to extend the theorem to all other basic parts of the economy.

The experience of the International Monetary Fund between 1947 and 1974 confirms the validity of the extended Walrasian theorem in the sense that it is impossible to reach and maintain conditions of stable equilibrium without Numeraire, no matter how hard liberalization policies are pushed in trade and capital movements among member countries.

In the Articles of Agreement approved at the Bretton Woods Conference in July 1944 the new international monetary system created by that Act was defined in terms of only 25 per cent Numeraire in form of gold or in gold-convertible U.S. dollars, and 75 per cent in anti-Numeraire, national, inconvertible paper money. Since Numeraire tends to establish equilibrium and anti-Numeraire creates disequilibrium, just by looking at the proportion of the mixture, one can see that the new international monetary system established in 1944 could be viewed as an inverted pyramid which could never support and maintain conditions of stable equilibrium in the long run. By 1944 we had not yet learned the correct lesson from history: the modern gold standard failed during the storm of the 1930's for the same reason that its domestic makeup was also a mixed system (like an inverted pyramid) where the proportion between Numeraire and anti-Numeraire was even more diluted. Lord Keynes estimated the mixture in the modern gold standard as being composed of about 10 per cent gold and 90 per cent credit money.

The recent experiment with SDR's (another form of anti-Numeraire) cannot be successful, because it runs counter to the extended theorem of general equilibrium. Again we shall learn the hard way that no reliable and lasting stability is possible without having the natural parameter of Numeraire.

2. *The Division of the I.M.F. into Two Independent Departments*

In order to create the conditions needed for stable general equilibrium, this plan recommends that the International Monetary Fund be divided into two independent departments:

a. The Monetary Department of the I.M.F., or in short, Department A of the I.M.F., concerned only with the creation of international liquidity reserves for the accounts of the member countries and only in form of Numeraire.

b. The Banking Department of the I.M.F., or in short, Department B of the I.M.F., concerned only with lending and borrowing of claims resulting from current surpluses in the balance of payments of member countries or other excess reserves transferred from Department A.

In other words, Department B, dealing in short-term claims resulting from real transactions, serves only as an intermediary institution between creditor and debtor nations. The real credit involved in these transactions should not be monetized, because that would mean creation of anti-Numeraire and implicity disequilibrium.

As long as the two departments are kept strictly separated in their activities, there is no danger of international financial crises similar to those encountered presently or in the past.

3. *The Introduction of a New, International Currency Unit Called "UNICO," Fully Backed and Freely Convertible*

The international financial community needs more than ever in 1974 a new, international monetary unit, fully backed in gold (i.e., Numeraire) and freely convertible so that complete confidence may be restored in international markets.

This plan recommends that the new international currency unit be called UNICO (*U*nited *N*ations *I*nternational *Co*mmodity) and be independent from any other existing national currency. It could be defined as equal to 43.75 grains of fine gold. The official parity of the new currency would be 10 Unicos for an ounce of gold.

The present gold reserves of the member countries shall be converted into Unicos and be transferred to Department A of the I.M.F.

Basic rule: No Unicos shall be issued unless and until 100 per cent backing in gold is deposited with Department A. The Unicos, therefore, will be pure Numeraire capable of efficiently performing monetary functions in international transactions of any sort.

Immediately available funds or international liquidity reserves necessary for final settlement of differences in the balance of payments of member countries will be provided through transfer of Unicos from one account to another at Department A of the Fund.

4. *The Monetization of Other Suitable Commodities in Addition to Gold*

There are two other problems to be considered here which may have a common solution. One is a distrust in the minds of many contemporary economists who fear that there is not enough gold in the world to provide a sufficient quantity of international liquidity reserves consistent with a balanced economic development. The other is a direct concern regarding developing countries which have little reserves and no gold mines.

To a certain extent the fear of contemporary economists is justified if we refer to the mixed framework of the old gold standard, which in its internal aspect corresponded to an inverted pyramid. Such a mixed system, it is true, nurtured financial instability within a given economy, an instability which thereafter was transmitted to international markets. The end result was significant gold movements from one country to another.

In a system of 100 per cent Numeraire as proposed in this plan, this criticism and the fear itself are no longer valid. *First,* the natural parameter of Numeraire does not permit the development of a financial crisis. *Second,* the system being stable, most of the real transactions are liquidated by the use of short-term credits, so that very seldom will gold move from one country to another.

To answer positively the criticism against the use of gold as a monetary standard and also to help developing countries, this plan proposes that Department A of the Fund organize its facilities to monetize a selected group of suitable commodities, such as silver, tin, copper, or sugar, coffee, tea or wheat, under certain conditions of standardization and proper facilities of warehousing. For any deposit of such commodities in a warehouse under the supervision of the I.M.F., a special kind of Unicos shall be issued, called "Commercial Unicos." These Unicos would also be 100 per cent covered and freely convertible, however only into the specified commodity. The price of the additional commodities accepted for monetization shall be expressed in terms of Numeraire, "Gold-Unicos."

This idea of monetization of other suitable commodities in addition to gold would give the developing countries first, an incentive to expand their economies in terms of employment and real income and, second, more economic independence by providing a direct source from which to create their own international liquidity reserves instead of borrowing them from more developed economies. Once the real income in developing countries has increased substantially through their own efforts, without getting into more external debt, the gap between rich and poor nations will diminish and the volume of international trade will expand.[1]

5. *The Introduction of a New, Heavier Currency Unit to Clean the Existing Inflation in Each Member Country of the I.M.F.*

The use of anti-Numeraire in form of paper money and monetized bank credit on a large scale in every member country of the I.M.F. has produced a growing wave of rising prices which now encircles the entire globe in the form of open or hidden inflations. The traditional monetary and fiscal policies are no longer capable of dealing successfully with the problem of inflation, because we have reached a distorted set of conditions where an open conflict has emerged between the goal of price stability and full employment. In addition, a conflict has emerged between the needs of the domestic economy and the requirement of the balance of payments. This new disturbing set of conditions is often called "stagflation" and seems to be insoluble by using traditional policies.

The national economies of today are confronted with a serious dilemma. On the one hand, inflation cannot further go unchecked, since it is eroding the foundation of every free, democratic society, and, on the other hand, if we try to apply rigorously anti-inflationary policies, the social and economic pains of higher unemployment (at a time when unemployment is already high) are menacing the fabric of a society, leading inevitably to social unrest. We are caught between two evils inflicting mortal wounds to the body of contemporary society.

This plan suggests that each member country of the International Monetary Fund introduce a new, heavier currency unit over a weekend and thus drain off completely the existing inflation, without any harm to its citizens or economy. In addition, to avoid the recurrence of inflation, it is necessary to switch over to a natural parameter of 100% Numeraire-type of currency system, where credit is not monetized but limited to the volume of existing real income in the economy.[2]

VI. Final Remarks: Where Do We Go from Here?

The challenge of our time is too great to be ignored; there is so much to lose in case of failure, and so much to gain in case of success! The whole free world, in fact all humanity, is at a crossroads, facing an impasse of an unprecedented nature. The attainment of a more stable and a better world, both in the West and the East, requires new thinking in terms of conditions of stable equilibrium and bold action to convert new, better ideas into realities.

This plan is different in many respects from all other proposals, many of which are based on status-quo thinking and existing institutions. The recommendations made here can be considered a breakthrough in the stalemate of our present-day dilemma, in the face of which our leaders seem to fear new thinking and changed institutions.

History cannot be held back to wait while we give matters a second thought, as events seem to run ahead of our ability to control them. By now we should be able to recognize our present errors and those of the past by exposing and rejecting the myth inherited from the 1930's that a modern government or an international organization like the International Monetary Fund can *successfully* manage a monetary and financial system based on anti-Numeraire in form of paper money and monetized bank credit. If there is anything crystal clear and truly impressive in the monetary history of this century, it is that paper money and monetized bank credit cannot be managed in such a way as to achieve and maintain price stability, full employment, social equity in the distribution of income and a balance of payments in order. This means that we sorely need a change in both thinking and the institutional organization.

This plan offers a means to eradicate monopolistic market strategy in international markets, and anti-Numeraire in the form of paper money and monetized bank credit, which are not only nurturing permanent instability but are now endangering human freedoms and the sense of justice of equity in human activity at the national and international levels. Against the first evil, the plan recommends an International Code of Ethics in Business and the reinforcement arm of an International Court of Economic Justice. Against the second evil, it recommends a reorganization of the International Monetary Fund based on Numeraire and other conditions of stable equilibrium.

We can no longer afford to delay action and repeat mistakes of the past while hoping for miracles in the future, which under status-quo thinking and the present institutional setup will never materialize now any more than they did in the past. The time is ripe to test new approaches and to take bold actions. This is the real challenge of our days.

Let us hope that by the power of new economic and financial light the response of today's leaders will be positive and constructive in opening a new era of more freedom, more justice and more stability, the sole and best guarantee for lasting peace and prosperity to all nations and all races.

Boston, Massachusetts
November 1974

NOTES

1. For more detail on this subject of long-run measures on how to achieve and preserve financial stability in international markets, see: A. N. Rugina, "A Reorganization Plan of the International Monetary Fund as Oriented Toward Conditions of Stable Equilibrium," *Economia Internazionale,* Vol. XXVI, No. 3-4, Genova (Italy), August-November 1973.
2. For more detail on this issue, see: A. N. Rugina, "An End to the Agony of the American Dollar? A Plan for Stable Equilibrium Conditions of the American Monetary System," *Rivista Internazionale di Scienze Economiche e Commerciali,* Vol. XVII, No. 1, Padova (Italy), January 1970.

CHAPTER II

The Nixon Administration (1969-1974)

"I warned our Government in 1965 and again in 1967 that in moving away from the gold-backing of our dollar and permitting private banks to create and destroy credit-money every day in competition with each other for the purpose of making an additional profit—a phenomenon about which our people have no idea—we actually push our financial system closer and closer to the British one and thus risk a similar drama. . . .

"I am taking the liberty of writing to you since, to my knowledge, *none* of your announced economic experts (with due respect to their recognized authority in the field) has a workable and consistent solution to this basic monetary and banking problem."

From a letter to President-Elect Nixon of November 29, 1968

"I especially want to call to your attention, Mr. President, that what is 'overheated' is not the economy as such but its finances. It would be a terrible and unforgivable mistake if our Government would allow the economy really to slow down. . . . Such an approach would nurture many other problems, and, in a way, the errors of the Hoover Administration would be repeated."

From a second letter to President Nixon, dated February 25, 1970

"If nothing else can destroy American capitalism and open the door to a government-controlled economy and society, the continuation of government deficit spending and the ever increasing national debt will do it, slowly perhaps, but surely."

From an open letter to President Nixon, dated December 31, 1973

1. LETTER TO THE PRESIDENT-ELECT

November 29, 1968

The Honorable Richard M. Nixon
President-Elect
Hotel Pierre
61st Street at Fifth Avenue
New York, N.Y.

Dear Mr. President:

The newspapers recently brought the information that you have already appointed a number of task forces to investigate the various most urgent problems but I could not find one, which I think is very important, namely the position of the American dollar here at home and in the international markets.

After more careful thought given to the various issues, may I call your attention to the fact that your Administration will be a success or failure depending very much on two factors:

1. A reasonable and workable solution to end the War in Vietnam as quickly as possible; without this, it is impossible to reunite the nation, as you promised in your victory speech. I shall come back to this subject.
2. A concrete, consistent and efficient program to drain off first the double inflation of U.S. dollars at home and abroad, and secondly, to institute the necessary reforms so that this double inflation may not return in the foreseeable future.

The rather imperfect and erratic functioning of our framework in the financial system inherited from the past (private banks and the F.R.S.) is at the root and center of our troubles with the inflation at home and the chronic deficit in the balance of the international payments. Yet our professional economists debate on anything else but not this subject.

I warned our Government in 1965 and again in 1967 that in moving away from the gold-backing of our dollar and permitting private banks to create and destroy money every day in competition with each other for the purpose of making an additional profit—a phenomenon about which our people have no idea—we actually push our financial system closer and closer to the British one and thus risk facing a similar drama.

The two enclosures were brought to the attention of President Johnson but the experts in Government opposed their consideration, even though in view of what happened in recent years, I was right, from my first official warnings in 1965.

I am taking the liberty of writing to you since, to my knowledge, *none* of your announced economic experts (with due respect to their recognized authority in the field) has a workable and consistent solution to this basic monetary and banking problem, and I would not like to see your Administration begin under constant pressure of a financial crisis, whose intensity in our type of society nobody could measure in advance. To avoid such a situation, may I suggest in the most sincere and serious manner that you personally consider this problem now before you take office in January.

Far from me is the idea of looking for a position in the Federal Government when I am writing this letter. I have been serving Governor John A. Volpe now for four years, but as soon as he leaves Boston, I will be glad to go back to my teaching, research and writing.

I have something to say that has not been said about how and why the foundation of this free Republic and free society has been eroding gradually in recent decades. From my direct observation and my own studies, our nation is already deep in a period of transition, and immense forces (the most powerful being our lack of or disregard of true knowledge in economics and finance) are pushing our country in the wrong direction. My function is to warn you as I warned President Johnson that we are not, as the French say "sur la bonne voie" (on the right road), and to offer a concrete, workable and consistent solution to our financial problems at home and abroad. And our basic problem is not in the economy or in the government per se, but rather in the partially inconsistent framework in our financial system.

A large part of our people, in fact the majority, favor the free enterprise system. But very few people understand that for a free enterprise system to function normally, i.e., not only to preserve freedom but also to add more justice in the distribution of income and more stability, we need a revamping of our monetary and banking system, *not* in the direction of getting more but rather fewer government regulations after a more solid and stable framework has been secured.

First of all may I suggest that without publicity you invite 10 or 12 top economists and financial analysts in the country and let them run a dialogue with you about what is wrong in our economy and finances, and what can be done to remedy the situation. I am sure that this would be an experience very valuable to you.

My view in the dialogue is that if we do not introduce as soon as possible a new, heavier American dollar (convertible at home and abroad) in order to clean first the terrible inflation at home and abroad which has reached the stage of an iceberg full of odors of putrefaction, then under a new, more intensified pressure from the international markets, we may be forced either to devaluate and open the dike of more inflation or to suffer the consequences of a murderous deflation, like the one in the 1930's.

I would like to suggest further that you appoint a "National Monetary and Banking Commission" composed of members of Congress and others to re-evaluate our banking and monetary laws and financial institutions and make recommendations for a more stable financial system.

With my best wishes, I thank you, Sir, and remain

Very respectfully yours,
Anghel N. Rugina

Enclosures: 2

2. A SECOND LETTER TO PRESIDENT NIXON

February 25, 1970

Honorable Richard M. Nixon
President of the United States
The White House
Washington, D.C. 20500

Dear Mr. President:

Because of the important argument on the present inflation, I have prepared a Memorandum which I would like to submit for your consideration: "On the Serious Situation of the American Economy and Finances."

There are a few basic issues raised in this Memorandum which in my opinion explain why the anti-inflationary policies of our Government during the last five years have not been successful.

I especially want to call to your attention, Mr. President, that what is "overheated" is not the economy as such but its finances. It would be a terrible and unforgivable mistake if our Government would allow the economy really to slow down, as the economic indicators of the last two quarters seem to show. Such an approach would nurture many other problems, and, in a way, the errors of the Hoover Administration would be repeated. On the contrary, the economy should be encouraged by all conceivable means to increase its investments (in real terms) because the rise in production is our best deterrent against inflation until we revise our financial system.

The attention of the Federal Government should be concentrated on the financial sector, where the real causes of our troubles are located, rather than on the economy. Our monetary and banking system and the immense fever of pure speculations on the securities market are the most important factors to be considered in the fight against inflation and to improve the balance of international payments.

Also enclosed is an article just published by an Italian journal, which is pertinent to the Memorandum: "An End to the Agony of the American Dollar?" which I authored.

My best wishes for complete success in solving the present problem of inflation.

Very sincerely yours,
Anghel N. Rugina

Enclosures

February 25, 1970

To: Honorable Richard M. Nixon
The President of the United States
The White House
Washington, D.C.

3. A MEMORANDUM ON THE SERIOUS SITUATION OF THE AMERICAN ECONOMY AND FINANCES

An Attempt to Establish a Reliable Diagnosis and Some Recommendations for Immediate Action

> The only thing necessary for the triumph of evil is that good men do nothing.
> —EDMUND BURKE

I. Introduction

As Chairman of the Board of Economic Advisors to the Governor of the Commonwealth of Massachusetts between 1965-1970, it was my duty to follow closely every day not only the development of the economy in our State but also what was happening in the rest of the American economy and its finances, including the international markets and finances.

The greatest blunder in the history of American finances during this century was committed in 1965 and in 1968, when the 25 per cent gold requirement was repealed for both deposits and notes created by the Federal Reserve System. In the Annual Report to Congress on the State of the Economy of January 30, 1970, the President stated correctly that "the inflation unleashed after mid-1965 had gathered powerful momentum by the time this Administration took office a year ago." Yet no further explanation was supplied on what actually happened in 1965, which opened the dike of a cumulative inflation! That event was nothing else than the request of the Johnson Administration to Congress for repeal of the 25 per cent gold requirement for deposits created by the Federal Reserve System. This is official money which goes into the private banking system and is used as reserves for doing regular banking business in extending and expanding bank credits in the economy.

I was one of those privileged to testify before the U.S. Senate Banking and Currency Committee at that time. As a former member of the Central Bank of Rumania, with some experience and knowledge in monetary problems, I warned the Committee not to recommend the proposed bill hastily, since "*I have sufficient reason to expect that the repeal of the 25 per cent gold requirement, in part or entirety, sooner or later will create more difficulties than we have now.* In other words, neither the domestic economy will recover completely, nor will the deficit in the balance of payments disappear."[1]

What occurred thereafter happened exactly as I foresaw. We now have more difficulties than in 1965. And the many social and economic evils created by inflation in the meantime have their roots in that piece of legislation of February 1965, which unleashed the forces of financial instability in the private as well as in the public sector. At that time, in very precise terms, I warned in writing President Johnson, the Chairman of the Board of Governors of the Federal Reserve System, the Chairman of the Council of Economic Advisors to the President, and the U.S. Secretary of the Treasury that we should not proceed with such a reform because "*the 25 per cent gold requirement is a brake which introduces a very definite limit to internal inflation.*"[2] Apparently, nobody took my warning seriously.

Five years later, in 1970, a "stagnant inflation" pervaded the finances and the economy of the whole country, with distortions, gaps, waste, a maldistribution of income, and with social inequities of an unprecedented magnitude expressed in the paradox "poverty in an affluent society." We have had a negative real growth in the economy for two quarters in a row; the level of industrial production and the volume of personal income (in real terms) have declined; the housing industry is in a desperate dilemma; the outlook for business profits is questionable, and the layoff of workers begun in the automobile industry is now spreading.

The balance of international payments does not look promising either. Since 1965 we have lost one-third of our gold stock, while the total amount of claims by foreigners upon the U.S. Treasury Department (supposedly payable in gold!) has doubled. It has just been announced that during 1969 we had a record of $7 billion deficit in the balance of payments.

This is not an encouraging picture of our economy, especially not in a year of Congressional elections. In my humble view it is high time to take a good look and evaluate the real situation. How good are our traditional tools of monetary and fiscal policies? Did they work in recent years? Are we satisfied with the given results?

We know by now too well that the imposition of the 10 per cent surcharge tax in June 1968, the last two increases of the official discount by the Federal Reserve System, and the open market transactions of the Fed not only have not dampened but, on the contrary, have intensified the stagnant inflation. The economic body of the nation no longer responds positively to the given medicine of monetary and fiscal policy. There must be something wrong which did not exist before. Indeed, as I mentioned earlier, the new element or microbe which has unleashed the forces of inflation is the paper-credit dollar let completely loose after 1965. As a result, nobody knows exactly where these invisible forces may lead us, since with a financial apparatus lacking definite brakes, a national economy is running wild in a sort of vacuum full of vicious circles and surprises.

I do not want to see the Nixon or any other Administration hit by a formidable shock or a facing up to an unmanageable situation. Playing the game of "wait and see" and applying "stop-and-go" type policies seem to be outdated for the kind of cumulative problems that we have today. The moral obligation of helping my adoptive country in whatever way I can has prompted me to write this Memorandum, which I hope will be of some value to our government and compensate for the frustrations I had with the previous (Johnson) Administration.

II. Diagnosis and the Most Pressing Problems

1. Not the American Economy but Its Finances Are Overheated

The relationship between the economy and its finances is somehow overlooked in the debate on the present-day inflation. Very often we read in the papers or we hear in lectures that "the economy is overheated," a statement that is not quite correct, scientifically. Actually during a prolonged inflation it is *not* the economy but its finances which have a fever. Indeed, the economy under such conditions is a sort of passive body which suffers from innumerable distortions and gaps, inflicted by the instrument used to make and evaluate decisions, that is, the monetary standard, or in our case the dollar—which is no longer reliable. The paper-credit dollar, especially after 1965, is rapidly depreciating in a zigzag fashion and faster than the time needed to make the necessary adjustments, in decisions such as investments and the division of the current income between present consumption and future needs or savings. The place where we can really see the overheating is in the immense volume of pure speculations in the securities market and in the fluctuations of the rates of interest in the money market. But this is happening in the channels of finance, where I think the major reason for our troubles lies today, and not in the body of the economy.

It makes a big difference whether in evaluating the problem of inflation we put the accent on the economy (the passive body) or on the financial aspect (the active element). In point of my observation there is nothing wrong in the economy judged in real terms, except the perennial struggle between big labor unions and big business executives as to who is to get the lion's share from whatever extra profits exist. If the American dollar were stable or made stable, there would be only normal, legitimate profits (equal to the cost of management), but no extra profits; thus the argument between unions and business could be settled peacefully. But this is secondary to the problem here under discussion.

If we want to resolve the problem of inflation we have to focus our attention on the finances and not on the economy as such. Indeed, *it would be a grave mistake with incalculable consequences for the present and the future, if we were to think and act with the hope that a reduction in the volume of investments (conceived in real terms), and consequently an increase in the rate of unemployment, could restore financial stability and a balanced rate of economic growth.* Such a course of action seems to me to be not only erroneous in principle but in practice a kind of Pandora's box, actually an invitation for more woes similar to those faced by the Hoover Administration in the early 1930's, but this time loaded with social dynamite. Leave the economy in peace and concentrate on immediate action in the financial field, as will be shown below, or do anything conceivable to preserve and increase the volume of investments (in real terms) until the financial problem created by the use of the paper-credit dollar has been solved.

2. *The Paradox of the Phillips Curve Not Applicable for Resolving Our Problem*

The younger generation of economists who learned only "new, Keynesian economics" are trapped by the paradox of the "Phillips curve," which, if interpreted literally, shows that our lives in the West are boxed into a strange contradiction in the capitalist system. The now famous Phillips curve indicates that a free, capitalist country faces a social dilemma in the sense that it has no other choice but to decide between having (1) a continuous inflation with maximum growth and high employment, or (2) no inflation, i.e., stable prices but with a lower growth and high rate of unemployment. The paradox exists because there appears to be no choice in seeking a way to escape from the dilemma expressed in the Phillips curve. The only road available is to choose between two evils—one economic (inflation) and the other social (unemployment). Here is a rather harsh destiny for Western society, if things really are so, as many prominent Keynesian economists in the country seem to believe.

Here is an example of thinking and a conclusion derived from the use of the Phillips curve and the "New Economics." Professor Paul A. Samuelson of the Massachusetts Institute of Technology has publicly asked, "How can President Nixon end the inflation?" He added to his question: "Let the answer be given, loud and clear, at the beginning: President Nixon cannot end the current inflation. All that he can hope to do is (1) keep it from growing worse, and (2) contrive a gradual slowdown of the economy's growth that will bring the 1969 rate of annual price increase of 5% down by the end of 1970 to 4%."[3]

If this be so, then the Nixon Administration and the economy at large has little choice but to suffer economic and social ills, since that is what the Phillips curve shows. But the author of this Memorandum thinks that it is not so, in the sense that the Phillips curve cannot be used as a guide to solve our problem. We do have some good policy options as soon as we free ourselves from the model of thinking inherited from Keynes, which now dominates, almost exclusively, the academic circles of this country.

In the original construction of the Phillips curve, the father of this tool of analysis, Professor A. W. Phillips, did not include in his model "the cost of living adjustments in wage rates," that is, the fluctuations due to changes in the value of the monetary standard, since his whole research was based on "money wage rates," and he thought—as he explicitly pointed out—"that cost of living adjustments will have little or no effect on the rate of change of money wage rates."[4]

In other words, the Phillips curve *does* exist, but only in a model where we assume a shaky monetary standard with wild fluctuations in value and cost of living, as, for instance, during an inflation in a system where paper-credit money prevails. But if we assume another model with a stable monetary standard (100% "Numeraire" as defined by Walras), that is, a currency convertible both at home and in foreign markets, then the Phillips curve simply does not and cannot exist. Under conditions of financial stability of the Walrasian type, technological innovations will bring a slow and gradual decline of prices, an increase of real income, higher consumption and capital formation based on voluntary savings, and, therefore, higher production and a gradually increasing volume of employment. There is no trace of the Phillips curve and the awful contradiction implied by its application if we make a decision to shift from the present unstable paper-credit money system into a financial setup which proves to have a stable equilibrium (in the

Walrasian sense). This, however, is not possible unless we restore conditions of unrestricted convertibility of the dollar at home and in the international markets.

3. *The Inflationary Psychology is Not a Cause but an Effect*

Often we hear statements that the causes of the ills of the inflation are in the people's minds, the so-called "inflationary psychology." Even the present policy of monetary restraint by the Federal Reserve System is associated with the goal of "beating the inflationary psychology" once and for all to the ground. Consumers, especially housewives in various parts of the country, are trying hard to hold down purchases, with the noble purpose of fighting inflation and supporting the President of the United States in the same struggle. This goodwill of the people is in fact based upon an illusion, as long as the monetary unit—the dollar—continues to depreciate every day, every hour of the day, as the result of an incessant increase in the supply of bank credit money which escapes from the indirect control of the F.R.S. to a significant degree. The roots of the inflation are not in the price system, which in itself is an instrument, like a mirror, where the motions of the real forces are registered and evaluated.

The real forces on the market come from producers and consumers, and their behavior will depend upon the form of the market (competition, monopoly, oligopoly, and so forth) and the financial conditions. Under conditions of stable equilibrium when official money is the 100 per cent Numeraire-money of Walras, or "neutral money," the behavior of both consumers and producers is *normal* in the sense that the effective demand for consumer goods and the effective demand for investment have the same Marshallian curve with a negative slope. We then have no problem.

Under conditions of financial disequilibrium or unstable equilibrium due to the use of paper-credit money, which automatically produces an inflation, the normal behavior of both consumers and producers changes into an abnormal one, in the sense that the same effective demand for consumer goods and for investment receives a positive slope. Indeed, during an inflation the consumers demand increases with rising prices, and the demand of business for investment rises when interest rates jump. This is exactly what has been happening in the United States, especially for the last five years. This phenomenon has no name but it could be represented, for the time being by what may be called inverted or non-Marshallian curves.

In any case the roots of the inflation are not in the minds of the people but in the financial system whenever official money is not 100 per cent Numeraire. In other words, whenever an inflation becomes persistent it generates conditions that force the people (regardless of whether they are consumers or producers) to change their behavior from normal to abnormal. The rationale is logically correct and the judgment of the people is sound. What is wrong lies in the financial system, which lacks a reliable monetary standard.

4. *The Monetization of Public Debt an Evil and a Great Danger for the Future of Any Free Society*

In this country we have not had a serious debate on the consequences of an ever-rising national debt. A single known economist, Professor James M. Buchanan, in his book *Public Principles of Public Debt* (1958), has questioned the Keynesian interpretation that there is no danger in the accumulation of public debt. But his book has received little attention from other professional economists. Yet a great issue is at stake in this subject. And probably the first mistake in the Nixon Administration was to ask Congress during the first month in office to raise the ceiling of the national debt by $12 billion, even though there was an excuse in the fact that this was inherited from the previous administration.

Why is national debt accumulation an evil, and what is the danger for any free society in the future? Under our present financial setup, national debt is monetized through the medium of private banks with the help of the Federal Reserve System. This is one major source of inflation with which we are now struggling desperately.

What is the danger for the future? At the end of World War II the national debt stood at around $200 billion. During the same generation this debt has increased to $377 billion, and this happened in a time of prosperity which enjoyed the longest boom in our economic history. Since 1929 the G.N.P. has increased by 9 times while the national debt has increased by 23 times. This growth in public debt cannot be considered normal. The danger is that, if it is continued unchecked, then one day the Federal Government will not be able to pay back anything, not even the interest. Since the Government cannot be declared bankrupt there would be no alternative but to nationalize the banks, including the people's savings, and other industries.

The situation speaks for itself. We have already reached the point where around $115 billion of the national debt is maturing each year. Since the U.S. Treasury is not in the position to pay any significant portion of this annually maturing debt, then, with the help of private banks supported by the F.R.S., this debt is refunded or postponed. Consequently, the cost has now reached the staggering amount of $15 billion per year just for interest. In the overall budget, the cost to service the national debt has become the second biggest item after national defense. But this is not all. *In the seventies we are approaching conditions when bigger and bigger chunks of the national debt will mature, and this in turn will exercise more and more pressure upon the money market; thus the interest rates will rise and the cost of servicing the national debt will mount.*

If we really want to stop inflation, the Federal Government must introduce a bill asking Congress to prohibit any further monetization of debt and to accept a gradual amortization of the existing debt over a period of time, e.g., 25 years, as a part of the annual budget. That would mean a significant release in the pressure on the money market, and the interest rates inevitably will go down, opening a new era of normal conditions in the public sector.

5. *The Monetization of Private Debt as an Evil and Great Danger for the Future of Any Free Society*

Very often we find in leading financial newspapers or in talks given by bankers or business executives the opinion that our Federal Government is the sole culprit in producing the present-day inflation, specifically by allowing deficits in the budget. If this reasoning were correct, the problem of inflation could and should be solved simply by balancing the government budget. But we know that simply balancing the public budget is not sufficient to solve the problem of inflation. It is certain that the Federal Government shares a responsibility for the present inflation, but is not the lone guilty party.

The other bigger source of the existing inflation lies in the monetization of debt for private purposes. When this is done to increase production, there appear some good results to mitigate the social harm. But when it is used to finance pure speculations in the securities market, there is only more social harm and the benefit of additional profits for a minority of speculators and other vested interests in the banking system.

I want to make it crystal clear that there is no question here of attacking our banking system, as do some radical thinkers in accusing bankers of being a part of the Establishment which controls and manipulates our society and economy. Having worked in a bank, I know how indispensable are the services of banks in a modern, civilized society. In their functions of administration and serving customers, American banks are without equal in the whole world.

My argument is that I question the wisdom at the foundation of our banking structure—namely, the laws regarding both private banks and the Federal Reserve System which are based on the fractional reserve principle of banking. I think both are very weak today since they are creating problems for our society and economy (specifically the existing inflation, with all the social and economic troubles at home and difficulties in the balance of payments) without being able to solve those problems correctly and in an equitable manner. I do not recommend diminishing in any way the independence of the Federal Reserve System. But what is the use of that independence if the Federal Reserve System —under present-day conditions—cannot control the supply of bank credit money in such a way as to have an equilibrium supply of money with no inflation and no deflation? If they had the formula or the technique, the F.R.S. would have applied it, at least during the last five years! As a former central banker I suspect, or, more truthfully, I *know* that the F.R.S. has no formula for calculating the equilibrium supply of paper money and credit monetized by private banks; therefore, their efforts to apply monetary policies in order to stop inflation are both useless and meaningless. If the Federal Reserve System were challenged in a court of justice on how they justify the prerogatives with which they are entrusted by law (to defend the stability of the dollar), I am afraid the F.R.S. would lose the case!

I do not condone further in any way the idea that the big banks have to be nationalized or propose to apply more controls on banks than we already have. None of our problems of today would be solved by nationalization; rather more grievances would be created. On the contrary, I want to see our private banking system enjoy the highest degree of independence which is consistent with the general requirement of social justice in not producing any harm either to the economy in whole or in part or to society. What I have in mind is to create that financial structure which helps the economy to reach conditions of stable equilibrium and full employment in the short as well as in the long run. This in practice would mean fewer banking controls and regulations than today.

The private banks of today, with the help of the F.R.S., are actually to an extent of 85 per cent *Issuance Banks,*—that is, private financial institutions which create money in the form of *pure bank deposits* as part of their lending business in competition with other banks and for the purpose of making an extra profit. These pure bank credits are covered by a small fraction of official money (reserves), which since 1965 means covered by nothing, because "official money" after the changes from 1965 to 1968 means empty figures in the books of the Federal Reserve System. No other institution in the country, not even the Federal Government, may conclude a contract of business without having the full amount of money. Yet commercial banks may grant a loan by having only a small fraction of the respective amount (the required reserves of an average 10 to 15%) and creating the missing difference of 85 to 90% in form of additional pure bank deposits. In this way, private banks for every additional $1 of reserves can and, under favorable conditions, do create $7 to $10 more. This is the *miracle* of modern banking through the *monetization of private and public debt.* But this is also a great social and economic evil because it initiates and spurs the forces of inflation. In turn this produces much social and economic harm and suffering to millions of innocent and industrious people who have no guilt except that they are at the bottom of the social scale. Obviously the banks realize an additional profit and extra financial power, which are not justified by performance. In the long run I believe it is in their own interest for bankers to study this problem and cooperate to find a solution fair to all concerned.

If we really want to stop inflation and restore stable equilibrium for both domestic economy and the balance of international payments, then, among other things, Congress should be prepared to pass a *Law for Social and Economic Justice* prohibiting monetization of public debt as well as private debt. This is the only equitable solution I can see to the conflict of interest between the banking practice to "monetize debt" and the social harm inflicted upon society through the ill effects of inflation.

Such legislation, by the way, would have precedence in modern history. During the eighteenth century, private banks printed their own money in the form of banknotes, which were put into circulation through lending business exactly as is done today with bank deposits. The British economist David Ricardo first observed that when private banks issued banknotes in competition with other banks, they automatically created conditions of a recurring inflation, with difficulties not only for the domestic economy but also for the balance of international payments. During the Napoleonic wars, due to a heavy loss of gold, Great Britain was forced to suspend the convertibility of the pound through the Bank Restriction Act of 1797. There was much discussion then of how to stop the loss of gold, and many were proposing to introduce controls of foreign trade and impose a gold embargo. Finally, Ricardo came up with the explanation that the loss of gold was due to the internal inflation produced by private banks which were free to issue notes in competition. Ricardo should get the credit for having observed first a "social evil" in the freedom of private banks to print their own money.

After a heated and prolonged argument on this subject between the followers of Ricardo (called the "Currency Principle") and the opposing view (called the "Banking School") during the first half of the nineteenth century, the British Parliament was finally convinced to pass the Robert Peel Act of 1844, which prohibited private banks from issuing notes. The European countries followed the British solution.

In the United States we had the same problem with private banks printing their own banknotes. The U.S. National Banking Act of 1863-65 tried to solve this problem by introducing a special tax of 10% on any private bank which wanted to continue the issuance of banknotes, with the exception of U.S. National Banks, which were put under government control in respect to capital and the privilege of issuing notes. Since this

10% tax was higher than the prevailing rates of interest in the market at the time, the provision of this law in reality meant a prohibition on the issuance of notes by private banks.

The theory of credit-money, however, was not yet well enough developed to allow people to see that banknotes were just one form of "monetization of debt" and that other forms might be possible, to which the private banks might shift as soon as the first form was prohibited. This is exactly what happened. Private banks in England, Europe and the United States bowed before the new legislation, but at the same time they gradually shifted to the issuance of bank deposits by popularizing the use of checks in the course of the same lending business as before. How important theory and science are for the correct solution to problems in real life can be seen in this particular case. The concept of credit-money was incomplete at the time. Consequently, the good purposes of the banking laws of the nineteenth century, prohibiting private banks from issuing their own money, never materialized because private banks continued to do the same thing under a different cloak. We are now suffering again from the ills of the same inevitable inflation produced through this old practice by private banks: "monetization of debt," regardless of what technique is used. But this practice must terminate, according to the requirement of "social and economic justice," which no longer can be ignored in the twentieth century.

The reform in question should not be viewed as the disbanding or neglect of banking business but only as the end of the malpractice of allowing banks to create their own money. In any case, the function "of issuing money" belongs by definition to the central bank, that is, to the Federal Reserve System, and should not be appropriated by any other institution, private or public. Such a reform would actually restore the Federal Reserve System to its proper functions.

There is enough business left for private banks in a modern, civilized society. Private banks could continue to administer a system of private credit granted specifically by private business but not to monetize it as they do today. If a given firm wants to grant credit up to a certain amount, this information could be channeled to a bank and the bank could be entrusted with selecting the customers who merit such credit. The point is that in this new order the banks would not monetize "bank credit" but would only be intermediaries between business and customers. The difference between the practice of today and the new method is enormous. With the new method, "credit" granted by business (direct or through the banks) would not change the supply of official money in circulation, and therefore we would not have the phenomenon of inflation. Today such credit goes into the banking system, and it is immediately monetized in form of additional bank deposits, which automatically fuel the machine of inflation.

The drawing of checks in official money would be restricted only to persons who really have a deposit in a bank, and the respective bank would be required by the new banking law to hold such deposits 100% covered in official money at all times. When a customer puts his money in a checking account in a bank, he does so because he knows that he has bills to be paid and will issue checks in the same amount. Thus reducing the balance, he will use his current income to replenish his balance. Since the bank will hold his account 100% covered in this new order, the supply of money in circulation will not be changed, because checks put into circulation by paying current bills will just match deposits of real income. In addition, this new rule would render impossible the phenomenon of a "run on the banks," which during crises of confidence creates great financial calamities in a country.

Under this new system of banking, the money market would be separated from the capital market, eliminating another problem of today's financial setup. Once the money market has been separated from the capital market, we enter into the territory of true financial stability. This is because the money market retains its proper function of supplying immediately available funds for liquidity (financial stability), while the capital market would perform its proper function, i.e., to supply medium- and long-term funds for investment purposes (economic growth and full employment).

6. *The Pure Speculation in the Securities Market as an Evil and Great Danger for the Future of Any Free Society*

This is probably the most sensitive and provocative subject in finance, since professional economists and people in general think that the Securities Exchange Act of 1934, and its reinforcement through the Securities and Exchange Commission, is probably the best arrangement we could have in a free country to avoid abuses and develop an orderly market in securities. Now it is true that the kind of abuses which existed in the market before the law of 1934 are today illegal and punishable by harsh penalties. Yet, in recent years, hardly a week has passed without a report in the *Wall Street Journal* and in the financial pages of daily papers that this or that well-known firm—with a reputation in the market—has been suspended for a given time from trading because of a violation of the law. These occurrences are a part of the *fever of speculation* which has dominated the market during the last two decades, in a situation similar to the experience of the 1920's, with the difference that this time the speculation is on a much larger scale. The brokerage firms cannot even cope with the administrative task of handling the paperwork associated with this giant speculative activity in the market.

The immense volume of trading for purely speculative reasons not only requires a mountain of paperwork but at the same time ties up a huge amount of funds which otherwise could be used in the economy for productive purposes. The phenomenon of higher and higher rates of interest, which has become a calamity for our government and economy, is associated with the ever-increasing demand for funds for speculative trading in securities and commodities. This in turn has something to do with our financial organization, where the money market is not separated from the capital market and ultimately with the fractional reserve principle of modern banking.

The social evil associated with *pure speculation* cannot be seen unless we understand the basic difference between two entirely different types of transactions which take place daily in the securities and commodities markets, both on the organized exchanges and the over-the-counter market.

1. The first is the common or regular kind of trading, where people who save some money want to invest it in some good stock or in bonds. The object of business in this case clearly is an actual or real buy of securities for investment purposes. On the other hand, the sellers dispose of these securities because they want cash for liquidity reasons. The effective demand for securities in this type of real trading can be represented in the language of a professional economist by a normal Marshallian curve with a negative slope.
2. The second type of trading is entirely different, in the sense that the object of business is no longer a real purchase but a nominal transaction, in reality a bet on a future price fluctuation.

Indeed, an "order to buy" put through a brokerage firm in this case is *not* the result of a plan or intention to make an investment in that security but rather a bet on that security—namely, that its price will go up and in the course of an immediate liquidation (sale) a "differential profit" would be realized. This is what the broker calls "to take a position" in a given security, which usually is the part of a bullish speculator. Conversely, an "order to sell" does not necessarily mean that the security is available in real terms and that the seller wants cash for liquidity purposes. In the second case an "order to sell" means that somebody wants to bet that the price of the respective security will fall, and consequently in the course of an immediate liquidation (purchase) he would realize a "differential profit." This is called by brokers "to get out of a position," which usually is exercised by a bearish speculator.

These are "pure speculations," actually nominal transactions or "as-if" type of trading which is conducted for the sole purpose of achieving a *differential profit.* Now where is the "social evil" in pure speculations? In using the language of a professional economist, the effective demand for speculative trading or for taking positions, an activity that has nothing to do with investment, can be represented only by a non-Marshallian or inverted curve which has a positive slope. On a bullish market, the higher the price of a given security (thinking in general of stock), the bigger the demand for bets to speculate in that security. But this is the characteristic similar if not identical to the abnormal behavior of consumers during an inflation when the demand curve also has a positive slope, as was mentioned earlier. Conversely, the curve representing the supply of bets by the bearish speculators, that is, orders to get out of a position, must have a negative slope, which again is equivalent to the abnormal behavior of producers in a prolonged inflation.

Under this set of conditions where pure speculations are free of any controls, and inverted or perverted curves of abnormal behavior prevail, we can never have a position of stable equilibrium in the securities market. Under conditions of stable equilibrium, fluctuations of prices are simple and finite. In our system of today, however, the price fluctuations of securities are cumulative and indeterminate, which is a characteristic of disequilibrium conditions similar to the price fluctuations of commodities and services during the business cycle phenomenon. The pure speculations are the real reason for the known gap between the "book value" and the "trading value" of a stock. In conclusion, here lies the explanation of why the prices of securities in a market presupposed to be free like ours in reality are artificially higher during a boom and artificially lower during a depression. During a boom the bullish speculators are stronger than the bearish speculators, and vice versa during a depression.

It is now clear that in *pure speculations,* which at first glance seem to be harmless, there is in fact a great "social evil" and danger for the future of any free society. Professional economists have missed the problem that in the securities market there are two entirely different types of transactions and that pure speculations represent abnormal forces which convert or induce a normal behavior into an abnormal one, represented by a demand curve with a positive slope. *First* of all, artificially higher or lower prices in the securities market have an inevitable adverse effect upon the economy in connection with booms and depressions where millions of innocent people are suffering the ill effects of an inflation or of a deflation. *Second,* an enormous amount of funds is always tied up in these pure speculations, whereas otherwise a large part of it would be used in a productive manner. *Third,* pure speculations offer an unfair opportunity to get rich through a kind of organized or *institutional gambling* which is not healthy for a free society, where a useful performance alone should be the basis of a normal accumulation of wealth, if the social question is to be avoided.

Such avoidance poses a wearisome problem because in our country people think that to make a buck or a million by "playing the market" is a part of our personal freedoms, even though, evidently, this is a misinterpretation, since the public at large is not aware of the *social evil* involved here and described above. Thus the first thing to do is to allow or induce economists and sociologists to argue pro and con about the nature of this social evil. Second, we do not even know exactly in a given day just how much trading was composed of "normal" transactions and how much were "pure speculations," because the architects of the Securities Exchange Act of 1934 were not aware of this problem. Therefore in accordance with the letter of the law there is no difference between the two.

To know the real magnitude of the problem, Congress should be convinced by the Administration in power to pass an amendment to the Securities Exchange Act ordering that pure speculations be separated from normal transactions. Standards have to be worked out for a delineation between the two types of transactions. One point could be to require that whenever someone put in an order to buy, he or the institution in question must take the security and pay the full price. When the order to sell is made, he or the institution must have the security in real terms and receive the full price. This and other conceivable measures could reduce the fever of speculation that is now plaguing the market.

Why should the betting on stock be prohibited when gambling activity is allowed in horse and dog races? Why should it be different with a bet on a given stock? The reason is at hand. The betting on horses and dogs does not change the price of a horse or a dog. The betting on securities, on the other hand, changes their value. Indeed the price of securities is determined by the relationship between the amount of bets that the price of the respective security will go up (bullish speculators) and the amount of bets that the price for the same security will go down (bearish speculators). When the group of the bullish speculators is stronger than the other group, the price for that security will go up regardless of the real situation of the corporation or of the economy at that particular moment, and vice versa when the bearish group is stronger. To have a really "orderly market" of securities with the possibility of equilibrium prices, we have to prohibit pure speculations in the organized securities and commodities markets as well as in over-the-counter markets.

7. The Main Culprit Is the Paper-Credit-Money System Embedded in Modern, Speculative Banking

The fever of "pure speculations" in the securities market as well as in the organized exchanges for commodities probably would not have assumed the proportions of becoming a social evil, as we know it in modern times, if the monetary system had been kept separated from the private banking system, or if the banking system (both private and central) had not been organized on the fractional reserve principle.

The greatest illusion as well as disillusion in the history of modern finances was the so-called "modern gold standard," which had two faces. At the international level it was 100% gold because gold could circulate freely from one country to another, and it was the sole international currency which was used to settle foreign claims in a definite and ultimate manner. At the domestic level, however, because of the application of the fractional reserve principle, incredible as it may sound, the same modern gold standard was diluted in a proportion of 80 to 90% credit money. This mixture of two bipolar types of money (gold money and credit money) caused us to succumb to the financial disaster of 1929-1934. The reason is that the use of credit money in a system of free markets creates conditions in which the inevitable inflation changes the normal behavior of consumers and producers into abnormal reactions as shown earlier.[5]

The Federal Reserve Act of 1913 was deficient in introducing a 40% gold standard at the central bank level without any concern that in a system of free markets gold money has a normal behavior, whereas credit money has an abnormal behavior in the sense that it is the culprit creating disequilibrium conditions. In 1945 a monetary amendment to the Federal Reserve Act reduced the 40% gold requirement to 25%, which meant a weakening of the already precarious foundation of the official dollar. The amendment of 1965 and 1968 repealed the requirement of 25% gold altogether; thus we have reached a monetary system based on 100% paper-credit money, a small portion of which, i.e., about 10-15%, is being issued by the Federal Reserve System and 85 to 90% issued by private commercial banks.

Where could this 100% unstable monetary system lead in view of the experience after World War II and especially that of the last five years? *Are we not courting a financial collapse or a government-controlled and -manipulated society in the next decade, ushered in by our inability to cope with the given financial and social problems?* If we might slip into a Stalinist type of society, why should we waste a vast amount of resources and sacrifice American lives fighting a supposed evil in distant foreign countries when here at home the same evil is nurtured and flourishes, gradually introducing a government-controlled society and economy? It just does not make sense! There is then a contradiction between what we do at home and what we recommend to other friendly nations abroad.

The truth is that we have problems of financial instability and lack of sufficient social justice in the distribution of income and wealth which we have not been able to solve up to this moment. The obstacle which barricades our efforts to solve these problems lies, I believe, in the use of an artificial monetary standard composed of a 100% paper-credit money. As long as we continue to maintain this artificial monetary standard, there is no hope for financial stability or social justice, and—who knows?—in the end we risk losing even the liberties which we now take for granted.

8. *The Federal Reserve System Lacks the Means and the Possibility to Control the Supply of Paper-Credit Money Efficiently*

The crux of the matter is in the question: Does or does not the Federal Reserve System have the means to calculate the equilibrium supply of paper money and monetized bank credit for the whole United States at any given time, and therefore have the ability successfully to exercise the prerogatives entrusted by law in order to defend the stability of the U.S. dollar at home and in international markets? If we were actually able to compute this magnitude with mathematical precision, we would know at the present time, for instance, how great the intensity of the existing inflation is, i.e., how large is the surplus of purchasing power in dollars at home and in foreign markets that has to be withdrawn in order to restore a balanced growth in the domestic economy and an equilibrium in the balance of international payments.

It is true that the Federal Reserve System has a number of tools, such as regulation of the official discount, the legal reserve requirements for member banks, the margin requirements for speculations in the securities market, and every other week the open-market transactions with the opportunity to sell or buy government securities, thus decreasing or increasing the supply of money in circulation. These tools, plus a number of other regulations, are the instruments for applying what is called "monetary policy."

What are the results of the monetary policy conducted by the Federal Reserve System, for instance, over the last five years (1965-1970) since the new forces of inflation have been launched, as the 1970 Economic Message to Congress by the President pointed out? I do not happen to take for granted that what the *New York Times* or any other major newspaper or magazine says is true merely because it was printed there. But the following quotation from an editorial in the

Times seems to be quite relevant to the problem under discussion: "*Fiscal and monetary restraints* have caused industrial production and housing to fall, pushed interest rates to record levels, and halted economic growth; but *they have not stopped inflation. On the contrary inflation has accelerated.* Consumer prices have risen 6 per cent in the past year compared with 4.7 per cent in 1968 and 3 per cent in 1967. Prices of crude industrial materials have increased by 11 per cent in the past year compared with less than 2 per cent the year before."[6] (Italics added.)

Although I do not want to appear intrusive or discourteous with the Chairman of the Board of Governors of the Federal Reserve System, Dr. Arthur F. Burns, I do think the American people need and deserve a very precise answer to the question raised above. It may be embarrassing for Chairman Burns and the distinguished members at the Board of Governors of the F.R.S., but for our country it is imperative to know the truth. And the truth is the sad story that the Federal Reserve System cannot control the supply of credit money in such a way to maintain conditions of stable equilibrium with full employment and price stability in the economy. This author warned the former Chairman of the Federal Reserve System, William McChesney Martin, as far back as 1965 that the System was not in a position to exercise monetary policy for economic stability as members of Congress and the public in general assume, but he did not heed this warning.

After five years of waiting I would like to present the same question as a challenge to anyone concerned, not only to the F.R.S. but also to the Council of Economic Advisors to the President, to the U.S. Treasury Department and to the many places in the country where economic and financial research is conducted on a continuous basis. The question, to repeat, is: *Can we calculate the equilibrium supply of paper-money and monetized credit for the whole country at any given time in such a way that the economy and the balance of payments are under conditions of stable equilibrium?* The professional economist knows further that this equilibrium supply of money has to be consistent with a number of other basic requirements such as a balanced division between the investments in the production of consumer goods (I_a) and the investments in the production of capital goods (I_b); that the new investments have to coincide with the aggregate of capital formation based on voluntary savings (personal and business, including government budgetary surpluses) conceived as an *ex ante* phenomenon; and that the prices of consumer goods $x_1, x_2, x_3, x_4 \ldots x_n$ as well as the prices for capital goods $y_1, y_2, y_3, y_4 \ldots y_n$ have to be equal to the least cost per unit of production. These are true equilibrium prices composed of the cost of the factors (nature, labor, capital, management and social organization or government) and computed at the point where the available human and natural resources are used to the optimum, where the marginal utilities of all factors are equal and where full employment with the highest possible real income per capita is achieved.

In accordance with my observations the magnitude of the equilibrium supply of paper-money and monetized credit, consistent with the basic requirements just mentioned, cannot possibly be computed in a free society. This inability should not plunge us into despair. The great economist of the nineteenth century, Leon Walras, taught us almost a century ago that if we organize a system of free markets and if the prices are expressed in terms of "Numeraire" (the monetary standard equal to a certain quantity of a selected commodity, e.g., 15 grains of gold equal to a dollar), the equilibrium supply of money and the general equilibrium for the economy are ipso facto realized through the free interactions between consumers and producers at home and in the foreign markets. All we need is not to waste precious time sweeping the bottom of the ocean to find a pebble dropped there accidentally, as is similarly done by our government in attempting to discover accidentally by fine tuning the "unique combination of monetary and fiscal policies" which for a moment, let us say a day, will stop inflation, but the next day the same forces of pure speculations and monetization of public and private debt would automatically drag the financial conditions and the economy back to where they were before. This pattern has been repeated so often in the past five, ten or twenty years that by now we should have been able to learn the correct lesson from history—namely, that the supply of paper-credit money cannot be controlled efficiently to avoid inflations or deflations.

I cannot take up more space here to demonstrate in further detail why the control of credit money from the practical point of view, as an institutional issue, is insoluble in a free society.[7]

The whole argument boils down to a fundamental question—*What should we do in a free society:* (1) *have the official money based 100% on Numeraire, e.g., gold or silver or any other suitable commodity, as Walras advised us,* or (2) *should we be satisfied with a nominal, artificial monetary standard of the type $1 is $1, as Lord Keynes recommended?*

9. *The Situation of Our Balance of International Payments Also Requires Immediate Action*

Today the United States faces difficulties similar to those experienced by Great Britain during the Napoleonic wars. Decidedly, the British people at that time suffered the consequences of an internal inflation and a continuous drain of gold, menacing the foundation of the official monetary system based on the gold pound sterling. The convertibility of the pound was suspended in 1797, as mentioned earlier, but the country was fortunate in having an economist of the caliber of David Ricardo, who warned in precise terms that the disorders came from the constitution of the private bank system where banks were printing their own banknotes in competition. This automatically implied a danger of inflation with all its dire consequences.

After a few decades of arguing back and forth on this subject, the British Parliament finally passed the Robert Peel Act of 1844, which, even though it did not solve the problem completely, nevertheless represents a sort of Magna Charta in monetary field of modern times, specifically indicating where the right solution lies, even for our time.

If one would take the time to read the almost insane quantity of material in the daily press and professional journals of economics and finance, all related to the subject of gold and the deficit in the U.S. balance of international payments, he would be struck by the fact that no word whatsoever is mentioned regarding the relationship between the free activity of private banks in creating bank deposits as money and the corollary, i.e., the internal inflation, which in turn foments the chronic deficit in the balance of payments. During 1969 the deficit reached a record level of $7 billion after the international accord of March 1968 had more or less frozen the free exit of gold from Fort Knox. We don't have a Ricardo, but we desperately need one; or if we have one, we are not willing to listen to him. Why this passive attitude of a nation in danger?

III. Recommendations

The *diagnosis* of the situation seems to be clear: We are suffering from the ill effects of a double inflation of dollars, one at home and the other in foreign markets.

The *task*, as I see it, is also a double one:

A. To clean or drain the existing double inflation, if possible to the very bottom, in an orderly fashion without creating other problems, and

B. To undertake the necessary reforms so that financial crises will not recur in the foreseeable future.

A. How to Drain the Existing Inflation

There are different methods of approach possible to this task:

1. The *first method* is to effect a parallel drainage at one and the same time, both at home and in foreign markets.

This is my recommendation, with the introduction of a new, heavier

U.S. dollar equal to 20 old dollars (as presented in the first draft of my plan to our government in 1965 and printed in the *Congressional Record*).

2. The *second* method is to attempt a gradual drainage over a longer or shorter period of time.

This seems to be the approach followed by the Federal Reserve System, the U.S. Treasury Department and the Council of Economic Advisors to the President. The program, however, is not clear, since the official purpose as announced is not to drain the inflation but just to stop its growth, which is not the same thing.

It is possible to conceive a more consistent program for a gradual strengthening of the paper dollar but *definitely not* through a continuation of the present tight-money policy, because this nurtures more and more miseries for the economy. I could visualize, for instance, a program stretched over five years with an exact schedule of gradually increasing the legal reserve requirements for all private banks without distinction (member and state banks) from the present level to say 90% reserves for all demand deposits, and the gradual decrease of the official discount, but keeping it always above the level of current interest rates on the market. Such a reform, once realized, would mean a separation of the money market from the capital market, and indirectly a restriction of pure speculations in the securities market.

On this road there are some good chances of moving things in the right direction, that is, toward conditions of relative equilibrium in the economy, even though this is still a far cry from the conditions of general stable equilibrium. Relief for the economy on this road will be significant but incomplete. The existing inflation would then be beaten to one ground, the Federal Reserve System. If the paper-credit-money order is preserved, even though the supply of money would then be concentrated in one hand—the Federal Reserve System—still the basic problem of how to calculate the equilibrium supply of paper money and monetized credit would remain unresolved. Yet it must be recognized that the relief achieved by following this approach would be incomparably better than merely waiting for dreams to become reality, as with the application of the traditional Keynesian policies employed thus far.

3. The *third method* is to languish along the road followed in recent decades while looking for a miracle combination, the famous "perfect mix," or "perfect tuning," recommended by the followers of the "New Economics," which consists of trying to play the game of monetary and fiscal policy until you hit the proper reaction which will stop inflation. Now we've been at this game for five years 1965-1970 (only since the last chronic inflation started!) with no positive results whatsoever, as so masterfully pointed out in the editorial from the *Times* quoted above! How long should we continue this play of gambling with the agony of the American dollar? *How long can the finances of this country endure*

the adverse effects of such illusionary policies? With a 98% probability I can predict that the result of the third method, which hopes only to stop but not to cure inflation, would result in a fiasco similar to those in the past for reasons described already.

A word is in order regarding the agitation created in recent years by Professor Milton Friedman (also a Keynesian economist but with a conservative tinge). He presents the problem as if all tribulations caused by the stagnant double inflation and the myriad social and economic gaps due to the use of paper-credit money would disappear if the Federal Reserve System could only be convinced to increase the supply of paper money and monetized credit by 4.5 or 5% annually, which would match the annual average increase in productivity. This is also an illusion, *first* because the supply of money in our country is 85 to 90% composed of credit money, which in itself is based on confidence—that is, something abstract in the mind of consumers and producers which may change abruptly every day and cannot be controlled by government in a free society. *Second,* he is not aware that credit money may appear not only on the deposit side of the balance sheet of a bank (and this alone appears in the official statistics of bank deposits in the banking system) but also on the debit (loans) side. Can we seriously imagine that the F.R.S. would be able to control each bank in the country to monetize no more and no less than 4.5 or 5% bank credit than the previous year? Professor Friedman's recommendation is related to the assumption that the increase in the total supply of credit money will be only on the credit side, while in reality this could also happen on the debit side. To accomplish the given goal by Friedman's recipe would mean such a rigorous check on the banking business that in fact it would be equal to the nationalization of banks. However, I would recommend that Professor Friedman be invited by the Federal Reserve System to conduct his experiment for a limited time, not for the whole United States but just for one single small state, such as Rhode Island, and see whether the inflation in that particular state would be cured. The appearance of conditions of stable equilibrium would be evident if the system of increasing the supply of paper-money and monetized credit money by 5% really works as Friedman proposes. But if he does not have the exact formula for calculating the equilibrium supply of money and the practical means to apply it for Rhode Island, the probability is 97% or more that his experiment will fail.

B. How Can We Eradicate the Danger of Inflation and Deflation in the Future?

My proposition is to scrap the bad parts of the existing financial system and regenerate it through the introduction of a 100% Numeraire-currency system (Walras) combined with the necessary reforms in private banking, the securities market and government finances. Here are the major points of the long-run solution:

1. The establishment of a new, heavier U.S. dollar freely convertible in gold, both at home and in the foreign markets.
2. We have enough gold at Fort Knox to cover the new, official dollar.
3. If we adopt a project of, for instance, only 50% Numeraire, the Federal Government should be required to have over a period of 10 or 15 years appropriations in the annual budget to buy gold at home or in foreign markets until the official dollar will be covered 100%.
4. The passing of a Law for Social and Economic Justice by Congress, which would outlaw the monetization of private and public debt.
5. The new monetary law should provide that the money market is to be kept separated from the capital markets.
6. An amendment to the Securities Exchange Act of 1934 should declare illegal the use of public facilities of organized exchanges or over-the-counter market for pure speculations.
7. The new monetary law should also provide a complete separation between the Treasury Department activity, the budget included, and the issuance of official money, which should remain an exclusive function of the Federal Reserve System and should be shared with no other institution, private or public.
8. The present arrangements with the International Monetary Fund and other international organizations must, of course, be adjusted to the new conditions, while making it clear to the international community that the new reforms would not constitute harm to any other nation or citizens of other countries.

Other issues could be brought up here, but for the time being those indicated above are sufficient to prove my point, which is that in order to extricate ourselves from the present morass we need new approaches, new thinking and new facilities. Following this road we can make our imperfect society of today a more perfect one of tomorrow and can give to the world an example of what it means to clean one's house of evils inherited from the past. The most valuable help or gift we can give to the contemporary world is this living example of a new, better society where man can live in freedom, social justice, and stability.

Respectfully submitted,
Anghel N. Rugina

NOTES

1. Gold Reserve Requirements. Hearings before the Committee on Banking and Currency, U.S. Senate, 89th Congress, First Session, February 1965, p. 198.
2. *Ibid.*, p. 199.
3. *The Boston Globe,* February 21, 1970, p. 7.
4. A. W. Phillips, "The Relation Between Unemployment and the Rate of Change of Money Wage Rates in the United Kingdom, 1861-1957," *Economica,* Vol. XXV, No. 100, November 1958, p. 283.
5. I attempted to explain the abnormal behavior of credit money as far back as 1949 in a German book, *Geldtypen und Geldordnungen. Fundamente für eine echte allgemeine Geld- und Wirtshaftstheorie* (W. Kohlhammer Verlag, Stuttgart, 1949).
6. *New York Times,* January 15, 1970.
7. I have done this in the German book mentioned before and in other works, more recently in an article, "An End to the Agony of the American Dollar? A Plan for Stable Equilibrium Conditions of the American Monetary System," *Revista Internazionale di Scienze Economiche e Commerciali,* Milano, Gennaio, 1970.

4. A THIRD LETTER TO PRESIDENT NIXON

March 27, 1972

Honorable Richard M. Nixon
The President of the United States
The White House
Washington, D.C.

Dear Mr. President:

In view of the situation that Phase II of the New Economic Policy is encountering difficulties in achieving the desired goals of price stability and full employment and that the realignment of foreign exchange rates on December 18, 1971 did not yet produce the expected results to bring the balance of payments on the road to equilibrium, I am taking the liberty of sending for your consideration two enclosed papers:

1. A Second Memorandum on the Serious Situation of the American Economy and Finances; and
2. A Plan for the Reorganization of the International Monetary Fund as Oriented Toward Conditions of Stable Equilibrium.

I hope that this material may be of some value to our Government in resolving the most urgent problems of our economy and the balance of payments.

May I strongly recommend to you, Mr. President, that the Bill just approved by Congress to raise the price of gold *not* be signed immediately because that would mean an automatic loss of about $1.6 billion gold,* which will compound the difficulty of a needed return to convertibility in the near future. Instead, an official statement should clarify the point that the delay was due to a reconsideration of the reopening of convertibility.

Wishing you complete success in dealing with these most pressing problems of today, I thank you for any consideration of the enclosed material, and I remain

Respectfully yours,
Anghel N. Rugina

* From the Memorandum: By raising the price of gold from $35.00 to $38.00 per ounce, we will automatically lose $1.6 billion in gold as a part of our subscription of capital to the International Monetary Fund and other international organizations.

March 25, 1972

To: Honorable Richard M. Nixon
The President of the United States
The White House
Washington, D.C.

5. A SECOND MEMORANDUM ON THE SERIOUS SITUATION OF THE AMERICAN ECONOMY AND FINANCES

On February 25, 1970 I sent to the White House a Memorandum with a detailed diagnosis and some recommendations for reforms and a new kind of policies oriented toward conditions of stable equilibrium. Two years later, in March of 1972, history appears to have confirmed the content of my 1970 Memorandum since the problems that we are facing now are the same but in a more intensified version. The identification of the issues merits to be recalled here again.

I. Diagnosis and Problems

1. Our major problems do not proceed from the economic sector of production, even though the issue of concentration of power in labor unions and big business management does represent disturbances, at times very expensive and unnecessary to the country. Even the war in Vietnam or demobilization of forces in Vietnam does not constitute a major reason for the difficulties that the American economy has been encountering since 1965.

Our main difficulties stem from the monetary, banking and financial framework of our system, which, after the amendments to the Federal

Reserve Act of 1965 and 1968, has become de facto and de jure a paper-credit-money system. Due to these two Amendments the gold dike holding back inflation was thrown open, and we have since been unable to plug it up. The American capitalist system in its present state cannot generate a position of stable equilibrium.

There is no tool of monetary and fiscal policy capable of creating stable equilibrium conditions in the American economy and its balance of payments as long as we insist upon maintaining a paper-credit-money system. Indeed, history has shown again and again in this country and in the rest of the world that paper-credit-money has an inherent and incurable instability.

Working with traditional policies, including price and wage controls, under the given circumstances, resembles shooting in the dark, or fishing in the Dead Sea. *In other words, a combination of price stability and full employment at home and a balance of payments in equilibrium is simply not possible, no matter what we do, as long as we do not change the monetary, banking and financial framework of our system in such a way as to correspond to conditions of stable equilibrium.* In this respect the American free enterprise system faces mortal dangers if the necessary reforms are not effected in time.

2. The trading off between inflation and unemployment, or the consequences of the Phillips curve, are inevitable if we do not undertake the changes needed to make the financial system stable. Under the conditions of stable equilibrium the Phillips curve cannot exist.

3. As yet unresolved is the double inflation of American dollars: one at home, and the other in international markets.

4. The principal causes for our financial traumas can be found in four different places:

a. The American private banking system is the major culprit because it represents the principal fountain or factory which provides fuel to the internal and external inflation in a proportion of 85 to 90 per cent, namely, through monetization of private and public debt.

b. The Federal Reserve System is helping with the creation of 10 to 15 per cent of primary reserves which enter into the private banking system. On the basis of these additional reserves private banks, through lending business, do create the residual 85 to 90 per cent of the total supply of money in circulation.

Since the 25 per cent gold requirement for deposits and notes of the F.R.S. was repealed in 1965 and 1968, the Federal Reserve System has no standard for orientation and no built-in brake for an efficient control of monetized bank credit in the economy.

c. The American securities market is oriented more toward pure speculations, i.e., how to acquire additional profits through artificial price fluctuations instead of looking for productive investments in the economy at a time when unemployment is so high.

A large portion of the monetized bank credit, directly or indirectly, is helping to finance a huge volume of pure speculations in the securities market, and pure speculations produce disequilibrium and consequently artificial price fluctuations, because only then can they make an extra profit. Government securities are no exception to this ordeal of pure speculations.

d. The ever-recurring deficits in the public budget and the ever-rising national debt constitute another major source of fuel to the murderous inflation, because they too put in motion the machine of monetization of bank credit.

5. The internal and external inflation is the end product of our inherently unstable financial system. It is a vicious cycle. The internal inflation produces deficits in the balance of payments, and the external inflation aggravates the domestic economy. When the U.S. government seriously tries to fight inflation at home, then the balance of payments worsens. If we attempt to eradicate the deficits in the balance of payments, then our efforts are crippled by a simultaneous rise of difficulties in the domestic economy.

It would appear as if there were no salvation for the American free enterprise system, if we accept the reading of the Phillips curve without seeing a better alternative. The Phillips-curve effect exists only if we prolong the status quo—that is, do nothing to correct the loopholes in the framework of our financial system. It is the main thesis of this and the previous Memorandum that with the necessary corrections in our monetary, banking and securities-market system, conditions of stable equilibrium could be quickly effected, and the Phillips curve or the trade-off between inflation and unemployment would have no application.

This is the diagnosis and the major problems, as I see them.

II. The New Economic Policy After August 15, 1971

If my diagnosis, as shown above, is correct, *the new economic policies after August 15, 1971,* including the suspension of convertibility and the introduction of wage and price controls, *do not and cannot work efficiently to achieve the principal goals of price stability, full employment and a balance of payments in equilibrium.* The basic reason is that the tools used in the new economic policies do not touch the four main evil sources mentioned before and from which our difficulties reappear. It is worthwhile to repeat these sources of disequilibrium: the private banking system, the Federal Reserve System, the securities market, and the recurring deficits in the public budget with the ever-rising national debt.

1. For reasons just mentioned, the suspension of convertibility and the 10 per cent surcharge tax on imports could not resolve our chronic deficit in the balance of payments. Conceived as emergency measures, there is some justification for them, but never as a solution to the problem in question.

With such measures, inconsistent with our previous official policy of liberalization of international trade and capital movements, we have unnecessarily irritated our friends, who are among the leaders of the free world. Meanwhile, we dropped the 10 per cent surcharge tax on imports, but we still have the other issue of convertibility, which is a thorn and stumbling block in the restoration of confidence and equilibrium in the international monetary system.

2. Neither was the devaluation of the American dollar a wise decision. By raising the price of gold from $35.00 to $38.00, we failed to realize immediately a substantial improvement in the balance of payments. In addition, if the devaluation bill approved by Congress is signed by the President, we will automatically lose $1.6 billion in gold as part of the depreciation of our subscription of capital to the International Monetary Fund and other international organizations. This substantial loss of gold will compound the difficulty of the return to convertibility in the near future. And this return is required for both the financial stability of our own economy and the equilibrium of the international monetary system.

In view of this situation, it is strongly recommended here that the devaluation bill not be signed immediately; instead an official statement should be made to clarify the point that the delay is due to a reconsideration of the reopening of the convertibility.

3. The wage and price controls, or what is called the incomes policy after August 15, 1971, did not have much chance of success from the beginning, even though at that time the majority of experts in both political parties thought that this might be the answer to our problems. In reality this was an illusion; as long as the principal factor producing inflation, or the machinery of monetizing bank credit, is feverishly at work, the wage and price controls cannot fulfill their function.

The open conflict between organized labor and the Pay Board was inevitable, even though some political considerations may have been involved in hastening the outcome. In this issue our government should remember an earlier British experiment, under the Wilson government, which ended in failure. Harold Wilson subsequently lost the elections.

The failure of the British experiment was not due to a total lack of understanding or cooperation on the part of British trade unions but rather to an inevitable conflict between the promised fruits of incomes policy to both organized labor and business management and the unpleasant realities after the application of this policy, which created myriad social inequities and disequilibrium gaps engineered by the same invisible machine of inflation-deflation of the modern banking apparatus.

The truth of the matter is that we are sitting on an inflationary iceberg, accumulated during the last three decades and growing continuously. Under these circumstances, neither wage and price controls nor any of the traditional policies can restore price stability, full employment and a balance of payments in equilibrium, no matter how much good will or technical skills is displayed by those entrusted with applying these policies.

If we do nothing to change and correct the deficiencies in the financial framework of our otherwise healthy and progressive system, there is no hope for salvation. As Dante stated symbolically in his *Inferno: "Lasciate ogni speranza voi che entrate [nell' inferno]!"* ("Abandon all hope, ye who enter [Hell]!") As an optimist, however, I believe that the unstable framework of our financial system can be restructured quickly upon conditions of stable equilibrium so that our free enterprise system may prove in time to be the best answer to the aspirations of man and humanity in our time.

What we need badly is to free ourselves of certain dubious financial and economic theories inherited from the 1930's, and to devote our energies and resources to new thinking and to the forging of new tools for policies consistent with our basic ideals of freedom, social justice and stability with lasting peace. In this spirit I offer my solutions for consideration.

III. The Task at Hand and New Tools for an Equilibrium Type of Policies

The task at hand can be divided into two separate targets or goals, which are complementary: One is to drain to the bottom the existing inflation, and the other is to initiate the necessary reforms in order to put our financial system under equilibrium conditions.

1. How Can We Drain the Existing Double Inflation?

The main problem we face is not merely to stop the pending inflation, but rather how to drain it first and at the same time take the required measures to assure that it will not recur.

(1) We can drain the inflationary iceberg in 24 hours, over a weekend, by the introduction of a new, heavier U.S. dollar. According to

the present conditions, we probably need to make 1 new, heavier dollar = 25 old dollars.

(2) On the conversion day, reduce by 25:1 all existing prices, incomes, all sorts of claims (domestic and foreign) and taxes.

(3) Foreign claims outstanding on C-day (in 1972 approximately 50 to 60 billion dollars) shall be reduced by 25:1, but for the definite settlement of these claims the gold price for that day should remain unchanged. In this way, with circa $2.5 billion in gold, we shall be able to compensate the huge amount of foreign claims.

(4) The justification for the reduction of foreign claims by 25:1 and the maintenance of the price for gold unchanged for the C-day, can be provided first by the fact that no inequity will be produced, since the same procedure will apply to domestic claims. In addition, foreigners will now have a choice of whether to accept the opportunity of investing in American ventures where a 100 per cent covered and convertible dollar will assure that its internal value will be equal to its external value. This opportunity did not exist before.

(5) For any foreign claims born after C-day, the official price of gold should be established in new, heavier dollars.

In this way the internal and external inflation will be wiped out by one single surgical monetary operation. At the same time the heavy foreign outstanding debt will also be partially liquidated.

2. *How Can We Restore and Maintain Conditions of Stable Equilibrium?*

After the existing double inflation has been drained, completely, on the same day a number of other necessary changes must take place.

(1) Announce the reopening of free convertibility of the U.S. dollar, both at home and in international markets. We shall have enough gold to support this convertibility if the bill of devaluation is not signed and if the price of gold during the day of conversion of old into new dollars remains the same.

(2) Any new official dollars put into circulation after C-day must have a 100 per cent gold backing.

The new official price of gold has to be established between a lower limit of 1.4 (which corresponds to the old price of $35.00) and a higher limit of 3.00 new dollars, so that the mining of new gold can be profitable.

(3) Besides the concept of 100 per cent backed official money, the other cornerstone of the new stable financial system lies in complete separation of the money market from the capital market, both at home and abroad.

The reason for this separation is that each market has its own function which it cannot fulfill unless it is located within its own boundaries. Indeed, the money market has to provide a sufficient amount of liquidity funds so that the current output and income in the economy are produced and distributed without serious difficulties. The capital market, on the other hand, has to concentrate exclusively on the function of capital formation and new investments necessary to secure a balanced rate of economic growth consistent with full employment.

(4) According to the basic rule of separation between money- and capital-markets, the banking business has to be divided into two separate and independent functions:

Department A of Demand Deposits and Checking Accounts

This Department A will receive regular demand deposits subject to the use of checks and hold 100 per cent reserves in official money at all times. In this case the checks in question will replace official money withdrawn from circulation but will not change the supply of money provided by the Federal Reserve System.

Taking the banking system as a whole this would mean that the money market is finally 100 percent liquid at all times, and therefore a financial crisis reminiscent of other times cannot materialize.

Department B of Savings and Investments

This Department B will handle all available capital formation in the form of voluntary savings to be matched by investment opportunities on short-, medium- and long-term bases.

A schedule of interest rates, arranged according to risk and the time element related to different investment opportunities, will insure that the volume of new investments is equal to the available amount of savings. This is one of the basic conditions for stable equilibrium. In this way the financial sector in equilibrium would avoid the vagaries of the business cycle phenomenon, for the economy.

The new banking law should specificially provide that the separation of banking business into two independent departments is required for American banks at home and/or their branches in foreign countries, as well as for foreign banks doing business in the United States and its territories.

(5) An additional piece of legislation should prohibit the monetization of debt for private or public purposes, in any form, since this is contrary to the public interest.

(6) Another cornerstone of the new stable financial system lies in the independence of the Federal Reserve System within the prerogatives and functions specified in the new revised Federal Reserve Act.

(7) The Federal Reserve System alone shall have the prerogatives of supplying the economy with new dollars at the official parity after the costs of minting and administration have been subtracted.

(8) Present-day manipulation of the official discount, as well as open-market transactions including margin requirements and other direct or indirect controls of the private banks by the F.R.S., shall be suspended indefinitely as being unnecessary in the new system.

(9) The present Office of the Comptroller of the Currency shall be reorganized in order to be consistent with the new system. Any regulation of private banking should be entrusted to this office. Perhaps its name should be changed, too, to "Comptroller of Banking."

(10) In order to dispel any doubts about the necessary and sufficient supply of money for keeping the national economy expanding at a balanced rate of growth consistent with the increase in population and the desire for progress, it is recommended that the Federal Reserve System immediately proceed to study the implementation of a national plan whereby in every state of the Union, an additional commodity other than gold, at the discretion of the people in that state, can be monetized into 100 per cent covered and convertible new Federal Reserve notes.

The monetization of these commodities shall take place at the prevailing market price expressed in new dollars, after the cost of warehousing and handling for a given period has been covered. This additional issue of money might be called "commercial" dollars. They would be 100 per cent covered and convertible into the respective commodity which serves as their backing.

(11) The commercial dollars, however, should not be confused with official dollars, which will be 100 per cent backed in gold. The official monetary standard, at home and in international transactions, is the gold dollar. The only price which is constant is the gold price. All other prices are expressed in terms of gold, because otherwise Gresham's Law would impede a normal functioning of the new system.

The Federal Reserve System, through a skilled regulation of the warehousing and administration costs involved in the monetization of commodities other than gold, shall follow the rule that the value of commercial dollars be equal or very close to the value of official dollars. This is not difficult to achieve as long as the free convertibility and monetization are preserved. In this way, even though officially there is no fixed ratio of conversion between the two forms of currency, nevertheless in actual circulation they will be equal.

(12) Since in the new regime only the Federal Reserve System may put new money into circulation, then at any given time we shall be able to know exactly the total supply of money in the economy, something which we cannot do today with precision.

(13) In order to eradicate the socially harmful "pure speculations," or at least to reduce them to a minimum, an amendment to the Securities Exchange Act should specifically require that all transactions undertaken in the organized markets or over the counter shall be 100 per cent covered at all times, both in terms of funds when the object of business was a purchase, and in terms of the respective securities when the transaction was a sale. In other words, "pure speculations," under a reasonable and clear definition, shall be declared illegal and illegitimate as being contrary to the public interest.

(14) In order to resolve the problem of mergers and conglomerates, that is, the issue of monopoly and concentration of undue economic power in a few hands located in large corporations, a special piece of legislation as an amendment to the antitrust law should be passed by Congress, which may be called the "Law of Omenia." *Omenia* is an untranslatable Romanian expression which means, approximately, human behavior in accordance with an unwritten Christian law of social and economic justice.

This amendment to the antitrust law should require that any kind of business, regardless of size, shall be conducted at the real cost of production or acquisition, plus a "normal rate of profit," defined as a compensation equal to the opportunity cost of management. Any additional, extra or differential profit over and above the "normal profit" shall be considered illegal and illegitimate and therefore be deposited in the general fund of the Social Security System.

The "Law of Omenia" would thus break any monopoly power and eradicate unearned profits, and in this way it would make impossible the existence of surplus-value, as defined by Karl Marx. Thus we may strengthen our free enterprise system by making it immune to the usual criticism from the socialist-Marxist camp. We may also put an end to the insatiable appetite for acquiring unjustified wealth, which creates social problems.

(15) Organized labor has to come under the same "Law of Omenia," and there will be no dispute with management, since in the new regime there will be no "administered prices" and no extra, unjustified profits. The great role of the labor unions would then be to make sure that the new system functions properly; specifically that business corporations do not get an extra profit, and that the work conditions are consistent with the requirements and opportunities of a civilized society.

IV. *Other Examples and Events to Be Remembered and Considered*

1. *The French Experiment of 1959*

The French government, in its financial reform of 1959, applied the concept of a new, heavier franc = 100 old francs, which helped to drain a good portion of the domestic inflation existing at that time. There were no difficulties in conducting the reform. France, which had a chronic deficit in her balance of payments for decades, reached an equilibrium in about six months through this reform. After that a surplus piled up until the rebellion of May 1968.

This author presented a plan in 1958 for the financial and economic stabilization of France, in which the use of a new, heavier franc was recommended. According to my calculations a more realistic ratio between the old and the new franc was about 10,000:1, rather than 100:1, which ultimately was used. As a result of this gap between the two ratios, a substantial layer of inflation still remained in the French economy, which later produced troubles. In addition, in my proposal I recommended that the convertibility should be extended to the internal and not only to the external franc.

The two weaknesses of the French experiment do not disprove but, on the contrary, confirm and reinforce the thesis of this plan that a new, heavier U.S. dollar with a realistic ratio can work quickly and efficiently to restore price stability and full employment at home and a balance of payments without troubles abroad.

2. *A New Message from the Socialist Community of the COMECON*

Representatives at the higher level of the COMECON countries (Eastern European countries plus the USSR) met in Bucharest, Romania, in July 1971, and, after long deliberations decided that both more active cooperation and integration of the national economies included in the socialist community as well as the acquisition of a larger share of international trade require the introduction of a "collective ruble" convertible in gold and followed by convertible currencies of all socialist member countries.

This decision by the socialist-Marxist countries of Eastern Europe resembles a symbolic "handwriting on the wall." This change in thinking and tactics, if not strategy, results from a historic confrontation between modern capitalism and socialism-communism at a time when the United States was forced to suspend the convertibility of its currency, the

American dollar, once the strongest currency in the entire world! This news should give our government officials as well as the entire profession of economists something to think about.

* * *

I firmly believe that through a reasonable experiment, that is, through rigorous and systematic corrections of the financial framework as outlined in this Memorandum as well as in the previous one, our imperfect capitalist system will receive a new image and in fact will be converted into a new social order that may be called "The Great Free, Just and Stable Society," or, briefly, "Social Liberalism," as distinguished from "laissez-faire capitalism" of the past or the troubled welfare state of today.

At this late hour we still have a chance to prepare the conditions for a better life for all our people who strongly desire and aspire to more freedom, more justice and more stability with lasting peace.

The realization of this plan would provide these conditions for a better life to all of our people, and thus offer a living example to other nations facing similar problems. The challenge is great, and the results will depend upon how well we shall use the chance still available to us! Let us hope for a positive and constructive answer to the challenge from those who have the power, the means and the responsibility to make this a better world, before other calamities overtake us.

Respectfully submitted:
Anghel N. Rugina

Boston, Massachusetts
March 1972

6. A LETTER TO THE SECRETARY OF THE TREASURY

January 19, 1972

Hon. John B. Connally
Secretary of the Treasury of the
United States
Washington, D.C.

Dear Sir:

One month after the signing of the Foreign Exchange Agreement on December 18, 1971, the news concerning the position of the U.S. dollar in international markets is not encouraging. The problem of how to restore confidence in the American dollar, that is, how to stop the internal inflation and bring about a normal equilibrium in the domestic economy as well as the balance of international payments is still open for debate.

In view of this situation, I am taking the liberty of sending you a short Memorandum together with five documents, all pertinent to the same monetary problem with which you have been struggling since you became Secretary of the Treasury.

I hope, Mr. Secretary, that the enclosed Memorandum and the other documents will be of some value to you and to our Government in helping to find and apply in time the correct solution to our monetary problem, which is complicating not only our own economy but also the functioning of the international monetary system, a vitally important element for the whole free world.

An answer would be most appreciated.

Respectfully yours,
Anghel N. Rugina

Enclosures: 6

January 19, 1972

To: Hon. John B. Connally
Secretary of the Treasury of the
United States
Washington, D.C.

7. A MEMORANDUM ON SOME NEW THINKING WITH ADEQUATE POLICIES FOR A DEFINITE SOLUTION TO THE CRISIS OF THE AMERICAN DOLLAR

Attached are the following five documents:

1. A Memorandum on the Serious Situation of the American Economy and Finances. An Attempt to Establish a Reliable Diagnosis and Some Recommendations for Immediate Action—sent to President Richard M. Nixon on February 25, 1970.
2. An End to the Agony of the American Dollar? A Plan for Stable Equilibrium Conditions of the American Monetary System (1970).
3. Monetization of Public and Private Debt as the Principal Fountain of Modern Inflation (1971).
4. Gold Reserve Requirements. Hearings before the Committee on Banking and Currency. U.S. Senate, 89th Congress, First Session. February 2-10, 1965. Statement of Dr. Anghel Rugina, Jamaica Plain, Mass.
5. "The American Dollar Is Crippled!" A Letter to the Editor of the *Boston Herald Traveler*, on February 5, 1971.

In all I was concerned with one and the same issue: the present financial difficulties and how to avoid them in order to open a new, brighter outlook for the American dollar.

What our government has done during the past decade does not seem to be consistent with the conditions of stable equilibrium, and this is the basic reason why the monetary policies, especially since 1965, have not worked, and in fact cannot work under the existing conditions to achieve the desired goals of stability and full employment.

In 1965 I warned President Lyndon B. Johnson that by repealing the 25% gold requirement for deposits with the Federal Reserve System as requested by the government at that time, the impending difficulties with the balance of payments and with the domestic inflation would increase rather than diminish.

In 1967 after the devaluation of the British pound, I again wrote to President Johnson, calling attention to the fact that we were also treading a dangerous path. But the experts who prevailed are those who, so to speak, are taking the bull by the tail,—in the sense that they are interested in *ways of more quickly achieving a fully government-controlled economy and society rather than in correcting the evils and malfunctioning of our existing system.* Thus, in 1968 the last foundation of the American dollar, namely, the 25% gold requirement for F.R.S. notes was removed. The financial situation, instead of improving, worsened.

After President Nixon was inaugurated in January 1969, I continued to follow the events in the monetary field closely, but in good faith I could not find any trace of a change in thinking or policies as compared with the previous administration. Then I wrote a long Memorandum (see Document No. 1) to President Nixon on February 25, 1970, which I transmitted through the office of Hon. John A. Volpe, Secretary of Transportation, with whom I worked earlier when he was Governor of the State of Massachusetts. I received a confirmation, but I am not certain that the content of this Memorandum ever came to the direct attention of the President.

I am convinced that you, Sir, President Nixon and other distinguished members of this Administration (as well as had President Johnson and some of his associates) sincerely want to improve the functioning of our mixed, but still free enterprise system. However, the methods and policies used so far, especially since 1965, are absolutely inconsistent with the goal of a free enterprise system, a view presumably shared by the majority of our people and elected and appointed officials. These *inconsistent methods of thinking,* in places where major monetary policies are shaped, and not the lack of response on the part of our economy, *constitute the real cause in recent years of our country being pushed into increasing difficulties which inevitably require more and more government intervention.* It is a gnawing conflict between "thinking" and "reality" that leads only into more disequilibrium, more gaps, more confusion, and more suffering for innocent millions of people without work or income.

The moment has come to make a critical reevaluation of all the policies followed during the past decade and to take the bull by the *horns* instead of toying with its tail. By now there is sufficient evidence to admit the following:

Truth No. 1 is that we are sitting at home on an inflationary iceberg and that the traditional methods and cures of monetary and fiscal policies will not work until the existing "stagnant" inflation has been drained to its roots.

Truth No. 2 is that the whole international monetary system is flooded by another inflation of American dollars, and that traditional policies do not and cannot work successfully as long as the first and this second inflation are not completely drained.

The realignment of foreign exchange rates, on December 18, 1971, cannot solve the double inflation in question because nothing in the agreement was conceived specifically for that purpose.

As I see it, the major task of our government in regard to the monetary issue is composed of two distinct parts:

I. *How to drain the double inflation by an instantaneous clinical operation so that no further harm will be produced at home and in the international markets?*

The inflation after World War I was tapered off haphazardly, without a plan or adequate procedures. We know that this later created impossible conditions between 1929 and 1934, and even thereafter.

The post-World War II inflation has not yet been touched, and by now is stale and malodorous. We must learn the right lesson from history; otherwise, as Santayana said, history will repeat itself. We should be able to reduce the existing inflation by a controlled experiment which, I think, can be achieved by the introduction of a new, heavier U.S. dollar, as I tried to prove in all the enclosed documents.

II. *How to create those stable equilibrium conditions for the immediate future, so that the domestic inflation and the chronic deficits in the balance of international payments will not recur?*

The fact of the matter, which is not discussed publicly, leads this writer to the conclusions that our major economic and financial troubles stem mainly from four factors:

1. Our monetary system as changed in recent times has no reliable mechanism in functioning.
2. Our banking system, based on the fractional reserve principle, has become the primary source of fuel for the factory of inflation.
3. Our securities market system, based mostly on pure speculations, attracts huge sums of funds which avoid the productive stream of

the economy, at the same time inducing the banking system to accelerate the monetization of private and public debt. This heaps more fuel into the mill of inflation.

4. Our national debt has reached a critical level and our government is cornered and cannot take the measures necessary to put the monetary-, banking- and securities-market system in order. The annual portion of the maturing debt has reached the staggering annual figure of approximately 120 billion dollars and may be even more. The private banks, with the mechanism of monetization of public debt and charging high interest rates, help to perpetuate an anachronistic state in our financial system. Indeed, more and more funds are used today to refund the public debt and spur the machine of inflation instead of being used for productive purposes in the economy, especially at a time when we have such a high level of unemployment.

In the enclosed documents I attempted to show what can be done in order to restore the stability of our monetary-, banking-, and securities-market system and also put an end to the chronic deficit in the balance of payments. Ultimately, we must face the realization that either we initiate the necessary reforms in time, or by allowing the situation to drift, we inevitably will slide toward a less efficient and more complicated, government-controlled economy.

At this rather confusing moment in history, the entire world watches our country to see what our next move will be as signals of more troubles for the U.S. dollar become apparent. In the *New York Times* of yesterday this statement appeared: "Dollar sets new lows on European markets." Today's newspapers bring the shocking news that the budgetary deficit for the current fiscal year may reach the sum of $30 to $40 billion. These are not encouraging facts for the position of the American dollar in international markets. It was also reported in the same newspapers that Hon. Paul A. Volcker, Under Secretary of the Treasury, mentioned at a news conference that the Nixon Administration soon will be forced to apply to Congress for "a very substantial increase in the debt ceiling," now temporarily at $430 billion.

There evidently exists a tormenting cycle here whereby the double inflation is eroding the foundation of our economy and our free society. When the Nixon Administration took office in 1969, the national debt stood at $365 billion. Over a period of only three years, the ceiling of the national debt was raised by $65 billion. This cannot be interpreted as a healthy state of affairs by foreign creditors. In addition, our balance of trade during 1971 will show a substantial deficit for the first time since the 1880's. Where do all these contradictions lead but to more problems if our government neglects to change, resolutely, its present course of dangerous drifting into a channel of new revival, encompassing stable equilibrium conditions?

In view of a realistic confrontation between the monetary and fiscal policies applied in recent years and the dismaying realities with which we are now faced, it is not difficult to predict that so long as our government insists in preserving the paper-inconvertible dollar as a basis for our financial system (especially from the point of view of economic relations with other nations) and the private banks continue to make use of the mechanism of monetization of private and public debt, there exists no chance or hope for a stable economy with full employment and an equilibrium in the balance of international payments.

I hope that this Memorandum, which strongly hints at the need for new thinking and new tools of analysis with adequate policies for a definite solution to the crisis of the American dollar, together with the other five enclosed documents, will find a hearing in the Treasury Department and other places where the decision-making process in monetary matters is located.

Respectfully submitted,
Anghel N. Rugina
Professor of Economics and Finance
Northeastern University, Boston, Massachusetts

1933-1973

8. AN OPEN LETTER TO PRESIDENT RICHARD M. NIXON ON DECEMBER 31, 1973

A REBUTTAL TO THE FAMOUS OPEN LETTER OF LORD KEYNES TO PRESIDENT FRANKLIN DELANO ROOSEVELT ON DECEMBER 30, 1933

NO EXACT FORMULA EXISTS TO COMPUTE AND MAINTAIN A STABLE EQUILIBRIUM SUPPLY OF PAPER MONEY AND MONETIZED BANK CREDIT

A New Approach to Avoid Possible Economic and Financial Disaster in the United States

An Open Letter to President Richard M. Nixon

Dear Mr. President:

Four decades ago, on December 30, 1933, the most prominent and influential economist of this century, John Maynard Keynes, addressed a long open letter[1] to the President of the United States, Franklin Delano

Roosevelt. That letter was like an "Economic Sermon on the Mount" which was faithfully accepted and applied, first by the Roosevelt Administration and subsequently by all incoming Presidents, until finally, under your Administration, all the recommendations contained in that document have been exhausted.

1. *The Voice of the Past: Recommendations of Keynes in 1933*

It is interesting and instructive to recall the contents of that letter because it contains the seeds for explaining many problems we are facing today. Lord Keynes wrote: "Dear Mr. President: You have made yourself the trustee for those in every country who seek to mend the evils of our condition by reasoned experiment within the framework of the existing social system. If you fail, rational change will be gravely prejudiced throughout the world, leaving orthodoxy and revolution to fight it out. But if you succeed, new and bolder methods will be tried everywhere, and we may date the first chapter of a new economic era from your accession to office."

There are two key propositions—"reasoned experiment" and "rational change"— which are Keynesian in nature, but in the above quotation they are not consistent with the qualification of "within the framework of the existing social system." From what we know from other sources and the rest of the letter, Keynes was not a conservative thinker, since he definitely wanted to change the capitalist system. Why then did he use that typically conservative expression? It may have been part of his strategy not to appear too radical in the eyes of the American people and their President. However, there is one point where Keynes the thinker was a conservative, namely, in accepting the institutional framework of modern banking and finance as a given datum without raising any questions about possible inconsistencies of structural nature. Indeed, he developed plans to change the monetary system and the economy at the national and international levels, but he never touched the structure or the practices of modern banking and finance. Was this attitude held because he foresaw that, following his propositions, banks, in the final analysis, would have to be nationalized, or did he not perceive in his thinking the real conflict between modern banking and finance, on the one hand, and a workable free enterprise system on the other? I am inclined to think that the latter interpretation is more plausible.

The task of the 1930's was formulated further in the same letter when Keynes stated to President Roosevelt: "You are engaged on a double task, recovery and reform—recovery from the slump, and the passage of those business and social reforms which are long overdue." The rest of the text, however, was devoted to the techniques of recovery rather than reforms. Keynes warned the President that "even wise and necessary reform may, in some respects, impede and complicate recovery. For it will upset the confidence of the business world." Again we can see the conservative side of Keynes' thinking. He conceived the problems of the time in terms of the status quo and did not question the financial framework of the prevailing system.

In order to attain economic recovery, in the same letter Keynes recommended the application of three special techniques:

a. "In the field of domestic policy, I put in the forefront, a large volume of loan expenditure under government auspices." This is what is called "government deficit spending."

b. "I put in the second place the maintenance of cheap and abundant credit, in particular the reduction of the long-term rate of interest."

c. In point of international transactions, his basic rule was that "the currency and exchange policy of a country should be entirely subservient to the aim of raising output and employment to the right level." This is what he called the "ideal managed currency." In continuation, he was in favor of devaluation of the dollar in terms of gold but not "returning to the gold standard at a new fixed ratio."

2. *The Historical Record Since the 1930's*

The Roosevelt Administration proceeded to devalue the dollar by 40% and rigorously followed government deficit spending and a plentiful supply of cheap credit by keeping artificially lower rates of interest, which in the early 1940's were below 2%. However, despite all these genuine Keynesian policies, the country could not escape another sharp recession in 1938, and the problem of mass unemployment was resolved not by the multiplier effect but by the mobilization of the economy for World War II. After the war the passing by the U.S. Congress of the Employment Act of 1946 made Keynesian thinking a permanent element of official policies of this country.

Your Administration, Mr. President, has faithfully continued to apply the same "Economic Sermon" by Keynes. What are the results of all your efforts and good intentions?

3. *Unemployment, Inflation and an Enormous Growth in National Debt.*

Unemployment, standing now at a national average of close to 5%, is not acceptable, especially when in many states unemployment runs over 6 or 7% and in certain large cities over 10 or 12% for minorities.

Your initial goal of "prosperity without inflation" is far from any hope of realization. During the last twelve months consumer prices have risen at an annual rate of 8.4%. We have to remember further that these are just average figures. In reality, prices for individual items and necessary daily services have increased during the past year by 30, 40 and even 50%. The magnitude of the failure appears in even stronger hues if we add to this dismal picture the less mentioned fact that between 1968, when your Administration first came to power, and December 1973 the national debt increased by more than $100 billion.

If nothing else can destroy American capitalism and open the door to a government-controlled economy and society, the continuation of government deficit spending and the ever-increasing national debt will do it, slowly perhaps, but surely.

4. The Suspension of the Convertibility, and the Energy Crisis

The suspension of the convertibility of the dollar in August 1971 and thus the official rejection of the international gold standard, with all respect to you and your advisors, Mr. President, I must say emphatically was not a wise decision, even though this happened to fulfill the last wish of Keynes. With that decision the American dollar became a paper currency and automatically lost its previous qualification for serving as a reliable international monetary unit. I dare say that the present energy crisis is, in reality, also an aftermath of the international crisis of the U.S. dollar, worsened after August 1971.

Before the suspension of the convertibility there was no serious talk of shortages of oil or other commodities traded in international markets, for the simple reason that there was no shortage beyond the natural degree of scarcity, for which a normal price was paid. The price of crude oil between 1960 and 1970, for example, was expressed in terms of stable gold dollars. That is why it stood at $1.80 per barrel for such a long period, and the available supply was sufficient to cover the effective demand, which increased by leaps and bounds after World War II. Even if after 1971 some new evidence had confirmed the existence of a shortage of oil, its price would have increased at a reasonable rate of 4 or 5% per year had we had a convertible gold dollar and no large overhang of dollars in foreign hands. But, alas, after August 15, 1971 the price of the same crude oil was measured in terms of a weak, depreciated paper dollar. And a paper currency, with no official backing in gold and declared inconvertible, simply cannot successfully fulfill the function of an objective standard for measuring prices on domestic and international markets.

Our troubles are not over yet! Future difficulties can easily be visualized and explained by the huge overhang of U.S. dollars in foreign hands, estimated at close to $100 billion. An influential Arab oil minister has already predicted that, during the spring of 1974, the price of oil could rise still higher. From Brazil the latest news is that the price of coffee, expressed in American dollars, will be increased by 13% during the first half of 1974. Very probably other commodities of international circulation will follow suit. Domestic prices cannot remain aloof from this international inflationary boost either.

5. *What Was Basically Wrong with Keynes' Recommendations?*

All these events and tribulations, which are not academic matters of interpretation but hard realities of life, clearly indicate that we are not on the right track! The "Economic Sermon" of Keynes proved not to be the right one for the needs and aspirations of the American people. First, the Keynesian idea that money does not need to be covered in gold or some other suitable commodity proved to be untenable and, in fact, false. If a monetary unit is to serve as a standard to measure prices, incomes, assets and liabilities, it must have value from within, exactly as a standard unit to measure distances must have length in itself. The other concept hailed by Keynes—that a modern government, through appropriate monetary and fiscal policies, including wage and price controls, is capable of properly managing the supply of paper money and monetized bank credit—also proved untenable. Third, the rule that the currency and foreign exchange policy should be "entirely subservient" to the goal of full employment is not valid either, since under equilibrium conditions any kind of policy must be consistent with, and not subservient to, any other major goal in the economy.

We had to learn the hard way that government is not able to manage the supply of uncovered money and credit so as to reach conditions of stable equilibrium with full employment. The myth that the Federal Reserve System can perform an appropriate "fine tuning" of the American economy and its necessary supply of purchasing power must be exposed publicly as well-guarded "empty magic." *The naked truth is that there is no mathematical formula and no practical means of calculating and maintaining an equilibrium supply of paper money and monetized bank credit at any given moment so as to satisfy the desired goals of full employment, price stability, maximum of social justice in the distribution of income and a balance of payments without deficits or surpluses.* I wish that those who have the responsibility for these matters in the Federal Government and the Federal Reserve System would have the courage finally to admit to you and the nation that an adequate "fine tuning" under the existing financial framework is not possible in practice, and that we should think of other better methods to solve the problems on hand.

6. *The Present-Day Task Is a Double One*

To further lament the past, the present or the scare of the future would not serve to improve our situation. The task, as I see it, is a double one:

First, we must immediately reduce the existing stagnant inflation of dollars at the national and international level to the lowest possible level, since it has reached such dangerous proportions and has continued too long.

Second, we must undertake the necessary reforms at once, specifically to make really stable the institutional framework of our monetary, banking and financial system, which in its present form (partly inherited from the past) runs counter to a workable free enterprise system.

7. *A New, Heavier Dollar (Convertible at Home and Abroad) Can Do It!*

As to the first task, as far back as 1965 I recommended to the Johnson Administration the introduction of a new, heavier U.S. dollar equal to 20 old dollars. According to my calculation at that time, this was sufficient to drain the domestic inflation to its bottom and to wipe out the dollar overhang in international markets. Having drained this double inflation, it is possible to restore the full convertibility of the dollar at home and abroad without absolutely any danger of losing more gold.

Of course, with the introduction of the new, heavier dollar, an immediate adjustment of all prices, incomes, assets and liabilities, both domestic and foreign, must take place in the same proportion of 1:20. It is understood that the full convertibility of the dollar cannot be restored unless the second task—the establishment of a stable framework for our financial system—is accomplished simultaneously with the first task.[2]

I take the liberty, Mr. President, of mentioning also that, through the good offices of Hon. John A. Volpe, then Secretary of Transportation, and later of Hon. Elliot L. Richardson, Secretary of Health, Education and Welfare, I tried to submit for your consideration two long Memoranda under the title "The Serious Situation of the American Economy and Finances." One was dated February 25, 1970, and the other March

25, 1972, but unfortunately I was not given a hearing. Since I am a firm believer in the virtues of a free society with a democratic form of government, I am trying again.

8. *An Obstacle but Also a New Hope*

I am aware, finally, of a major obstacle to my proposal, namely, that it runs counter to the heritage of Lord Keynes, as passed over to a very strong Establishment of "New Economics" and to enormous vested interests in the world of modern banking and finance, which, ironically, in the 1930's were against and now are for Keynesian ideas. But I know, on the other hand, that American capitalism today is at a crossroads. There is so much fallout in terms of already accumulated instability and social inequities that modern banking and finance, being enmeshed in the real causes of these troubles, cannot survive and preserve their independence in facing the mounting social pressures of tomorrow.

There is no intent here to tarnish the memory of Keynes, who in good faith thought that more active government intervention in economic life was the right solution to the dilemma of his time: a chronic deflation with mass unemployment versus a hands-off concept of government. However, our experiment with his ideas for four decades has resulted in another dilemma: a chronic inflation with high unemployment rates, plus cumulative deficits in the balance of payments, versus a neo-mercantilist type of government ever thirsting for more and more powers and devouring a progressively larger portion of the national income without resolving the pertinent problems. *We have reached a stage where a deep conflict is emerging between what the professional experts recommend to government and what the people really want.*

In this country the vast majority of the people desire freedom; want to work in peace without government intervention, direct controls and regulations; wish to see justice in the distribution of national income and wealth; yearn for a decent life in tranquility and stability so that they can plan for the future with more assurance that what they save for rainy days may not be eroded through inflation or confiscated through unjust government overtaxation.

Entering 1974 we need a new spirit and dedication in public as well as in private life: We must not mesmerize ourselves with the thought that we never had it so good, even though we should be thankful that in certain respects we enjoy more material goods than many other nations. But that is not enough for a safe and better future. We must accept the true challenge of our time, i.e., a reform of the framework of our monetary, banking and financial system in accordance with conditions of general stable equilibrium so that we may be able to curb in time the forces of erosion and create the environment for the realization of the eternal American dream: "The Great, Free, Just and Stable Society."

Everyday many millions of Americans, as well as people in the rest of the free world, attentively and anxiously watch what the President of the United States is doing or saying, because they sense correctly that the future of the free world, in the final analysis, depends on the strength, stability and morale of the United States of America. If I remember correctly, it was Lincoln who said that if this country ever goes down, it will not be from external enemies but from internal decay. It is a good warning and deserves to be mentioned at a time when the inconvertible paper dollar, under the shield of theories that in practice proved to be invalid, promotes by deception the danger of economic and financial ruin from within.

Very respectfully yours,
Anghel N. Rugina,
Professor of Economics and Finance
Northeastern University, Boston, Massachusetts

Boston, Massachusetts
December 31, 1973

NOTES

1. Published in the *New York Times,* December 31, 1933.
2. For more detail, may I refer to my article "An End to the Agony of American Dollar? A Plan for Stable Equilibrium Conditions of the American Monetary System," published in *Rivista Internazionale di Scienze Economiche e Commerciale* in January 1970.

CHAPTER III

The Johnson Administration (1965-1968)

"For three years I have tried in vain to convince our Government that the problem of losing gold and the perennial deficit in the balance of international payments would not and cannot be solved by the repeal of the 25 per cent gold requirement and/or by the introduction of voluntary or involuntary controls and regulations in our financial and economic relations with other countries.

"We are sitting at home on an inflationary iceberg, granted created during World War II but ever increasing since then. I call it a "stagnant inflation" which has now pervaded and infected the whole economic body of our nation, and it is grossly malodorous.

"The international monetary system is also sitting on a similar inflationary iceberg of American dollars, created through our generosity in aiding other countries after World War II by granting foreign aid in dollars convertible in gold when it was not absolutely necessary.

"The problem we face today, therefore, is a double inflation, one of internal and the other of external dollars. One does not need to have a Ph.D. in Economics to understand that the big question under these circumstances is to discover a method that would help us drain this double inflation to the bottom and correct our monetary and banking system so that this phenomenon will not recur in the future."

An open letter to President Johnson of February 26, 1968

1. FIRST LETTER TO PRESIDENT JOHNSON

January 21, 1965

Hon. Lyndon B. Johnson
President of the United States
The White House
Washington, D.C.

Dear Mr. President:

This is a rather unusual gift from the world of ideas which I prepared for your Inauguration Day. Your mention of the "Great Society" coincides exactly with my many years of teaching and writing devoted to the study and explanation of the great ideal of humanity—a free, just and stable society.

Then the State of the Union Message to Congress came and you mentioned specifically: "We seek to establish a harmony between man and society which will allow each of us to enlarge the meaning of his life and all of us to elevate the quality of our civilization. . . . The Great Society asks not how much, but how good; not only how to create wealth but how to use it; not only how fast we are going, but where we are headed. . . ." To give full meaning to the term "Great Society," we should add the word "Free" so that there may be no doubt about what we want and what is to be realized.

The big problems lie ahead of us, namely to discover those practical means, reforms and policies leading to the realization and preservation of Freedom, Justice and Stability for all. Enclosed is a "Plan for the Stabilization of the U.S. Dollar. The Monetary System for the Great Free Society." I hope that it will be of some value to you and our Government.

Very respectfully yours,
Anghel Rugina
Professor of Economics & Finance
Northeastern University

2. A SECOND LETTER TO PRESIDENT JOHNSON

March 15, 1966

Honorable Lyndon B. Johnson
President of the United States
The White House
Washington, D.C. 20500

Dear Mr. President:

Recently a number of prominent economists have asked for an immediate tax increase, supposedly to halt the danger of inflation. Pressure from many areas would seem to indicate that such action is useful, desirable and has to be done now.

The purpose of this letter is first to signal a warning that the proposed tax increase, like the recent hike in interest rates, may end in higher costs of production and thus higher prices, and in our monetary and banking system automatically also in a bigger supply of money. The proposition of higher taxes—besides being a burden to the people—would in reality become a new form of "cost-push" inflation with all the known troubles both for the domestic economy and the balance of international payments.

May I present, Mr. President, for your consideration the enclosed plan for a new, multiple U.S. Dollar which could solve the danger of domestic inflation, put an end to the deficit in the balance of international payments and provide the basis for additional non-inflationary funds for the many projects of the Great Society.

Very respectfully yours,
Anghel N. Rugina

ANR:iar

3. A THIRD LETTER TO PRESIDENT JOHNSON

November 25, 1967

Honorable Lyndon B. Johnson
President of the United States
The White House
Washington, D.C. 20500

Dear Mr. President:

In view of the international tension in the free world's financial markets and based on the fact that we have no reliable instruments to detect in advance where such tension may lead, may I take the liberty of presenting for your consideration the enclosed plan for:

"A New, Heavier U.S. Dollar as a Realistic Solution to Both Domestic Inflation and the Balance of International Payments Problem."

The time of old tools and analysis of the 1930's era has passed. I hope that my plan offers some new perspectives for the development of new thinking and better solutions to the financial problems of today.

Very respectfully yours,
Anghel N. Rugina

4. AN OPEN LETTER TO THE PRESIDENT OF THE UNITED STATES

February 26, 1968

Hon. Lyndon B. Johnson
President of the United States
The White House
Washington, D.C. 20500

Dear Mr. President:

For three years I have tried in vain to convince our Government that the problem of losing gold and the perennial deficit in the balance of international payments would not and cannot be solved by the repeal of the 25% gold requirement and/or by the introduction of voluntary or involuntary controls and regulations in our financial and economic relations with other countries.

Recently the newspapers stated that a new Committee on Price Stability has begun work to explore areas of economic inefficiency which supposedly are a cause for sharp individual price rises. Very good, but again the approach is not adequate and sufficient to solve the two basic problems at hand: (1) a domestic inflation with a tendency for most of the prices to go up, and (2) a chronic deficit in the balance of payments with a continuous loss of gold. To my knowledge no prominent economist in or out of government has pointed out precisely that these two problems are the inescapable result of certain basic deficiencies in our monetary and banking system which we take for granted instead of seeking means to correct them without creating further problems.

We are sitting at home on an inflationary iceberg, granted created during World War II but ever increasing since then. I call it a "stagnant inflation" which has now pervaded and infected the whole economic body of our nation, and it is already grossly malodorous. This peculiar type of inflation that the economists have not yet studied is tricky in behavior: with a little more inflation big chunks of the accumulated monetary iceberg are coming to the surface to show up adversity; with a slight deflation big chunks of the same monetary monster are sinking and creating additional problems.

The international monetary system is also sitting on a similar inflationary iceberg of American dollars, created through our generosity in aiding other countries after World War II by granting foreign aid in dollars convertible in gold when it was not absolutely necessary. A part of the war in Korea and now also in Vietnam was financed through the same unsafe method of using dollars convertible in gold, whereas the power and position of our economy in the world would have made possible the application of some other device with domestic dollars.

The problem we face today, therefore, is a double inflation, one of internal and the other of external dollars. One does not need to have a Ph.D. in Economics to understand that the big question under these circumstances is to discover a method that would help to drain this double inflation to the bottom and correct our monetary and banking system so that this phenomenon will not recur in the future.

In February 1965 I testified before the U.S. Senate Banking and Currency Committee, and I presented to you before appearing there a "Plan for the Stabilization of the U.S. Dollar. The Monetary System for the Great Free Society," with my letter of January 21, 1965.

I renewed my proposal in a letter of March 15, 1966, with an enclosed "Plan for a New, Multiple U.S. Dollar" which proposed to "solve the danger of domestic inflation, put an end to the deficit in the balance of international payments and provide the basis for additional non-inflationary funds for the many projects of the Great Society."

Finally, in the course of the international tension in the free world's financial markets due to the British devaluation last year, on November 25, 1967, I sent to you again for your consideration the present plan with the recommendation to introduce: "A New, Heavier U.S. Dollar as a Realistic Solution to Both Domestic Inflation and the Balance of International Payments Problem."

I did not seem to get anywhere because of strong opposition to my plan from the Treasury Department, from the Board of Governors of the Federal Reserve System and from the Council of Economic Advisors to the President. I thought perhaps they might have a better alternative that could not be made public, and for this reason I resigned myself somewhat not to insist further on a hearing of my plan.

Since first presenting my plan in January 1965, this country has lost about $4 billion gold; the chronic deficit in the balance of payments has not ceased and no better alternative plan has been presented by the above-mentioned authorities except the recent program of involuntary controls of the capital movement and the most controversial tax on American tourists, both measures announcing the beginning of a government-controlled economy and society. Topping this program, the other most controversial proposal of a 10% tax surcharge is not going to make any of our citizens happy, and in addition I am afraid it will lead to more inflation and more tribulations.

In the enclosed paper, "A Rebuttal in the Dialogue of the Century," I took time to explain my proposal and to show that the objections raised by the U.S. Treasury Department are not adequate to invalidate the diagnosis and the recommendations made in the last version of my plan. Soon I shall prove on paper that the objections raised by the Board of Governors of the Federal Reserve System and the Council of Economic Advisors also are groundless, so far as my plan is concerned.

Under these circumstances I cannot have peace of mind knowing that I am right, yet my solutions have been rejected unjustly since 1965—during which time $4 billion gold has been taken from us by foreign creditors at such a cheap price. I am sure, Mr. President, were you a private citizen as in my case and having a positive, correct solution, you would feel the same way: sad, frustrated and disillusioned that scientific truth in such an important issue does not prevail in the appropriate places and at the right time. I know, Sir, that you personally have no fault since you must rely upon the advice of available experts. It is my own profession which should be indicted for present-day troubles; we reached a stage of a pure monopoly of just one model of thinking which we inherited from the British economist John M. Keynes. This model is not suitable to solve correctly the basic problems of our time. Great Britain since the 1930's has followed faithfully the doctrine and the medicine of a paper- and bank-credit money system that Keynes so cleverly called "managed currency." But where is that country today? Why should the United States repeat the British experiment which proved to be a total failure?

It is not only that the chronic deficit and the loss of gold will continue but also all programs which you like so much, as the "War on Poverty" and others, will be in jeopardy. The main reason and stumbling block lie in the inflationary iceberg mentioned before, which is the product of certain basic deficiencies in our monetary and banking system. The thirty million Americans at the bottom of the social and economic ladder cannot achieve their financial independence among other reasons because the same stagnant inflation is continuously chopping away their already meager income. The "cheating of the masses" through inflation is a contradiction in our system, and it must be solved before more violence of the poor flares up. This social side of the issue can be solved effectively and at no extra cost through the application of my plan.

In order to clarify the entire issue, may I ask you, Mr. President, to call on the Treasury Department, the Commerce Department, the Bureau of the Budget, the Board of Governors of the Federal Reserve System and the Council of Economic Advisors to have a joint meeting at the highest level and discuss the pros and cons of introducing a new, heavier dollar as a possible solution to our basic problem of the day.

At the same time I respectfully ask you, Sir, for a private audience to explain the merits of my plan.

Respectfully yours,
Anghel N. Rugina

5. HEARINGS BEFORE THE U.S. SENATE BANKING AND CURRENCY COMMITTEE ON FEBRUARY 9, 1965

GOLD RESERVE REQUIREMENTS

Extract From
HEARINGS Before The
COMMITTEE ON BANKING AND CURRENCY
UNITED STATES SENATE
Eighty-Ninth Congress
First Session
On
S. 797, S. 743, and S. 814
Bills to Amend or Eliminate The Federal Reserve
Bank Gold Reserve Requirements

February 2, 3, 4, 9, and 10, 1965

THE CHAIRMAN. We have Dr. Anghel Rugina, from Jamaica Plain, Mass. He is a professor at Northeastern University, Boston.

STATEMENT OF DR. ANGHEL RUGINA, JAMAICA PLAIN, MASS.

DR. RUGINA. Mr. Chairman and honored members of this committee, I am grateful that you called me to testify against the Government proposition. In many countries this privilege does not exist.

I am a former immigrant who came to the United States in 1950. I became a citizen in 1955, and I think it is an honor to my institution where I am teaching, Northeastern University in Boston, to have the privilege to testify before your Committee.

I hope with your permission, Mr. Chairman, that all my three papers, which I presented previously, will be included in the record so that I do not need to repeat what I have developed there.

THE CHAIRMAN. How many pages would you like to have inserted in the record?

DR. RUGINA. I think altogether there are about 45 typewritten pages.

THE CHAIRMAN. Is there any objection? The Chair hears none. They will be printed in the record.

DR. RUGINA. Thank you.

Why do I think that the bill to repeal in part the 25 per cent gold requirement should be at least tabled for a while until more deliberations can take place?

(1) It is based upon a monetary theory of uncovered paper money versus gold money which was refuted 150 years ago by David Ricardo in the Bullion Report of 1810.

(2) It is based upon a more recent monetary theory, the so-called "managed currency," by Lord Keynes which is the same thing, i.e., paper money controlled by the government which was applied in England since September 1931 and which by now, it is clear to all, is a failure.

(3) The Douglas bill, with great respect due to the Senator from Illinois, himself a peer in the economic field, I think will not solve either of the two basic problems we do have now:

(a) One, the American economy is not growing at a sufficient rate to give an opportunity for any American to work and earn a decent income; (b) to stop the deficit in the balance of payments and the loss of gold.

I have sufficient reason to expect that the repeal of the 25 percent gold requirement, in part or entirety, sooner or later will create more difficulties than we have now. In other words, neither will the domestic economy recover completely, nor will the deficit in the balance of payments disappear.

What is my diagnosis of the present situation of the American dollar which is moving toward a critical situation?

(1) We are now living under conditions where there is a conflict between domestic and foreign considerations. The well-known instrument of monetary policy, i.e., the manipulation of the official discount is out of order; it is useless.

Indeed, if the Federal Reserve System would decide to raise the official discount in order to improve the balance of payments, that rise of the official discount cannot take place without having more difficulties in the domestic economy. Vice versa, if the FRS would decide to decrease the official discount and try to help domestic economy with so many projects of the Great Society, it cannot do it without creating more difficulties with the balance of payments. In this respect, I think, we are stuck.

(2) We have already reached the point where foreign countries with which we trade are most happy when the United States has a deficit in the balance of payments and a steady loss of gold. This is not only disequilibrium but a contradiction which is unbearable to us in the long run. If we do nothing to cope with this condition, then the United States will have the same destiny as Great Britain, on the road to financial bankruptcy.

(3) The external dollar is convertible in gold and has an official value stable since 1934, when the price of gold was fixed at $35. The external dollar, in other words, is a 100 percent guaranteed gold dollar. The internal dollar is not convertible and the value fluctuates every day; yet the 25 percent gold requirement is a brake which introduces a very definite limit to internal inflation.

The existence in the same country of two monetary units (one convertible and the other not) constitutes a split monetary system and is a contradiction in terms.

First, there is a problem of justice. Why should foreigners enjoy the privilege of stable money whereas American citizens are not allowed this privilege since 1934?

Second, whenever there are foreign crises, foreign holders of American dollars have no choice but to ask for gold since the internal dollar is depreciated as compared with the external dollar.

This situation of a double-faced or split-dollar system does not and cannot go on indefinitely without more serious consequences.

Great Britain has experienced this double-faced monetary system between 1931 and 1965. By now should we not have learned the right lesson? Should we repeat the British experiment? Any political leader of this country should have a clear-cut answer to these questions.

(4) The International Monetary Fund and other similar agreements

(so-called "swaps" operations) with the European central bankers, which own the largest share of outstanding claims upon the U.S. Government, cannot solve the problem we have at hand either.

All these agreements are artificial things, goodwill arrangements for postponing a problem. The truth, as I see it, is that there is no substitute for a weak dollar other than a strong and stable dollar.

The outstanding claims in the hands of foreigners are very close to a proportion of 2 to 1 as compared with our gold stock. You cannot cover $2 claims with $1 actual money. It is as simple as that.

Sure, not all creditors will ask for gold at one and the same time. However, this depends upon the conditions in the world markets. If we want to attract some creditors to give up their privilege of converting dollars in gold, then we should offer them a higher rate of interest for investing in this country. But as I said before, that would mean a tight money policy by the F.R.S., which is unacceptable to our own Government and our own economy, as President Johnson mentioned again and again. And I think, on this particular point, the President is right.

What is the primary cause of all these troubles? In accordance with my research we have a double inflation, an inflation of internal dollars and another inflation of external dollars. How these two inflations came into existence is a long story which I cannot go into at this time. The fact is that these two inflations exist at the same time. creating the contradictions mentioned before.

Our government experts are definitely wrong when they say that we have been living under conditions of almost perfect stability since the late fifties or early sixties. The truth of the matter is that we live under conditions of what I call a "stagnant inflation." It is *a stagnant inflation* since at this moment the 25 percent gold requirement forces the F.R.S. to stop a continuation of this inflation, both at home and abroad. But once this gold requirement has been removed then we shall face a fast growing and cumulative inflation.

This stagnant inflation impedes a normal rate of capital formation through voluntary savings. Inflation is the true reason why the American people cannot save enough to assure a normal capital accumulation. Inflation is also the major reason for chronic unemployment; of course, there are other reasons, too.

In foreign trade, because of this *internal inflation,* we cannot export enough to cover the deficit in the balance of international payments. The artificial need for more liquidity in the world markets is created by the American inflation. Inflation has this peculiar effect of feeding itself in the desire to want more and more money. And this is valid both for domestic and foreign inflations.

Solution: I think there is no other solution but to disinflate the supply of dollars at home and abroad. I propose the revaluation of the internal dollar to put it on the same platform with the external dollar, that is, 100 percent gold, stable money. As a result of this, a reunification of our monetary and banking system will be accomplished. I would like to call your attention to the fact that the problem is very difficult, because it is not alone a monetary problem. It is also a banking problem.

How to do it without getting into more difficulties and without producing any deflation? I tried to prove this in my three papers which I submitted previously. Contrary to what Keynesian economists say, gold money is not the enemy but rather a friend to free men and free nations. Modern history has proved again and again that paper money is the true enemy of free men and free institutions through the evil forces of inflation and deflation.

My wish is to ask you to appeal to your conscience and to beg you not to let this bill go to the floor of the Senate until all other alternatives have been presented and debated upon in a public forum. If I be allowed, I would recommend to you that you call here 10 or 12 of the country's top economists and give them a chance to argue the issue. All you need to do is to watch because in the course of such an open dialogue, you will see where the truth is. I shall be at your disposal any time, because I say, and these are my last words: It is not personal opinion, but the truth which should be the basis for your decision.

Thank you!

The papers by Dr. Rugina follow:

1. Preliminaries and Transitory Measures Toward a Complete Stabilization of the U.S. Dollar;

2. A Plan for the Stabilization of the U.S. Dollar. The Monetary System for the "Great Free Society" and

3. A Plan for the Stabilization of the U.S. Banking System for the "Great Free Society."

Note: Since the content of these papers was used to draft the two long Memoranda to President Nixon and also in the article "Monetization of Public and Private Debt as the Principal Fountain of Modern Inflation," which is included in Part Two, there was no need to reproduce them here. They are in the Congressional Record of the Senate Banking and Currency Committee of February 2-10, 1965. Instead, another paper entitled "The Problem of a Stable Monetary and Banking System in the United States: A Historical Review of the Issue," dating the same time and used during the Johnson Administration, was added.

6. THE PROBLEM OF A STABLE MONETARY AND BANKING SYSTEM IN THE UNITED STATES

A Historical Review of the Issue

1. U.S. First Monetary System

The quest for a stable monetary and banking system goes back to the beginning of the nation. The circulation of a multitude of foreign currencies of different qualities disturbed the founding fathers. The first President asked his Secretary of the Treasury, Alexander Hamilton, on April 15, 1790 to work on the project of an American monetary system.

During the same year on December 13, 1790 Hamilton made a report to the House of Representatives proposing the establishment of the first Bank of the United States. It started to operate in 1791 with an initial capital of $10 million, partly subscribed by the Federal Government ($2 million) and the rest by the public. It had the privilege of issuing banknotes up to its capital. The charter extended for 20 years, but in 1811 was not renewed. The reasons for lack of renewal were in part political.

At that time private banks chartered by the states also enjoyed the privilege of issuing their own banknotes. Since the first Bank of the United States was assigned the task of collecting taxes for the Federal Government, the management of the Bank accepted as deposits or in payment of federal taxes only those notes which came from state banks maintaining permanent and unconditional convertibility.

In 1816 the Second Bank of the United States was chartered for 20 years, but in 1836 its charter again was not renewed. During the tenure of these two federally chartered banks the famous "battle of the banks" developed. At the center was a monetary argument: convertible (dear, hard) vs. non-convertible, paper (cheap, soft) money. But this is—as we shall see later—the same thing as the problem of stable vs. unstable currency. Unfortunately other political reasons and even a constitutional issue about the legitimacy of the Federal Government granting such a charter have distracted the attention of the public from the real issue which, as I said, was stable vs. unstable money.

On January 28, 1791 Hamilton presented in his Report a recommendation for the adoption of a bimetallic system[1] as the monetary standard of the United States. The Congress accepted his proposal and passed the Mint Act of April 2, 1792. The gold dollar was equated to 24.75 grains of fine gold and the silver dollar to 371.25 grains of fine silver. This means an official ratio of 15:1 between the two metals.

By selecting two official standards our first monetary system was condemned *ab initio* to face insurmountable difficulties. Indeed, with a bimetallic system, whenever the market value of one of the two metals rises, the other metal automatically becomes cheaper or is overvalued. Gresham's law says that cheaper or overvalued money, under such circumstances, will drive the dearer or undervalued money off the market. The original reasons for Hamilton's money-system design are not determinable now. In any case they were not determined by the central idea of having a stable monetary unit. But we should not rush in with a value judgment. We have to remember that Hamilton was only 33 years old when he developed this project, and I am not sure that in 1791 the concept of a stable monetary system was well established as a definite criterion. About two decades later, David Ricardo raised the problem of unstable money in the form of partially covered notes issued by private banks. It should be noted, however, that in the original Report of January 28, 1791 Hamilton described very well the dangers involved in a bimetallic system.[2] As it happened, the historical conditions were such that both gold and silver coins were pushed out of circulation by paper (unsecured banknotes) money of less value, evidence again of the Gresham law in action. At the end of this first monetary experiment, in 1816, the United States faced in fact approximately in the same situation as before the Mint Act of 1792.

New discoveries of silver in Mexico in the first decade of the 1800's made the American silver dollars appear overvalued compared to gold ones, and thus the official ratio of 15:1 between the two metals was disturbed. By 1834 an amendment to the Mint Act changed the ratio to 16:1, but the results cannot be considered an efficient solution to the given problem. As a matter of fact and principle there is no adequate solution to the problem of bimetallic money system malfunction when the intermetal price ratio changes from the pre-set level because of free market forces.

The new gold discoveries in California in 1848 created conditions leading to the overvaluation of gold and the undervaluation of silver. The Coinage Act of 1853 reduced the weight of all fractional silver coins by 6.9% and limited the legal-tender power of the silver dollar to the amount of $5.00. This legal provision changed the position of the silver dollar from an official standard to a subsidiary coin. In fact, but not in law, the United States shifted to a monometallic system in 1853, or, as some economists argue, as early as 1834, when cheapened gold coins started to drive the relatively more valuable silver coins out of circulation.

The establishment of the First and the Second Bank of the United States, mentioned earlier, did not solve the problem of monetary instability inherent in our first bimetallic system. The battle of the banks ended by 1836 with the victory of the state-chartered banks. At times there were as many as 3,000 to 4,000 different forms of notes issued by private banks chartered by the states.

2. *The Currency Principle vs. the Banking School of Money-System Design*

During the first half of the nineteenth century there was a sharp dispute in England between two opposing schools of monetary thought. The so-called *Currency Principle* initiated by David Ricardo defended the view that, if private banks are allowed to issue unsecured banknotes in competition with each other and/or with a commodity-backed central bank money, the result would be an overissue and an inevitable inflation of unsecured money. On the other hand, a group composed mainly of bankers under the banner of the *Banking School* argued that this was not so because notes were put in circulation with the granting of a loan and were automatically withdrawn with the repayment of the respective loan.

Ricardo and his followers took the position that private banks, in their legitimate search for the highest profit, issue more notes than those withdrawn when the conditions on the market were optimistic. In real life the repeated evidence of an inflation also proved empirically that the first school of thought (Ricardo's) was correct. In 1844 the British Parliament passed Robert Peel's Act, which prohibited private banks from issuing notes as before. The privilege was given only to the Bank of England.

3. *The U.S. National Banking Act of 1863-65*

From 1792 to 1836 the United States also had the problem of unsecured private banknotes issued in competition with secured notes of the First and Second Bank of the United States. Later paper money was issued during the Civil War, the well-known "greenbacks." Their convertibility to gold or silver was suspended in 1862. After the Civil War a solution was sought for the problem of the rapidly inflating money supply. The U.S. National Banking Act of 1863-65 was drafted with the purpose of securing a uniform banknote currency under the control of the Federal Government. The Office of the Comptroller of the Currency was established for this purpose. Only the U.S. National Banks chartered by the Federal Government received the privilege of issuing notes. An amendment to the National Banking Act in 1865 required a tax of 10% upon notes issued by any other bank but a National Bank. The result was an indirect prohibition of notes issued by private banks chartered by the states.

Unfortunately, when judged in the perspective of history, both the British Peel Act of 1844 and the U.S. National Banking Act of 1863-65 have failed to provide stable monetary and banking systems. The major weak point was the fact that both monetary acts contemplated only one form of credit money—namely, partially covered *bank notes*—issued by private banks. There is, however, another significant form of credit money, which is called *bank deposits* or simply credit money, on which a borrower may draw a check. As soon as Peel's Act and the U.S. National Banking Act were passed, the British and the American private banks continued the same kind of business as before, this time shifting the granting of credits to the form of "demand deposits" with the privilege of drawing checks. In fact the use of checks as a payment instrument continuously grew in importance as a result of the passage of those two monetary laws. The ingenious observation and reasoning of Ricardo, and the courageous battles of sound-money proponents leading to the passage of Peel's Act in England and the National Banking Act in America, have been almost forgotten in our time. We stand in 1964 with the same problem of monetary and banking system instability in England and America that was diagnosed so accurately by Ricardo just over 150 years ago. But let us continue with this historical investigation.

4. *The Limping Gold-Silver Standard in the United States (1878-1900)*

The convertibility of greenbacks into gold was reintroduced by the Specie Resumption Act of 1875 and was to start on January 1, 1879. The U.S. Treasury Department was authorized to get some budgetary surpluses in the interim years ahead and accumulate a sufficient gold reserve to make the convertibility possible at the time specified in the Act of 1875.

What about the silver as an official standard? In the Coinage Act of 1873 the silver dollar was not even mentioned on a list of coins that the Mint was authorized to strike. Yet the Bland-Allison Act of 1878 and the Sherman Act of 1890 directed the Treasury Department to buy a certain quantity of silver at the official rate of the old parity 16:1 ($1.29 per fine ounce) when on the free market the price of silver by 1876 was $1.15 per fine ounce.

The two silver Acts confused the nature of our monetary system. In fact, we were on neither a bimetallic nor a monometallic system. This is what in literature was called the *Limping Standard.* It existed between 1878 and 1900. In the 1890's an argument occurred about silver and gold, and the final victory at the polls was in favor of gold. Thus the United States officially introduced the Gold Standard in 1900, abandoning silver and bimetallic currency convertibility for good.

5. *The First Experience with Legal Reserve Requirements*

The National Banking Act of 1863 also introduced legal reserve requirements into our money system. It divided the U.S. National Banks into three categories: Central Reserves City banks, Reserves City banks and Country banks. Banks in the first category were located in New York City and Chicago, and their legal reserve requirement was to maintain in cash 25% or more of their total demand-and-time-deposit liabilities. The second category of banks, located in 16 other (smaller) cities, were required the same rate of 25%, but only half in cash and the other half in interbank deposits with correspondent banks of the first group. These qualified interbank deposits earned the current rate of interest. Country banks made up the third category and were required to maintain at least 15% in reserve made up $\frac{2}{5}$ths in cash and $\frac{3}{5}$ths in interbank deposits. The result of this reform was an enormous concentration of reserves in form of interbank deposits in New York City and Chicago. And this produced such super liquidity at times in the two big cities that bankers at times succumbed to temptation and used these deposit funds to play the stock market. Also, any change of mood in the rest of the country could at another time force the outside banks to put pressure on the big-city banks and withdraw large parts of the interbank deposits. The big-city bankers under such circumstances had no choice but to liquidate on short notice positions taken in stock market speculations. This was the major reason for the money market liquidity crisis and panics like those in 1873, 1890, 1893 and 1907.

The last panic of that era in Wall Street (1907) created a mood for a reform of the banking system in the country. The Knickerbrocker Trust Company collapsed and all New York banks suspended convertibility of their demand-deposit liabilities into gold-backed notes (currency). At that time deposits in the American banks were approximately $15 billion, whereas the circulation of notes by all National Banks was less than $1 billion. The notes of the U.S. National Banks were, as already mentioned, only partially (maximum 25%) covered by gold. During the money panics of that era people tried to convert their "bank deposits" into U.S. banknotes and these notes into gold coins, an operation which, by a simple consideration of the figures just mentioned, was impossible. Thus panics were manifestations of the same money system problem Ricardo described a century before, only this time related to the overissue of "bank deposits."

6. *The Establishment of the Federal Reserve System in 1913*

To cope with problems created by the U.S. National Banks, the National Monetary Commission of 1912 recommended to Congress the establishment of the Federal Reserve System. This proposal was implemented by the Federal Reserve Act of 1913. The privilege of issuing notes was taken from the National Banks and entrusted to the new institution. U.S. National Banks and any state bank willing to accept the reserve requirement controls imposed by the new Central Bank were granted membership privilege in the Federal Reserve System, on the condition that they purchase part of its capital stock. Once this new money system went into operation, member banks were required to keep reserves at the Central Bank in proportion to their deposits. Deposits at the Central Bank were backed 40% in gold and 60% in securities of private nature.

The former U.S. National Banks, with the new name of *member banks,* would do the same thing as the private banks after Peel's Act in England, or the state banks after the U.S. National Banking Act, namely, concentrate on granting loans in the form of *bank deposits* instead of notes as before 1913. The new monetary system made it possible, depending upon the reserve requirement of, say, 20% or 16%, for member banks to grant credits and thus create private "bank-deposit" money, to a multiple of 5 or 6 times the amount of actual funds, respectively the aggregate of reserves in official money.

The Federal Reserve Act of 1913 further provided that the current obligations of the F.R.S. in form of outstanding notes and deposits should be covered by 40% in gold and the rest in commercial paper. This meant that in reality the Central Bank could create reserves for member banks amounting to 2.5 times the supply of gold reserves. Obviously, this new money system has operated after 1913 with a strange mixture of gold money and credit money emanating from both the Central Bank and the private member banks. This means in real terms that the total supply of money created by the Federal Reserve System, including member banks, could fluctuate from 1 unit gold reserve to between 12.5 and 15 times that amount at the limit. The lay public and even many trained economists believed that we had a gold standard, when in reality we were on a mixed monetary system with approximately 10% gold and 90% credit money, issued in part by the Federal Reserve Banks and in larger part by member banks.

How could such a mixed monetary and banking system ever be stable if the observation of Ricardo is held to be correct; namely, that the issue of partially covered notes to which we have to add bank deposits is a major source of a permanent danger of inflation and deflation? This fundamental problem was not thoroughly discussed when in 1913 the Federal Reserve Act was passed. Isn't it true today that in our country the Board of Governors of the F.R.S. and the Federal Government are at one time struggling with an inflationary pressure and at another time with a deflationary reaction? Is this not the best proof that Ricardo's observation is still valid?

7. *The Fruits of the Central Bank Reform of 1913*

One may ask: What are the results of the reform of our Central Bank System in 1913, judged by the history of the last fifty years? After a relatively short contraction of the supply of credit money in the early 1920's and the postwar depression of 1921, an unprecedented wave of speculations on the stock market developed. This created the fabulous boom of the 1920's, which brought the country to the inevitable financial and economic disaster of October 1929.

Some financial experts and professors of economics later accused the members of the Federal Reserve Board between 1929 and 1933 of being responsible for *not* having acted at the right time and in the right proportion and direction. This accusation, in the opinion of this author, is baseless if we consider it from the scientific point of view. The truth of the matter is immediately revealed if we consider two points. *First,* I know of no economists who possess the wisdom and the necessary objective tools to be used in measuring in advance the right time, the right proportion and the right direction for money-supply change. Only after the hurricane of depression did we hear about such hero economists accusing the management of the Federal Reserve System for not having proposed and applied wise or proper monetary policies in time. In fact, in a free society nobody has or could have such an all-comprehensive wisdom and really objective tools. The decisions of the F.R.S., or any other Central Bank of the modern era, were based on the presupposed good judgment of the officials involved and the method of trial and error. But this is evidently not sufficient to correctly solve problems of this nature related to the behavior of millions of free and independent individuals.

Second, and to the crux of the matter, the factor which produced the financial and economic catastrophe of 1929 to 1933 was not the alleged unwise or incorrect management of the Federal Reserve System, but rather the superabundant use of credit money, which in periods of general economic optimism is encouraged by the mixed design of our monetary system. As previously mentioned, the Federal Reserve Act of 1913 has created a system in which the money supply could fluctuate from 1 to 15 times in relation to the available gold reserves. If the observation of Ricardo and other classical economists is true that gold money is relatively stable but credit money is absolutely unstable on a free market,[3] then the evidence of where the ultimate cause of the evil lies is clear. I accept the view that "pure speculations" on the stock and commodity markets, as defined by Nicholas Kaldor,[4] are a great potential force creating economic disturbances when let loose as they are by rapid increases and decreases in cheap credit money. Without cheap credit money the evil of pure speculations would not materialize or affect the market in the same way as today. Indeed, in a 100% commodity (gold) money system, the rate of interest would be determined by the marginal productivity of capital and would be *higher* than under a system of only 10% gold and 90% credit money. This higher rate of interest alone would automatically restrict pure speculations simply because under such conditions the risk appears greater than in a system of artificially lower rates of interest.

Furthermore, in a system of 100% gold money, the inherent stability does not offer a chance for pure speculations to become remunerative on a large scale. In other words, in a well-organized commodity money system the phenomenon of the business cycle, with boom and depression as we know them, could not exist, for the obvious reason that unsecured bank deposit credit expansion and credit contraction are unknown in this system. We may therefore conclude that the final responsibility for the financial and economic tragedy of the 1930's lies with the ill-conceived Federal Reserve Act of 1913, which allowed the supply of credit money through our central and private banking system to fluctuate at the maximum to 15 times the available quantity of official standard or legal tender, to which, in accordance with the law and banking practice, all money was convertible.

8. *The Real Issue During the 1930's*

An economic catastrophe like that of 1929 should have precipitated a thorough study of alternative forms of money-system design, particularly inasmuch as we had been forewarned by Ricardo and others that such events are linked to the kind of mixed system then in operation. The real issue was the same as that raised by Ricardo, only this time in a double fashion.

The *first* question raised should have been: Can we let private banks issue credit money in form of "bank deposits" when we know that this kind of money on a free market produced the phenomenon of upward cumulative price movements (credit expansion) relative to the commodity base and/or downward price change, commodity-relative (credit contraction)? This phenomenon of cumulative price fluctuations was very precisely described as far back as 1898 by the Swedish economist Knut Wicksell.[5] Of course, this question, when posed in terms of private-bank-generated credit money known as "banknotes," had already been answered in the negative in England and America by Robert Peel's Act of 1844 and the U.S. National Banking Act of 1863-65, respectively. Should we or could we apply a different standard of evaluation and judgment about our present-day form of credit money simply because it is called "bank deposits," if we seriously want to solve the problem of monetary and economic stability for the long run without the risk of producing additional evils inherent in a government-regulated economy? Were the issue raised by Ricardo undusted, certainly the public would again ask to outlaw the second form of credit money.

The *second* question should have been: Can we let the Central Bank, respectively the Federal Reserve System, issue the same type of credit money in the form of partially covered notes and deposits for the account of private banks or the government, if we know that such license leads to the uncontrollable inflation/deflation convulsions that Wicksell described? Again the answer would be no. And again one must conclude that the depression of the 1930's provided evidence once again that a free market economy is not well served by a system based on monetized credit on a large scale. If we want to live in a free society and enjoy the fruits of a free and stable economy, then our money and banking system must be redesigned.

The closing of the private banks in 1933, the Emergency Banking Act, the Devaluation of the U.S. dollar in 1934, the establishment of the FDIC and the central Banking Reform of 1935 giving more powers to the Board of Governors of the F.R.S. to control private banking and to a certain extent even speculations on the stock market—all these effect-countereffect or compensatory-type policies rationalized by the Keynesian doctrine were just palliatives, heaping wet blankets on a raging fire. The other kind of policies prompted by cause-and-effect analysis, and which has as its goal the eradication of the roots of the evil, to eliminate as far as humanly possible the causes of the fire, was not considered at that time, simply because the adequate analysis of Ricardo and Wicksell were no longer popular. The popular (institutionally acceptable) ideas of the great new economist—Lord Keynes were to dominate the spirit of the time. Among others, the fascinating British economist threw into the arena of professional thinking the idea that "gold money" was a sort of pure evil, the agent which had produced economic instability and the great depression.

The truth of the matter is just the opposite; the real cause of the great depression was *not* the existence of gold money in circulation but rather the rapid expansion and subsequent contraction made possible, in fact facilitated, by our credit-money system. In the light of history the position of Keynes in this particular issue is revealed to be out of order. Nevertheless his authority was accepted without any adequate challenge, and thus the attention of other economists and the public in general was shifted in the wrong direction, and the design of our mixed monetary system—the crux of the matter—was left unaltered, little different from the way it stood a hundred years before.

Today we know that devaluation of a currency is not necessarily the correct solution for eradicating existing monetary and economic troubles. Many people, bankers and even professional economists, think that having a system of a collective insurance of bank deposits through the FDIC secures a stable banking system. I do not deny that the FDIC represents a relative form of security but it is more psychological than real. Indeed, all the reserves accumulated by the FDIC in the 1950's were equivalent to only 2% of the total of current bank deposits. In the case of a serious "run on the banks," when people in large numbers feel that something is wrong in the economy or in the financial sector and are anxious to convert bank deposits to official "money," the reserves of the FDIC would not be a solid guarantee.

9. *The Reorganization of the Federal Reserve System in 1935*

At this point we can ask: "What about the additional powers given to the reorganized Board of Governors of the F.R.S. in the reform of 1935? Are they a solution in the right direction? "One would answer, in good conscience, that the supplementary powers concentrated in the hands of the Board of Governors does represent an improvement over the previous conditions only in the sense of establishing another palliative that might help to avoid getting into a depression of the same magnitude as that of the 1930's. But the mere existence of these extra powers does not prevent the American economy from experiencing difficulties created by booms (credit expansion, inflation) and depressions (credit contraction, deflation) of relatively smaller magnitude repeated at shorter intervals. The intensity of the business-cycle phenomenon, because of the shorter periods, may be even more harmful than before. When the business cycle is of longer duration, then the businessmen and consumers in general have a little more time to adjust their decisions so as to avoid ill effects up to a certain point. However, when the cycle becomes shorter, and nobody knows the exact degree, then decisions and adjustments in the business world become more difficult. Under such circumstances to be cautious and ready to change investment decisions is literally a must. From here there is one step to the phenomenon of excess capacity and idle resources, even though other factors like overtaxation of profits or undue pressure by organized labor unions may magnify these conditions.

I think these are the types of problems we have in the United States in the late 1950's and early 1960's. The duration of the business cycle is definitely shorter, but its intensity is much stronger than before the 1930's. I am convinced that placing more powers in the hands of the Federal Reserve System or the government does not and cannot solve the kind of problems involved here. In a free society of today we have a serious and fundamental issue in determining the equilibrium supply of money at the point where there is neither inflation nor deflation and a full employment of available resources, without government interference, is achieved.

The history of the United States, especially during the last three decades, has proved that concentration of prerogatives and powers in the hands of governmental agencies has not solved any of the basic issues related to the business-cycle phenomenon and other vital problems. Under these circumstances there must be something wrong in the approach and/or the tools of analysis used. As mentioned earlier, there are two basically different types of policies: (1) Those oriented by the quest for the causes of the evil, and how to eradicate those causes so that the respective evil will not reappear in the future. (These are the classical, cause-and-effect, *ex-ante*, or qualitative policies.) (2) Those oriented by the exclusive concern about the effects of the evil and how to counteract those effects so that the evil will appear less harmful than otherwise. (These are the contemporary, effect-countereffect, *ex-post* or quantitative policies.)

Since the 1930's we have been concerned almost exclusively with experimenting with the application of the second type of policies. If we have any respect for scientific observation and truth, then we ought to accept the fact that we are not using the proper diagnosis or the suitable policy tools. The quantitative approach, even though promoted by the most famous economist of recent times, Lord Keynes, is not sufficient to solve our problems. The history of the United States, in particular, during the last decades has proved this conclusion beyond doubt.

10. The Validity of Keynesian Policies Questioned

The use of effect-countereffect or compensatory form of policy is a major part of the Keynesian heritage. In fact, the basic view of Keynes was that a free society of the capitalistic type has internal contradications which, among other things, produce the phenomenon of involuntary unemployment. So far as this phenomenon exists, the vast majority of economists would agree that it is an evil. If so, then Keynes and any of his disciples would draw the conclusion that all we need to do is to quantify or estimate the evil and let the government create extra employment by indirect means (holding an artificially lower rate of interest to encourage private investment) or direct measures such as public works programs. Whether an artificially lower rate of interest in the long run would prevent another evil, an insufficient capital formation,[6] is put aside as not being relevant when unemployment dominates the picture. The same is true of public works programs. If the government does not have the funds, the Keynesian recipe is the famous formula of government deficit spending. But this formula in the long run creates another evil, the ever-increasing national debt,[7] which, besides being an enormous burden for the current budget, threatens the whole country with the danger of financial bankruptcy.

We have to remember that in the United States the budgetary means of maintaining the national debt alone, i.e., simple refunding with no repayment from the principal, requires $10 billion annually, an amount second only to the national defense. One must understand that there is a serious issue at stake here. The Keynesian economist refuses to think about the national debt and sticks with his concern over unemployment. But unemployment, by the use of these contemporary effect-countereffect policies, remains unresolved in the long run.

Keynesian dogma was so strong, even as far back as 1938, that the recession of that year did not cause other economists in general to question the new theory and its application. It is interesting to ask why the American economists did not begin to question the validity of the Keynesian policies when they saw that the problem of unemployment, inherited from the great depression, was eliminated a decade later by war mobilization, *not* by the presupposed efficiency of the Keynesian full-employment policies. This, however, is an academic question which does not solve the problem with which we are concerned. In order to see the problem we need a change in the spirit of the time.

The quantitative approach is important, but in order to be fruitful in its use, it must be reevaluated as a tool in the service of the cause-and-effect or qualitative analysis and diagnosis. The solution seems evident, but that is not enough. The problem also requires the consensus of peers in the field and of public opinion, which has been so greatly misinformed and misguided during the past decades. Schumpeter used to say that it is difficult enough to develop a concept or a theory, but even more difficult to convince colleagues in the profession that what you offer is really relevant. Under that consideration, the truth as one sees it first has to be expressed in a clear-cut manner to achieve final victory over untruth.

The scare of a postwar depression in the United States, diffused at the international level by a Russian economist, Eugen Varga, and accepted by a group of prominent American economists led by Schumpeter, was so skillfully manipulated by Keynesian experts in charge of advice in high places that the country ended up with two more basic reforms moving in the wrong direction. I say "in the wrong direction" because I feel that, if the American people were informed correctly and consulted according to the democratic process, then I am sure that the vast majority would be for a free society and a workable free economy and against a government-controlled society and economy.

The first reform to move in the wrong direction was the Monetary Act of 1945, wherein the requirement of 40% coverage, in gold certificates, of the outstanding amount of notes and deposits of the Federal Reserve System was reduced to only 25%. This piece of legislation in practice meant that the framework of the American monetary system was diluted to a greater extent than before and made even more unstable. Indeed, after 1945 the F.R.S. could increase the supply of official reserves, that is, funds for the private banking system, at a maximum of 4 times the amount of gold certificates, instead of 2.5 as before. Since the private banking system accordingly is creating $6 in credit money for every $1 official reserves, it is easy to see how, after the monetary reform of 1945, the total supply of money in this country can fluctuate from 1 to 24 times the aggregate of gold certificates.

This much greater instability of our monetary and banking system created by the law of 1945 inevitably required more control of the banking system and of the economy. The second reform to move in the wrong direction had as its major purpose the furnishing of tools for this extra control of the economy, even though officially the legislators thought in good conscience that this reform was made to serve a good cause (not to let happen what Eugen Varga and other prominent economists were talking about). This was the Employment Act of 1946. The U.S. Government assumed by law the task and the powers to "promote maximum employment, production and purchasing power." The language of this law is purely in Keynesian terminology. The Employment Act of 1946 sets as its goal a "maximum" employment, production and supply of money without qualification. The truth of the matter is that the pursuit of such a goal without any qualification might end with conditions of maximum inflation, either real or potential, or maximum instability of the monetary standard by which we measure the performance of both individual and national economy, the private as well as the public sector. It might also end with the danger of ever-increasing national debt coupled with the specter of financial collapse. Poor financial conditions within a domestic economy sooner or later will also uncover difficulties in the balance of international payments. But, at the time the Employment Act was passed, the professional economists in high places were Keynesian disciples. Their advice was fully accepted.

11. The Precarious Boom of the 1950's

The legendary boom of the 1950's in America again impeded professional economists, not committed to the Keynesian dogma, in getting to the roots of the problem. The price paid for that legendary boom was double. First, the national debt has increased continuously without legitimate cause since the end of the Korean War. Second, again without a legitimate cause, the U.S. balance of international payments has been deteriorating steadily with a large loss of gold. It is almost incredible that the United States in such a short period of time and under conditions of supposed prosperity changed from a creditor nation to the status of a debtor country. What further proof do we need, and how much longer must we wait, to see that something is fundamentally wrong in the method of analysis and the policies we have been using during the last decades?

Added to these problems, we have, in the 1960's, another national headache—chronic unemployment, not of alarming magnitude but enough to make the whole system look unstable. From certain conservative circles we often hear that the pressure exercised by the labor unions and the excessive level of taxation of corporate profits (52%) have created an unfavorable climate for business. It is no longer profitable or advisable to follow investment plans where the expected rate of profit just covers the cost of capital. This can explain, to a large extent, though not completely, why the American economy at present has not grown sufficiently to make full economic use of our available resources in manpower, capital and other factors. Even if the labor unions were stripped by law of whatever monopolistic power they have or practice, and even if the Federal Government were to drastically reduce the corporate profit taxes, we would still *not* have any guarantee that our economy would automatically function normally or achieve stability with full employment, if we preserve a monetary and banking system where the supply of money can fluctuate drastically in both directions—expansion or contraction.

The inherent instability of our domestic dollar, which is an all-pervasive malady, is able at any time to contaminate the whole economy and cause it to move in artificial paths, sometimes too fast (a boom) and other times too slow (a recession or depression). The consequences of this zigzag pattern of economic activity are not only financial and economic but also social and even political in nature. I think that these abnormalities are not an inevitable product of a free society, as, for instance, Keynes thought, but rather the inevitable result of using credit money, which, by its nature and function, does not fit with free decisions which characterize a free country.[8]

12. *A Proposed Reform Leading to Even More Troubles*

There is at this time (1964) a proposed law in Congress to get rid of the 25% requirement in gold certificates reserves behind the outstanding liabilities in form of deposits of the Federal Reserve System.

If such a law should ever be passed, the 24-times limit in the fluctuations of the total supply of credit money would go into an indefinite limit or, in practical terms, into the territory of arbitrary policies. The Board of Governors of the Federal Reserve System would have no legal guide in their decisions. Today, whatever monetary policies are followed by the F.R.S., the supply of official money cannot come too close to the legal provision of 25% requirement in gold certificates. If this legal restriction is removed, then private decisions and public policies would operate in a vacuum. At one stroke the whole monetary and banking system would be converted to a completely shaky order. It would establish conditions to realize the final dream of Lord Keynes, namely, to give up gold altogether and introduce a thoroughly "managed currency" by the central government.

It is rather strange that some prominent American bankers support such a reform. They probably think naively that if there is no reserve requirement for the Federal Reserve System then the same thing should be applied for private banks. That would mean that the business of creating "credit money" in the form of bank deposits and charging a regular rate of interest would become completely a private affair of the bankers. In reality this is an illusion. Without high reserve requirements for both private and central bank systems, the whole monetary and banking framework becomes so inconsistent and unstable in respect to decisions by the people and those who control the system, that, with the passing of time and due to so many difficulties, a radical change in the structure of our society, economy and form of government is inevitable.

The proposed law (1964) to eliminate the 25% gold certificates reserve is also associated with our difficulties in the balance of international payments. Here there is another illusion. There are many views regarding the issue of explaining the loss of gold and its consequences. However, as soon as there were sufficient evidence that this law would be passed, the international confidence in the strength of the U.S. dollar would gradually erode. We now have approximately $15.5 billion of gold reserves. The total amount of foreign claims on this gold is over $25 billion (1964). Foreign creditors, except those who rushed to get the gold in time, could then one day introduce procedures of bankruptcy against the U.S. Government or simply refuse to accept American dollars. This, I hope, will never happen.

A new devaluation of the U.S. dollar now, when we are a debtor nation, cannot be accomplished without other dangerous consequences. In 1934 we were a creditor nation; therefore, we were not required to give account to anyone for that first devaluation of the dollar. Now in the 1960's the situation is entirely different. We have to ask the creditors what they think about such an operation if we want to see the U.S. dollar still used as international currency.

This abnormal situation of today (1964) is expressed by the fact that the U.S. dollar inside the country is "paper money," fluctuating with the issue of private bank credit money, while outside it is "gold money" with an official value not changed since 1934. This split or divided standard cannot be continued indefinitely without unpleasant consequences. The gap between the "domestic" and the "foreign" dollar (supposedly one and the same currency) is so big that in the long run no props are sufficient to perpetuate this imbalanced situation. The U.S. mixed unstable domestic monetary and banking system is responsible for this to a large extent.

This is the historical reassessment of the problem of a stable monetary and banking system in the United States. The next step for a reasonable solution requires two more investigations. One is the proof that a 100% commodity money system does supply a sufficient quantity of money for a normal functioning of a free economy tending toward full employment; and is stable without the need of steady government guidance and control either directly or through the Federal Reserve System. The other investigation should be concerned only with the practical issue of how and under what institutional changes we can move from the present situation in the new stable monetary and banking system without being exposed to other kinds of trouble.

Boston, Massachusetts
January 1964

NOTES

1. For the original Report of the Establishment of a Mint see: *Alexander Hamilton and the Founding of the Nation,* edited by Richard B. Morris (New York: The Dial Press, 1957), pp. 355-57.
2. *Ibid.*
3. For an explanation in detail see: Anghel Rugina, *Geldtypen und Geldordnungen. Fundamente für eine echte allgemeine Geld- und Wirtschaftstheorie* (Stuttgart: W. Kohlhammer Verlag, 1949), especially part three; and Anghel Rugina, "Programme de Stabilisation Économique, Financière et Sociale pour la France. Conditions d'etablissement d'une économie et d'une société libre et stable en France," *Revue d'Économie Politique,* Mars-Avril 1959.
4. Nicholas Kaldor, "Speculation and Economic Stability," *The Review of Economic Studies,* vol. VII, no. 1, October 1939.

5. Knut Wicksell, *Geldzins und Guterpreise,* 1898.
6. Simon Kuznets, *Capital in the American Economy. Its Formation and Financing.* A study of the National Bureau of Economic Research (Princeton University Press, 1961).
7. James M. Buchanan, *Public Principles of Public Debt. A Defense and Restatement* (Richard D. Irwin, Inc., 1958).
8. Anghel Rugina, "Und es kann doch 'neutrales' Gold geben! Eine Antwort an Herrn Prof. Dr. Fritz W. Meyer, Bonn," *Weltwirtschaftliches Archiv,* Band 67, Heft 2, 1951.

Part Two: Pure Economics
Matters of Theory

Chapter IV

The Economics of Stable Equilibrium

The virtues and benefits of a free society and economy with a truly democratic government are unlimited. The vagaries and calamities are limited and are due in modern times largely to an inadequate monetary, banking and financial system.

Commodity money, or what Walras called Numeraire, once brought humanity from a primitive stage to civilization, as Fr. von Wieser, an economist of the Vienna School, correctly observed.

Paper-, fiat- and credit-money and their corollaries are now menacing the future of man and humanity with a new, more sophisticated form of slavery—*Government-controlled economy and society.* Paper money deceives political leaders, economic experts and the people in general. While on the surface it appears relatively cheap and easy to manipulate, nevertheless, by its nature and function, it gradually inflicts enormous harm to society and produces unacceptably high social costs. And the high social costs are: instability, widespread social inequities and the necessity of curtailing human freedoms by concentration of illegitimate powers in the hands of modern government.

1. NATIONAL PURPOSE: THE THIRD ROAD OF SOCIAL LIBERALISM*

A "NEW SOCIETY" OF TOMORROW BASED ON FREEDOM, SOCIAL JUSTICE AND STABILITY

"Since order is the absolute requisite of civilized life, we must stick to the order that is, until there is a reasonable agreement on changes that will be on balance beneficial."

FRANK H. KNIGHT

1. *Introduction: New Tools for Old Problems*

The really basic problems in sociology, economics and political science do not change too much with the passing of time if we refer to a given period in history. What actually may change are the methods and techniques, the analytical tools and the reasoning used in trying to solve them.

It is true that the application of some new tools can help us not only to solve old problems better but also to raise new issues. However, the new issues very often represent old problems that were overlooked, forgotten or not yet solved.

I think that in general we could have an agreement among scientists about the really basic issues in all social sciences. In fact, considering the whole modern era we shall find scientists preoccupied with one or the other of the following two kinds of problems:

First, the quest for stability in terms of stable equilibrium in a framework where we assume the exclusive existence of normal phenomena (Walras-Pareto-Marshall models);

Second, the study of any system or conditions that are deviations from the stable equilibrium, namely, abnormal phenomena which may be both the cause and/or the effect of instability (Marx-Freud-Keynes models).

---

*This article was published in *Acta Scientiarum Socialium.* Societas Academica Dacoromana, Munich, West Germany, 1971.

What often is not clear among scientists of the last decades is the fact that all classical thinkers, with very few exceptions, were concerned exclusively with problems of stability of the stable-equilibrium type. This is the spirit and the methodological framework in which the so-called classical laws and heritage should be comprehended. Contemporary scientists, on the other hand, have devoted themselves almost exclusively to the study of instability issues (e.g., in economics, the analysis of boom and depression or of inflation and deflation) and definitely have come up with brand-new results partially, or even totally, unknown to classical thinkers.

Unfortunately, it was not pointed out from the beginning that the new research and subsequent results, in themselves, have absolutely nothing to do with the classical laws. In practice, however, the new results were presented in such a manner and form as if they were opposing and thus contradicting the validity of the classical laws. One of the major arguments of this article is to raise the issue that this kind of thinking does constitute a gross methodological error of incalculable consequences for the future of all social sciences, not to mention the future of the United States and the rest of the free world, in the course of application of policies based on the recommendations of scientists who are committing this fundamental error.

To sharpen the argument I shall repeat that the results of classical sociology, economics and political science *organically* are valid only in the model of a free and stable society and economy conceived as an ideal world toward which we should strive. Contemporary studies in the same fields are concentrated upon issues (theoretical and practical) of instability raised by a unique set of conditions prevalent in the modern-day world. These two worlds should be kept separate and judged on their own merits: One, the *real* world we live in; and the other, the *ideal* world we should aspire to reach if we want genuine progress.

In this direction there is one *fact* which cannot be changed because it is a self-evident truth: The ideal world of stability (the classical model) and the real world of instability (the contemporary model) are located toward the limit of two polar systems. Therefore, from the methodological point of view it is not permissible to use results from the latter model in order to invalidate results from the first model, or *vice versa.* Strangely enough, just this kind of negative work was done on a large scale during the past decades, with no other results than to confuse the minds of young generations about the real issue. Furthermore, the classical standards in education and culture based on respect for ideal values in human life and society were lowered to the point of spiritual nihilism, spiritual anarchy, and spiritual indifference or apathy where youngsters with no sense for values are ready even to betray their own country.[1]

To confuse and make a settlement of the real issue even more difficult, other scientists have suggested that a new "grand neo-classical synthesis" is possible, and thus they believe the argument would be solved forever. This project would again be succumbing to the same methodological error. Indeed, to take results from the study of a world of instability (contemporary model) and to adjust them to results coming from the search of a world of stability (classical model) is an impossible operation which cannot be done unless by the use of some "hocus-pocus" methods of reasoning. To have recourse for the same purpose to the opposite technique of arbitrarily amending classical laws in such a way as to make them fit the new results, in my opinion, oversteps the boundaries of scientific work and reaches the point where intellectual integrity appears to vacillate.

To my way of thinking it is high time to deal seriously with this kind of basic methodological issues. This article contains some new ideas in this direction. Obviously, such an immense task cannot be accomplished in a single article. I hope that I shall have a chance to continue the debate raised here at some other time.

The reader is cautioned that the language and the spirit of this article are somewhat of a departure from the prevailing manner and techniques used in social and economic research of today. That does not imply that I am a heretic who negates the results of new economics, sociology and political science. Such a reactionary position is far removed from the true attitude of this author.

I certainly agree that contemporary research in the areas mentioned has enriched all social sciences with invaluable new material. What has puzzled me for a number of years is that, with all this immense new research, the basic problems were solved neither in theory nor in practice to a degree of reasonable acceptance. On the contrary, the new research makes the old problems become increasingly complicated, until one day, alas, as in the allegorical world of Orwell's *1984* everybody will doubt everything and no one will any longer believe in what we today call science or scientific truth.

Judging this situation by the use of common sense alone, one can visualize that something must be wrong in the whole affair. Take, for instance, in economics the basic problems of what determines the rate of rent, wages, interest, profit or taxation. I am sure that fifty years ago an economist with academic training would have answered precisely that in a free economy (of Walras' or Marshall's model) the principle of marginal utility and productivity was the major determinant. How many economists of today would subscribe to the above answer as correct beyond doubt? I understand that the classical thinkers were not cautious enough to point out that their so-called "natural laws" were valid *only* for a free and stable economy and society and nowhere else, especially *not* in the muddled conditions of real life even in those days. But that does not mean that their results were not true in the model on which they worked as men of science.

Conclusively, I feel that the confusion of today and our incapacity to solve the basic problems, both in theory and practice, among other things are due to the methodological break with the classical values and way of thinking. My real, basic position represents an effort to construct the missing link between the past and the present. In other words, I am looking for a bridge between the classical heritage and the contemporary new economics, sociology and political science.

My new tools may appear oversimplified to some sophisticated readers. In fact, no mathematical formula and no quantitative approach is used. Instead the new tools are of purely conceptual nature and belong to what is called qualitative analysis. I would like, however, to stress that there is no contradiction between quantitative and qualitative analysis unless in a given problem one method or the other was misused. As a matter of fact, the end results of the two analytical methods should be the same in principle. Whenever they are not the same, then the issue of why they are not should be investigated.

I have tried to express my concepts and reasoning in a definitely explicit fashion in order to avoid any possibility of misrepresentation or confusion. Furthermore, by so doing I kept myself in line with the "simplicity postulate," or the principle of simplicity as applied in natural sciences. One of the most prominent thinkers of this century, the British physicist Sir James Jeans, put it this way: "When two hypotheses are possible, we provisionally choose that which our minds adjudge to be the simpler, on the supposition that this is the more likely to lead in the direction of the truth."[2]

With this introduction let us go now to the main subject of this article.

2. *The Three Basic Laws of Consistency*

If we look with an analytical eye at the United States of America or at any other country in the world today or at any other time in history where organized social life existed, among many other things we can find one striking characteristic: Human societies, like nature, are composed of *stable* and *unstable* elements, institutions, practices, customs, and habits. Of course, in some communities we shall find more and in other communities less of the first or the latter type. But that does not change the nature of the argument I would like to raise, namely, the existence of stable and unstable elements in the real world in which we live. This I consider to be a matter of fact which is evident to anybody without difficulty as soon as his attention is called to it.

That is the central observation with which I am starting, and since I do not see any possible argument to negate its veracity, I consider it as a sort of scientific axiom of the self-evident type.

From and around this axiom an attempt will be made in this article to show that, with the help of some new analytical tools, we are able to see the real nature and solution to almost all the major problems of our time. If only we had enough civic responsibility, courage and wisdom to purge our modern society of all, or at least most, of the unstable institutions and practices and at the same time to reinforce and consolidate the stable ones! There is the key for another, brighter future of a "New America," as well as any other country where people want to live under conditions of freedom, social justice and stability. This is the old but also the new American dream!

• • •

What is a "stable" and what is an "unstable" element in the composition of a civilized human society? This is a sort of Hamletian question of "to be or not to be" which has to be carried out in sociology, political science, law, economics and finance, and all social and cultural disciplines. I realize the difficulty of the task I have set for myself, but I shall try to keep my concepts so clear-cut that I hope in the end to be able to survive any possible major criticism.

Perhaps the first thing to do is to point out that an "element" as conceived here may take various forms in real life, such as: individual unit (person or thing), effect, phenomenon, force, principle, institution, value, procedure, practice, behavior, and so forth. It is almost anything of the type of an entity in a human society which can be defined and has its own identity. It is an indivisible and autonomous particle, force or principle (some visible and some invisible) of a community of men living in an organized society. It is true that as a concept these *social elements* are by definition similar to the chemical elements in the composition of the physical universe.

1. The first problem consists of the question: What is a "stable" element as defined above? To answer this problem, I used the classical concept of "self-mechanism" (i.e., self-coordination, self-control, self-preservation, self-development, self-action, self-existence), and also the contemporary concept of "built-in stabilizer," both in the sense of an inherent quality of everything which can stand by itself in a very definite

space-time framework. I shall call the framework "system," "order," or using the contemporary terminology of "model." Thus any element of a human society is stable when, under the assumption of a very definite time-space framework, it can stand, develop, and exist by itself. In other words, a stable element is consistent with or within itself. This I call the *first law of consistency,* and it refers to the internal structure of an element.

A pictorial representation of the first law of consistency is conceived in figure 1.

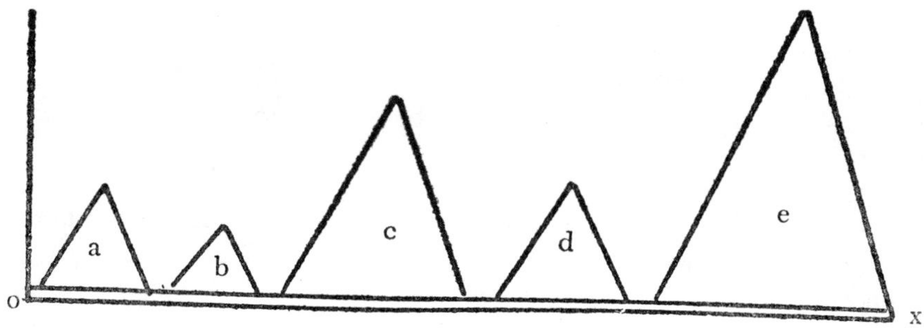

FIGURE 1

Because the first law of consistency is fulfilled, *a, b, c, d,* and *e* are stable elements.

We should now consider further that very definite framework. First of all, we must get into the habit of thinking in terms of a definite space-time framework as a system, in order not only to do correct logical reasoning, but also to be realistic and not to get lost in pure speculations. Indeed, without assuming a space-time framework nothing exists or can be realistically conceived.

In figure 1 the axis "*o x*" can be used to represent the space-time framework which I would now like to define.

The same classical concept of "self-mechanism" or "built-in stabilizer" has to be applied also to the space-time framework. Thus a social framework is stable whenever it can stand by itself, and it will stand by itself whenever it is consistent with and within itself. I call this the *second law of consistency.*

Viewing figure 2 it seems almost self-evident that the framework in question is stable, and therefore it is able to provide a solid foundation where the elements *a, b, c, d* and *e* from figure 1 can preserve their inherent stability. If, however, figure 2 were to be inclined to either side, then the stability of those individual elements of figure 1 would be jeopardized beyond any doubt.

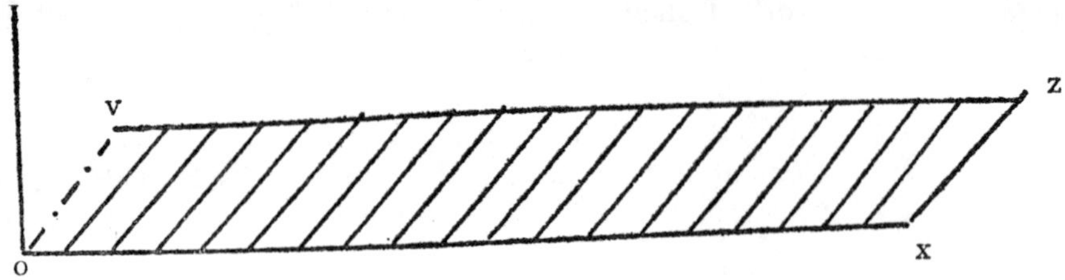

FIGURE 2

We can see now the organic relationship between the first and the second law of consistency. Individual elements are *truly* stable only when they have consistency in themselves and are located in an adequate space-time framework which is also consistent with itself. The organic relationship between the two could be considered the *third law of consistency.*

2. Let us raise the second problem: What is an "unstable" element in a given human society? The answer is not so difficult if the solution to the first problem is correct. I shall assume in good faith that it is so. Then simple, logical reasoning can help to solve the second problem. By the application of the so-called polar-types technique, an unstable element or framework in its pure form has to be the reciprocal of a stable one. Thus an element is unstable whenever it cannot stand by itself. The first reason for instability may lie in its own nature, simply because it does not fulfill the first law of consistency. In other words, it is not consistent in its internal structure.

This situation can be represented in the following manner:

Elements *m, n, o* and *p* are unstable (inconsistent) in their own nature, even though the space-time framework in which they are located is stable.

Finally, it is possible that an element cannot stand by itself, not due to its own nature but because it was located in an unstable system.

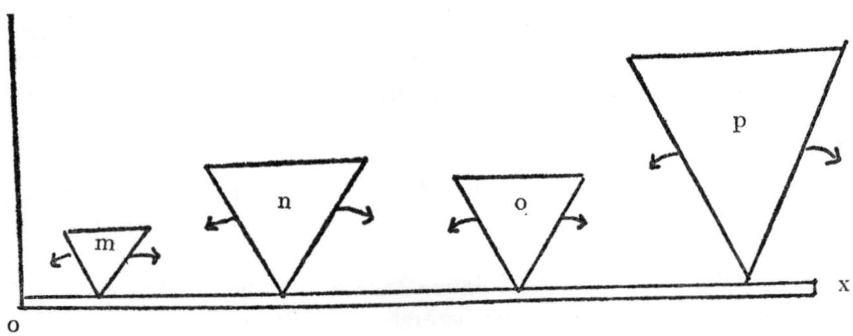

FIGURE 3

We can figure out various types of unstable frameworks. The pure form, as mentioned before, should be the reciprocal figure 1.

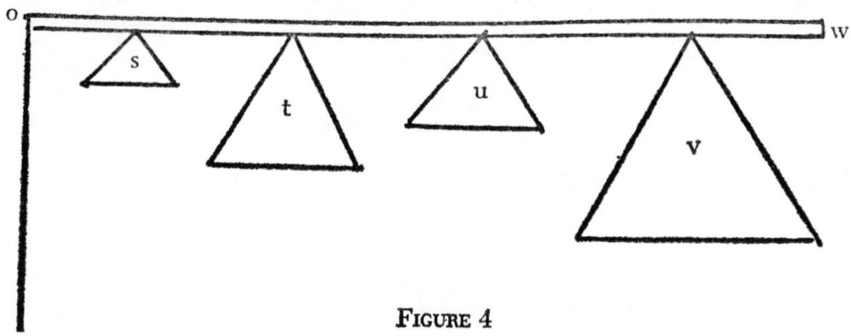

FIGURE 4

Elements *s, t, u* and *v* appear to be stable in their own structure, but because they are located in an upside-down type of framework (*o w*), they cannot behave in accordance with their own nature as stable elements. They will fall down by the nature of things and produce disturbances, and possibly chaos and disorder. In conclusion, the framework of figure 4 has inherent instability.

Of course, thinking in contemporary terms, we could construe conditions where elements *s, t, u* and *v* would not directly fall down but continue to exist in an abnormal way. For instance, suppose that an extraneous and sufficiently strong power keeps them bound to the "*o w*" axis regardless of their natural tendency. This is the classical case of the application of the principle of central planning and control in a totalitarian regime, of the right or of the left. Given such a case, we should then view figure 4 from the other side (viz. from the top), and the same elements would now appear unstable. This proof is valid to refute the argument of enemies of free society who think that their framework is a normal and stable one. Indeed, figure 4 indicates that regardless from what direction we view it (front, back, south or north), the conclusion is the same: There is an inconsistency between the nature of individual elements and the framework. Thus the third law of consistency is broken, and therefore the instability of Model 4 is inherent.

Applying the second law of consistency, we discover more precisely the cause of instability, namely, in the nature of the system. One important point to remember is that strict application of the principle of central planning and control in Model 4 can maintain the existence of the system indefinitely (more exactly, as long as the extraneous force of absolute power can be used to the full extent!), but that does not mean that the unstable *nature* of the framework was changed.

Just because a government with unlimited powers is absolutely necessary to keep Model 4 in existence, is *ipso facto* the proof and self-evidence that the system represented in figure 4 has inherent, but in a totalitarian regime hidden, instability. Perhaps the latter regime could be represented in figure 4-a.

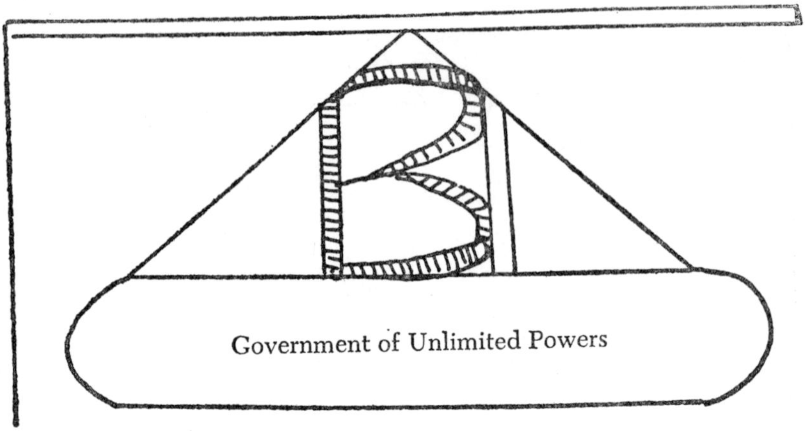

FIGURE 4-a

The individual elements *s, t, u* and *v* through the use of force (compulsory cooperation) were pressed into a monolithic structure supported by an absolute form of government with *B* representing the "Big-Brother" power, so masterfully described by George Orwell in his now classic work *1984.*

Finally, it is possible that the framework has inclined toward just one side or the other, as in the pictorial representation in figure 5.

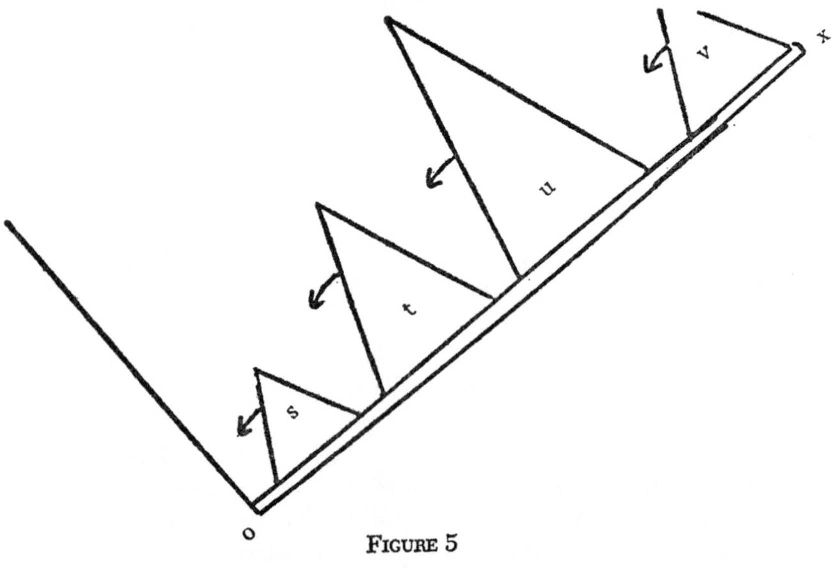

FIGURE 5

From the sketch it is self-evident that stable elements in an unstable system cannot preserve their stability.

3. *Table "A" with Stable and Table "B" with Unstable Elements*

Having settled the strictly methodological issue, the great task ahead is to make a thorough analysis of modern societies and evolve a Table "A" with stable and a Table "B" with unstable elements. To construct these tables is a laborious, sometimes hazardous and even treacherous task. Besides presenting a stern challenge, to wade through it successfully one needs patience, skill and above all an undogmatic mind. I shall give a sample of such tables as I have completed in my workshop over a number of years, noting that they are not by any means complete. Of importance is not the number of elements in one table or the other, but rather the new kind of analysis where we look for something very definite, namely, what is stable and what is unstable.

The construction of such tables for the entire structure of a modern society represents a life work not only for one but for a whole generation of men of science. It is a *new approach* and a *new vision* because we no longer merely face realities and become bewildered by their immense complexity. We now have a scope, a meaning of *what* to look for and *why*, and a little candle which throws light on the road ahead.

Here are samples of the two tables:

I. SOCIAL FIELD

TABLE "A" OF STABLE ELEMENTS	TABLE "B" OF UNSTABLE ELEMENTS
1. Individual freedom as a legitimate, natural right.	1. Total or partial negation of freedom of the individual.
2. Justice of fair (equitable) shares.	2. Injustice of equal or unequal shares.
3. Natural (normal) inequality in the distribution of income and wealth as a result of differentiated human performance.	3. Forced (artificial) equality or inequality in the distribution of income and wealth.
4. Voluntary (free) cooperation.	4. Imposed (compulsory) cooperation.
5. Stable equilibrium.	5. Disequilibrium (open or hidden) or unstable equilibrium.

6. Peace (social-, class-, race-, ideology tolerance and understanding).	6. War (open or hidden) (class-, social-, ideological struggle and subversion).
7. Natural order in the sense of derived from the nature of things, respectively from conditions of stable equilibrium.	7. Disorder (open or hidden) (anarchy and riots) or an imposed artificial order.

II. POLITICAL FIELD

1. The voice of the majority recognized and respected.	1. The voice of a minority or of a single despot or dictator prevails.
2. The rights of the minorities preserved.	2. Little or no concern about the rights of the majority and minorities.
3. Free (openly repeated) elections.	3. Lack of or make-believe (fake) elections.
4. Government by consent.	4. Government by social coercion.
5. Government of limited (delegated) powers.	5. Government of unlimited (inherent, absolute) powers.
6. Division of public powers.	6. Undue concentration of public and/or private powers.
7. True, genuine democracy.	7. True, genuine dictatorship or despotism.

III. ECONOMIC FIELD

1. Free and fair competition.	1. Monopoly (private or public) inclusive oligopoly and unfair competition of any form.
2. Private and public ownership based on actual performance of the same value.	2. Private and public ownership based on sheer power, abuse of confidence or pure speculation.
3. Free, personal choice in consumption.	3. Restricted or no personal choice in consumption.
4. Private decisions in regard to investments in the production of private goods.	4. Government decisions (in part or totally) of private investments.
5. Free foreign trade.	5. Private or public monopolies in foreign trade.
6. Free foreign exchange market.	6. Government-controlled foreign exchange market.

7. Prices = least ATC inclusive a normal rate of profit. ATC = Average total cost per unit of output composed of paid or imputed rent, wages, interest, taxes and a normal rate of profit equal to the cost of management.	7. Prices greater than ATC with an unjustified profit differential or an overcharge due to inefficiency; prices smaller than ATC with a loss to the economy.

IV. FINANCIAL FIELD—PRIVATE FINANCE

1. Natural (commodity) money, Numeraire.	1. Nominal (credit, fiat) money, anti-Numeraire.
2. Separation between money- and capital markets.	2. Little or no separation between money- and capital markets.
3. Natural (real) capital based on voluntary savings.	3. Nominal (artificial) capital based on forced savings.
4. Natural (real) rate of interest.	4. Nominal (artificial) rate of interest.
5. New investments = voluntary savings.	5. New investments greater or smaller than voluntary savings.
6. Free, independent central bank.	6. State- or government-controlled central bank system.
7. Natural (real) transactions on the stock-, exchange- and commodities markets in the sense of outright buying and selling.	7. Nominal (artificial) transactions on the stock-, exchange- and commodities markets in the sense of bets on price fluctuations in the future or pure speculations.

V. FINANCIAL FIELD—PUBLIC FINANCE

1. Separation of the public sector (government administration) from the private sector of the economy.	1. Little or no separation between the public and the private sector of the economy.
2. The issue of money separated from the public budget.	2. Administration of the public budget intermingled with the issue of money.
3. Decentralization of public administration in accordance with the nature of issues: national, regional and local.	3. Centralization of public administration in the sense that all issues in principle are resolved at or controlled by the national government.

4. The existence of national, regional and local budgets as independent entities.	4. All budgets are affiliated directly with and are dependent on or subordinated to the national budget.
5. All public revenues at their original source are shared in a fair (equitable) proportion among the central, regional and local governments.	5. All or most of public revenues are centralized into the hands of the national government, which can spend them at its discretion.
6. Voluntary taxation in the sense that public budgets are submitted to a referendum, once in each legislative period (be it two, four or five years) and are accepted by the voice of a qualified majority.	6. Compulsory taxation or taxation by coercion in the sense that the executive power of government decides upon the amount of expenditures and, with or without the consent of the legislative branch, the people are forced to pay that amount.
7. Public debt is separated from the issue of money in the sense that there is no monetization of public or private debt.	7. The issue of money is not separated from the public debt in the sense that public debt may be monetized when the needs of the government require.
8. Public sector in equilibrium in the sense that the marginal cost of public services is equal to the marginal utility of public services as determined under point 6 above.	8. Public sector in disequilibrium or under conditions of unstable equilibrium because the marginal cost of public services does not correspond to their marginal utility.

As previously mentioned, these tables should be interpreted as a sample of the results of my work. To me everything is clear. The story of how these tables were developed may be of interest to the reader.

Tables "A" and "B" were conceived in a rudimentary form as far back as 1945. For their conceptual nurture I owe very much to the late well-known German economist Professor Walter Eucken, with whom I was working at the time at the University of Freiburg i. Br. Unfortunately, he died early and did not have a chance to see the applicability of the tables to the full extent. Because of Eucken's theoretical approach, I became interested in Max Weber's concept of ideal types (*Idealtypen*) used in sociology. Further work on Keynes', von Wieser's and Fr. Knapp's nominal (credit) theory of money, and also on Menger's, Walras', Marshall's real (commodity) theory of money, opened my eyes to see that commodity (real) and credit (nominal artificial) money are two polar types of money which organically belong to two opposite forms of economic systems. From that moment on, the road was largely open for the development of the present tables.

The concept of stable and unstable elements was used first in the analysis of monetary, banking and business field in a work published in German.[3] By 1957 the tables were completed to their present form, and it was evident that as a method of analysis they were suitable to the entire study of human societies. In 1958 I used them again to work out a plan for social, economic and financial stabilization of France, part of which was published in French in 1959.[4]

For those who would like to follow this type of work, I would recommend not rushing into generalizations of the easy-thinking manner: "Now I have it, or from now on I know it!" The three laws of consistency are clear and quite simple, but their application to each individual case of analysis is an intricate and delicate operation. To avoid an arbitrary classification in the tables, we need also a composite standard of basic principles to make the decision a matter close to self-evidence. That will be the primary line of testing which I shall treat soon.

Further, may I call attention to the enormous difficulties which arise when we undertake the analysis of an institution of our days that at first glance stands as an entity, and yet, by scratching below the surface with the new tools, we find that a part of it is stable, whereas the balance is unstable. This mixed nature of many modern institutions constitutes the great puzzle: progress and instability at the same time. The main trouble in our time does not come so much from "modern" man but rather from unstable institutions of the aforementioned mixed type, which transform normal behavior into abnormal actions. It would be desirable, therefore, if more of us would turn our eyes from men's behavior to the nature of modern institutions whenever the behavior seems abnormal. However, one warning should be heeded: We should not hasten to declare a whole institution unstable when in reality part of it is sound and perhaps indispensable to the welfare of the respective community or nation.

4. *The Method of Thinking in Organic Models*

How can we use these tables for a more thorough and fruitful study of human societies? I think the best approach is to link them with the contemporary method of thinking and research called "models." A *model* by definition is a set of assumptions defining a logical framework where we search to solve a given problem. These assumptions are often the result of more or less arbitrary decisions or simply the choice of the researcher. Thus, if the researcher belongs to a certain school of thought, his models will be related to the doctrine of that school. Of course, if he would point out right at the beginning of any study to which school of thought he belongs, there would be no problem. Unfortunately, in practice—and I refer to the free world!—very few are or would be willing to do so. My proposition of "organic models" has the purpose of making the present technique of models a much more definite, more realistic, and therefore more reliable instrument of study. At this point I am interested in basic macro-models.

In reviewing the development of the social and economic sciences, macro-models are nothing but the classical concept of economic and social system. Certainly, a given problem may be related either to the system as a whole (macro-analysis) or to individual units within the system (micro-analysis). Thus the term "model" as used here is interchangeable with the classical concept of "system" or "order." It is also interchangeable with the previously used term "space-time framework."

I shall try now to make use of "organic" models defined as reasonably possible combinations of elements designated in Table A and Table B, first with each combination located in its adequate space-time framework.

How many such organic models are possible? This fundamental problem, in itself of a methodological nature, has not yet been solved, at least not in so clear a manner that we are able to see all the consequences to the very end. The two tables are very helpful in ferreting out the long-awaited solution to this first-rank problem.

Assuming that the elements of the two tables are placed in their right category, here are the possible combinations:

First, we can devise a model of a society composed of 100% stable elements. It is a pure and wholly consistent world of permanent and perfect equilibrium. I shall call this M1-type of society, where only natural (finite) fluctuations are possible as distinguished from artificial (cumulative) changes in the mixed modern world.

Second, we can imagine the opposite model of a society, composed of 100% unstable elements. It is a wholly inconsistent world of permanent and perfect disequilibrium, either in an open or hidden form. I shall call this M2-type of society.

Third, we can think of mixed models as those in which both stable and unstable elements exist side by side. A mixed model represents a world of ambiguous status, where the struggle between stable and unstable elements automatically creates a blurred picture of a society almost continuously in trouble, depending on how big the proportion of unstable elements is. At one time it appears to be stable, but in reality it is so only by accident (due to the law of probability), namely, in a temporary stage of unstable equilibrium. Shortly thereafter the same society is moving (sometimes rapidly, sometimes slowly) into a disequilibrium position either of an artificially inflated prosperity (boom with inflation) or of an again artificially but this time disinflated economic activity (depression, or slump with deflation). In a mixed model, which represents the modern world we live in, it is almost impossible to discern any causality law in the classical sense. The principle of uncertainty (Heisenberg) is in its own domain here. The changes up and down are very similar to the kangaroo type of jumps or chain reaction within the atom of a radioactive (i.e., unstable) element, as was masterfully observed by the famous Danish physicist Niels Bohr.

In conclusion, we may say that any mixed combination in human societies as well as in nature has problems of inherent instability, of course, not of the same intensity as in the world of M2. I shall use M3 to designate any kind of mixed model.

The difficulty of working with an M3 model is that there is an unlimited number of mixed models possible. And since we cannot use the concept of infinity (∞) in solving specific problems, we must find a way to avoid using it. With this in mind, I propose to select from the infinitely vast number of possible mixed systems only three representative models:

M3-Type A, where both stable and unstable elements are present but the stable ones prevail. This is the model of a mixed world running in the direction of M1.

M3-Type B, where again both kinds of elements are represented but the unstable ones have the upper hand. This is the model of a mixed world going in the direction of M2.

M3-Type C, where both kinds of elements are represented in a 50:50 proportion. This model shows a mixed world which is located just halfway between M1 and M2. This is the model which is characterized by the existence of an unstable equilibrium (Pareto's concept). The well-known Italian sociologist and economist Vilfredo Pareto seems to have given the best definition of unstable equilibrium: "It [the equilibrium] is unstable at the limit when the conditions of equilibrium are not valid except for changes infinitely small."[5] This is valid for the M3-Type C model of 50:50 proportion.

5. *Is a Unified Field Theory for All Social Sciences Possible?*

I believe that the study of these five basic models can give us the foundation for a unified set of general theories to cover the entire field of sociology, economics and political science. A unified field theory in the sense of a unique, general theory for the study of human societies in all their potential forms is an impossible thing by definition, first of all because M1 and M2 are two polar types of models. Thus, whatever concepts or theorems we may discover—assuming they are correct—if and when they are valid in M1, by definition they are invalid in M2, and vice versa. The same thing is true about the elements of Tables A and B.

A given element, *x*, can be either stable (A) or unstable (B) but not both; consequently, it can belong first either to M1 or M2. Therefore, it is clear that an element from M2 transplanted in M1 creates problems of instability exactly as an element from M1 moved into M2 represents a source of trouble in M2.

We can go further and say that M3-Type A and M3-Type B in a way also represent two polar types of systems or worlds. Accordingly, whatever concepts and theorems we may forge, they can never be absolutely valid in the same manner in M3-Type A and M3-Type B. Concepts and theorems are tools which help us to understand realities located in a very definite space-time framework of M1, M2 or the M3 types. It is just as necessary to have suitably adequate tools for the solving of problems in a given model as it is to have the right key to open a particular locked drawer in order to ascertain its contents.

Among natural scientists, it is known that Einstein in his later years contemplated developing one single "Unified Field Theory" capable of explaining the entire physical universe at the macro- and micro-level, i.e., the gravitational as well as the electromagnetic field. He attempted to achieve this, but finally he was forced to concede that the job could not be done. It is interesting to remember his reasoning: "In order to constuct a theory," he said, "it is not enough to have a clear conception of the goal. One must also have a formal point of view which will sufficiently restrict the unlimited variety of possibilities. So far this has not been found; accordingly, the field theory has not succeeded in furnishing a foundation for the whole of physics."[6] The methodological problem here is to find a technique or a mode of thinking in which the use of the concept of infinity or "the unlimited variety of possibilities" (Einstein) offers no impediment in reaching a final conclusion.

That was Einstein's point of view on why we cannot have a unique "unified field theory" for the physical sciences.

Working with the same kind of problem in social sciences, I came to the same conclusion but with a different sort of reasoning. *First,* to my surprise and joy I discovered a methodological link between natural and social sciences, a link that represents a common foundation that eventually may open the road for the unification of all sciences. This common foundation lies in the fact that both the physical and the social universe are of a dual nature in the sense that they are composed of stable and unstable elements. *Second,* this duality creates the natural conditions wherein the number of possible combinations is, in theory, unlimited. The difference between the physical and the social universe is one more of degree than nature, if we think about the issue methodologically. Indeed, in the physical universe we know, the stable elements prevail in a largely definite proportion, and this answers the question of why here on earth we can live with the least amount of natural disturbances. In human societies this proportion is much less definite and fluctuates more wildly than the disturbances in the physical universe, a conclusion that becomes evident if we take a look at the social, economic and political history of all nations, especially in this century.

What Einstein very probably did not see is the observation that, using the bipolar technique, the "unlimited variety of possibilities" is flanked by two pure models at the limit: the M1 of 100% stable elements and M2 of 100% unstable elements. These two pure models cannot stand together at the same time and in the same space. In the physical universe it is the case of matter versus antimatter and in human societies freedom versus coercion through a government of absolute powers. Now it also becomes clear why we cannot possibly have one single general theory, and this referring both to nature and to human life: at the limit the two parts cannot be connected.

The end result is that by the use of the bipolar technique, the infinity or, as Einstein put it, "the unlimited variety of possibilities," no longer stands in the way of constructing a number of relevant and consistent sets of general theories, which for social sciences in this article were limited to five. This theoretical apparatus, will, I hope resolve the antinomy raised by Einstein in the physical sciences, which I think has the same validity for social sciences. I cannot here go into the issue of how to proceed in the physical sciences, but I think that the natural scientists could take care of that as soon as they become aware that the prevailing research of today, almost exclusively in dealing with radioactive (unstable) elements, cannot lead straight to a conclusion valid for both matter and antimatter. There is here a problem of methodology, and Einstein was right in seeing that this issue has to be resolved first and independent of the subject matter, or, as he put it, a "formal point of view" of pure logic necessary to master the subject thoroughly.

We have to give up the dream of developing just one single general theory for the study of all economic, social or political systems. This is an impossible operation from the methodological point of view. What we can and should do is develop a set of at least five unified general theories, each one specifically valid in M1, M2, M3-Type A, M3-Type B, and M3-Type C. There would no longer be any confusion about a given concept or theorem inherited from the past or forged in the present, because all we would have to do is check up and determine the right model or system to which it organically belongs.

In this respect, the five basic models can perform unimaginable feats. *First,* if we take any country or community which ever existed and reached the stage of civilized, organized life, with the help of these models we are able to say precisely just what type of society was.

Sociologists, historians, anthropologists and archeologists who are engaged in this type of work would be happy to use this unfaltering compass.

Secondly, if we select any concept or any theorem—assuming it is correct—from any thinker or school of thought, past or present, we shall detect that it is truly valid only in M1, in M2 or in one of the M3's. How many arguments—some of them insoluble up until now—can in this way finally rest in peace when we show exactly in which model or world they are really true! We shall discover, for instance, that a major part of the classical doctrine in sociology, economics and political science is completely valid in a world of M1-Type or close to it and nowhere else. Likewise, we can prove beyond doubt that the Stalinist concept of central planning is true and valid in the M2 world or close to it and nowhere else. Finally, the much disputed Keynesian doctrine can be proved to be valid in an M3-type system and nowhere else.

Certainly there are many more aspects related to the application of the Tables A and B and the five organic models. I shall try to focus a little more light upon M1 in order to make its application more feasible and more meaningful.

6. *Is "Social Liberalism" a Utopia or the Neglected Solution for the Problems of the World of Today?*

M1 represents a really free, just, and stable society and economy in a stage of permanent and perfect equilibrium since it is composed exclusively of 100% stable elements and institutions, located in a stable framework.

The mention of "permanent and perfect equilibrium" may easily arouse this question in the reader's mind: "Is M1 not a utopia and, therefore, we should not waste time studying it?" My answer is definitely *not,* of course in realistic terms thinking about a system close to M1.

Personally I do not think that my generation will live long enough to see or go through a natural evolutionary process of education and culture to reach the stage described by Teilhard de Chardin as the attainment of the cultural point Omega, which is the final step of maturity and self-achievement of man conceived both as an individual and as a social unit in the best possible framework of society.[7] I am disturbed by the further question that the last evolutionary stage of man conceived by Teilhard de Chardin as possible, in reality may never be reached for all members of human societies in the future, if the relatively unstable framework of today's society (I refer first to the Western world) is not made stable. But this is a different problem. I am solely interested now in whether or not M1 is utopia by definition. Again I say *no,* because M1, compared with the concept of a utopia, still remains in the domain of the possible.

By definition, *utopia* represents a type of society where the so-called "state of nature" prevails. In the state of nature there is:

1. no form of government whatsoever;
2. a status of absolute freedom where each one is his own master;
3. no taxation;
4. no private property;
5. no money;
6. no banking; and
7. no stock market.

Webster's Dictionary defines *utopia* as "an imaginary island described by Sir Thomas More in a work of the same title published in 1516 in which the inhabitants lived in the enjoyment of social and political perfection."[8] It is the picture of a fairly primitive type of society with no accumulation of capital and no technological or economic progress.

There is nothing of a similar nature in M1. Only the perspective of our time might induce one to feel that M1 could be a dream. That feeling dissolves into an optical illusion because of the immense distance between the miserable conditions of the M3-Type B society in which we live today in the West and the enticingly wonderful world of M1. We in the West have almost lost the hope of imagining that such a world as M1 is desirable and possible, not to mention the sad destiny of mankind in that part of the world under conditions of despotism of some form or another, where people fear even to dream of a society with natural freedom. But, as previously stated, there is absolutely nothing utopian in M1 because this is, rather, the most advanced organized form of free society. It is the best imaginable social and economic framework for the full, complete development of man. M1 is truly the complete picture of the highest ideal of social organization called "*the good society*." It has an authentically democratic form of government of limited powers where major decisions are ultimately determined by what Jefferson called the "natural law of the voice of majority." In M1 there is private property but its source is equal to 100% services and contributions to society performed by the owner in order to be such. The exclusive use of real (commodity) money, savings and investment type of banks, and a certain form of stock market are also major features of M1.

Finally, M1 is an intricately complicated machinery of a society which is constructed only from consistent (solid-stable) elements and institutions. M1 does not function in accordance with some arbitrary decisions by government planning and control, or by the voice of a privileged few, by past history or chance, or simply by social customs or habits. The

M1-type of society operates by the interaction of a number of basic institutions and principles which are constructed in such a way that the vast voluntary cooperation of normal, free men ends in a status of steady progress under conditions of permanent and perfect stability. There is no utopia here but rather the most rigorous application of certain principles which act in perpetual motion in one direction, that is to reach and preserve general stable equilibrium (in the social, political, financial and economic fields). For any residuum of unstable elements there will be deviations from normal fluctuations.

7. *Basic Principles of a Future Free, Just and Stable Society*

The M1-type of society composed exclusively of stable elements of Table A represents in general terms the same ideal world conceived by the classical thinkers, but this time explicitly defined and set up as an ultimate goal for the realization of the long-awaited "good society" of tomorrow. It is also the best possible framework of social order, forged to create the necessary conditions for a natural evolutionary process indispensable in the development of the Omega-type of man described by Teilhard de Chardin. There is no utopia in M1 but rather a positive, noble ideal for which it is worthwhile struggling.

We should never confuse this ideal world of M1 as the most desirable end with the real world in which we live. The great task and responsibility not only of men of social science, political leaders and intellectuals, but also of any citizen in a free democratic country is to compare the actual conditions with the ideal world of M1 and find out just how far we are from the ultimate goal. M1 could be a north star for which we in the West should mobilize all our spiritual energies and material forces. For the younger generation of today with its diminishing sense of values this could be a fountain from which to draw the full meaning of life, and a chance to devote all their energies and good qualities to an ideal task. M1, as the free and stable society, can be opposed efficiently to any type of mass society, welfare state or collectivism which now menaces the freedom and dignity of man everywhere.

The judicious reader has covered enough by now to remark: "It's nice to be in Heaven, but how do you get there?" By proper judgment and effective action everyone can get on the right path. Personally, I am convinced that M1 is definitely a possible order, because the stable blocs from which it is constructed (elements of Table A) are actual parts of the real world in which we live. The major task is just to separate from them the unstable blocs, destroy them completely and take care that in the future no new or old unstable elements will spring up to produce troubles. Consolidate the old stable blocs and make additional new ones of the same nature, and there you have the complete picture of M1-type of society. Thus, the ideal system of M1 is not something from another world like the prophetic concept of Heaven but rather the best possible world we can organize here on earth.

The greatest difficulty in the realization of the M1-type of society is the proper judgment about the classification of the stable elements in Table A. If we make a mistake there, then the negative results in practice would create an atmosphere of doubt, suspicion and even resentment. The archenemies of a free society would immediately put the blame on M1 as a whole and thereby try to discredit the possibility of having complete stability within this system.

People should be taught two things. *First,* M1 is a product of the human mind and action, and, since we all are under the destiny of human imperfection, we should be tolerant and have understanding that, in striving toward M1, we might have some visible imperfections. But the good architects of M1 will take care of those imperfections in due time, realizing that they, and all of us, are human and not supernatural. *Second,* people should be educated to understand that even an M3-Type A society as close as possible to M1 is a hundred times better than any sort of capitalism, welfare state, socialism, communism or fascism as we have known them in this century.

How can we be sure that any particular element included in Table A is really stable in the framework of a free society? When I first started the construction of the tables in 1945 during the last days of World War II, my first element in Table A was the real (commodity) money, and in Table B, its counterpart, the nominal (credit-fiat) money. Why they are two divergent types of money I explained in detail in my German book mentioned earlier. I discovered further that these two polar types of money organically belonged to two other also divergent economic and political systems. That was the light which helped me to see that there is an organic relationship within a given monetary, banking, economic, political and social system. Then I checked the history of ancient, medieval, and modern times up to the present and was lucky to unearth enough evidence to verify that the relationship just mentioned was a working principle.

I needed finally some definite means of testing to be certain that my new tools and reasoning were really strong enough to make the classification of the elements a matter of close self-evidence. In my original testing I used a composite-standard of three basic principles which I could now represent in this simple manner:

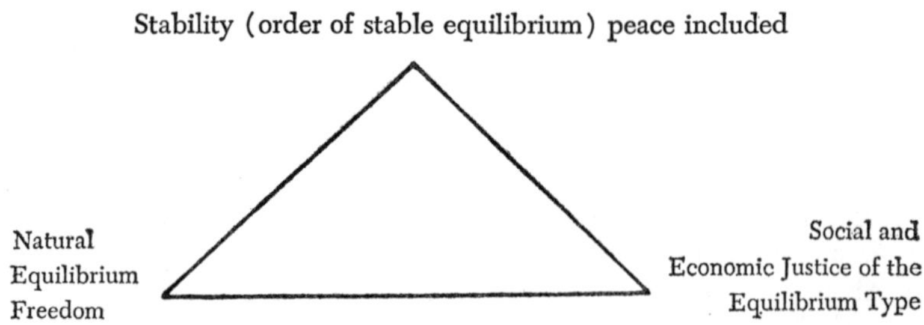

When I was developing this composite standard, I was handicapped by the fact that in the literature of the last decades there was an amazing lack of consistency in the treatment of these fundamental principles and values. In the West we are supposed to stand, defend and even die for these principles, and yet how many directly contradictory statements about them are publicized everywhere and even taught in schools. No wonder we are so confused and weak in the spirit when great issues come up for debate. Among other things, I think the same methodological break with the classical heritage is responsible for the deplorable status of Western culture at this moment, so full of contradictions and ambiguities—a culture dominated by the ideas of sex, absurdity, despair and an "easy life" of little distinction.

The absolute concept of freedom, as preached in the *"laissez-faire"* capitalism era, is untenable in any form of organized free society. It was inferred that the limit of this kind of freedom was at the point where the freedom of our neighbor begins. That is correct but not enough, because the action of an individual may produce ill effects upon the community as a whole, effects which are not directly visible to the next-door neighbor. In defining the concept of freedom, we have therefore to consider in the same balance both the individual and the society in which he lives. At the point where there is *no* conflict of interest—a neutral line—between man and his community; this is the natural limit of what I call equilibrium freedom.

The question of finding the neutral line of freedom led me to the development of the new, equilibrium concept of freedom. In the light of this concept the natural limits of freedom are in the other two basic principles of justice and stability (order, peace). Indeed, complete freedom can exist only in a social framework where justice and stability are guaranteed. The same equilibrium concept was applied to define the natural limits of justice and stability, and the results were perfect. Justice without freedom and stability, again, cannot exist. Thus, the latter two principles are its natural limits. Finally, stability without freedom and justice cannot exist either; therefore, its limits are in the other two principles.

There is much more to say about the three basic principles conceived as equilibrium concepts. Again I must postpone an ample discussion regarding them for another time. As soon as I completed the rough draft of the three basic principles, I applied them to test the validity of the first elements of Tables A and B. The results proved satisfactory with no contradictions.

After additional work on these tables and their applicability, I arrived at a second composite standard where I increased the number of principles from three to twelve, which are as follows:

1. natural (neutral) freedom;
2. justice of equitable shares;
3. government of limited powers;
4. the voice of the majority;
5. real (commodity) money, or Numeraire;
6. savings and investment banking;
7. referendum on public expenditure and public debt;
8. decentralization of public administration;
9. real transactions on the stock market;
10. daily business conducted at the price = ATC (average total cost per unit of output), where a normal rate of profit was included as the cost for management imputed or paid out;
11. Collective security (international peace with adequate defense organization);
12. Stability from within (order of stable equilibrium conditions).

For a complete clarification of these principles, considerable more work is necessary, which I do not dare to begin here. In any case, the first original standard, plus this enlarged version, seems to me to be sufficient for making a decision of whether or not a given element, institution or framework is stable as a whole or in part.

* * *

Naturally, I realize that at this moment I am treading over an unusually sensitive, delicate and, for a scientist, somewhat dangerous area. We are now in the realm of the so-called "judgment of values." Famous men of science have argued, especially at the beginning of this century, about this problem. A good number of them concluded that this area was "off limits." "Be neutral or uncommited" if you want to remain a man of science. That was the order of the day for scientists of fifty years ago. In fact, when I state that a certain element is stable and another unstable, I am on the precipice of saying, This is "right and good," whereas the other is "wrong and bad"! I must bow to the acceptance of this conclusion unavoidably as a matter of principle, although aware of the provocative challenge I am facing when I recall the position of men of science just pointed out before.

In preparing Tables A and B, I have not simply trespassed the boundaries of ethics as a science, but rather I have included thoroughly the ethical point of view, which is evident in the inclusion of the principle of social and economic justice in both composite standards. We must further assess that the ethics of M1 is contrary to the ethics of M2, whereas the ethics of M3 has some part of M1 and other parts of M2. My sincere hope is that the two tables and the two composite standards will help solve the old argument about the neutrality of a man of science.

It is not imperative for a man of social, political or economic science to take an active part in politics and run through the streets crying, "I like democracy, and I dislike dictatorship. I like free society, and I dislike centrally planned society!" The mission of a man of science, as I see it, is to reveal the whole unadorned truth as it grows from the study of M1, M2 or any kind of M3-type of society. He need not tell the people in what direction to point the compass, or what to do in their daily life, but to say honestly that if they travel in the direction of M1, M2 or M3 they should expect as inevitable certain specific consequences.

The relevance of M1 is immense if we consider that the vast majority of people in the United States and in the rest of the world want to live in freedom, justice and stability. The composite standard of the 12 principles is a sort of *new Twelve Commandments* which indicate the road and spotlight where and how to run our domestic and foreign affairs in order to escape the miseries of today and avoid a possible suicide or gradual decay of tomorrow.

To reach M1, or at least something approximating the M3-Type A close to M1, demands foresight, understanding, and above all, imagination, sacrifice and devotion to the cause of freedom, justice and stability with peace. A brighter future for our nation and for the entire humanity lies in M1. Either we shall be able to move into M1 during the coming decades, or we are taking a chance with our destiny. We may survive, despite of all our present-day problems, but also we may lose our freedoms and live under one of many forms of M2-type of tyranny.

8. *Conclusion: A Badly Needed Methodological Bridge Between the Thinking of the Past and That of the Present*

What are the merits and the weak points of the classical heritage in the light of the results of this article?

The *first* most notable contribution of classical thinkers in all fields lies in their unprecendented gift of possessing enough imagination to discover that, as in the physical universe, there is also possible in the social universe a type of society and economy which has a self-functioning mechanism. This was the idea of a free society combined with a free economy and a democratic form of government of limited powers, which is in principle what I have presented under M1.

The *second* significant contribution was their logical power to formulate the natural laws in such a way as to convince the majority of their contemporary fellowmen that this was the best possible social framework in which to live.

The *third* contribution of a more negative than positive value was in convincing the political men of the time to accept the concept of a hands-off policy, or *laissez-faire,* which in practice meant that government power was reduced to a minimum. In the theoretical field, finally, besides the unique performance of Quesnay, Adam Smith and J. B. Say, the most important classical contribution was accomplished by the French-Swiss economist, Leon Walras, when in the 1870's he worked out the general equilibrium theorem for this type of society and economy, and expressed it in both a conceptual and a mathematical form. Walras succeeded in this enormous feat only by having in mind a model equal to M1 which is wholly consistent; therefore, pure mathematics can be applied here on a large scale successfully.

The *first* salient methodological weakness of all classical thinkers was that they did not point out precisely that their natural laws were valid solely for an ideal model of specific conditions which was not to be confused with the actual conditions existing in the society of their days. In other words, they did not see the basic practical task of reforming the existing institutions to the point where they would be consistent with the ideal conditions of model M1. There was a reason why they all missed this task completely, and this exposes the *second* weak point.

All classical thinkers were of the opinion that freedom alone was sufficient to build up a free, stable society. They believed that, given individual and national freedom, the classical laws would function automatically and take care of every possible contingency. This unqualified optimism was definitely false, but not the classical laws as such. It is a pity that later the classical laws and not this numbing optimism were criticized as being untrue. Hence, an unprecedented state of confusion arose regarding the classical laws, leaving as a residuum a completely unjustified doubt about their validity both in theory and practice. This is the most regrettable injustice in the present evaluation and presentation of the classical heritage. Nevertheless, the weak point remains true: The classical thinkers did not see that the fabric of a modern free and stable society is much more complicated than a wheelbarrow. The list of the aforementioned 12 principles and all elements of Table A lucidly illustrate the point I wish to make. It took a number of crises over a period of more than a century, together with the depression of the 1930's, to cure us of the super-optimism that freedom alone can make and maintain a free and stable society

The *third* weakness, I think, was in their belief that the number of stable elements and institutions in a society with freedom is by the nature of things much bigger than the number of unstable elements. Therefore, in the end they thought that the forces of stability would prevail over those of instability (as is, for instance, the case in M3-Type A), and thus equilibrium would be secured by a sort of invisible hand. That again was an unfortunate error. They failed to see that, in human societies, the number of unstable elements may grow over a period of time, and that, in a given country with freedom, they may greatly outnumber the stable elements. Moreover, and far more important, they did not realize that the number of mixed systems, in one of which the modern world actually lives, was infinitely vast. Consequently, the complete picture of model M1 as developed in this paper was not seen by the classical thinkers in its entire perspective as compared with all other possible systems. They did not detect the truth that a free and stable society is a type of "*rara-avis*" land which does not evolve by itself, even if we would wait millions of years and granted that freedom would be miraculously preserved for that length of time. A free and stable society is similar to an immortal piece of art which is constructed from the best materials (stable blocks), handled by the best skills and in accordance with the best plans worked out with perceptive wisdom, patience and understanding. It is the most beautiful and most comfortable world to live in, but I might repeat that it will not come about by itself even if all citizens were saints. Suffice it to say that when the system is unstable in its own nature, even saintlike human beings of goodwill and intentions are impeded in their efforts to accomplish the good they want.

In conclusion, M1 type of society goes in the direction of complementing and integrating the classical heritage in order to make it usable for today and tomorrow. I call this regime "Social Liberalism."[9] It is a new kind of liberalism altogether different from the liberal experiment of the nineteenth century, well known under the name of "*laissez-faire* capitalism." On the whole, it is based not only on freedom, but also on social and economic justice, and stability of equilibrium. The freedom of the individual is weighed and balanced with the needs of the society. Thus, "Social Liberalism" appears to be a suitable designation for the national purpose in America or anywhere in the free world.

* * *

As soon as we have decided that "Social Liberalism" is the national goal, the paramount task ahead is of a practical nature—namely, *how* to shift from the present capitalistic system of the M3-Type B into the "new order" by the use of peaceful, democratic means and without additional troubles.

The conservative approach would be to make a gradual change, step by step. The truly liberal approach would be more inclined to make the shift all at once as a single, large-scale operation, and as soon as possible. The choice between the conservative and the liberal approach should be presented by the political parties to the people for direct consideration and final decision.

In any case we should be extremely cautious in our actions and what we plan to do for tomorrow. A rush to introduce inconsistent reforms by the back door may prove to be even more harmful than merely fighting to preserve the *status quo* and/or waiting for miracles. Thus, I think we might well take to heart the thought of Professor Frank H. Knight, a most respected dean of American sociology and economics:

"Since order is the absolute requisite of civilized life, we must stick to the order that is, until there is a reasonable agreement on changes that will be on balance beneficial."[10]

NOTES

1. The same issue raised in the area of psychology by Richard La Piere in *The Freudian Ethic. An Analysis of the Subversion of American Character.* (New York: Duell, Sloan and Pearce, 1959).

   For the latter part of the statement see: Eugene Kinkead, *In Every War but One* (New York: W. W. Norton & Co., 1959).
2. Sir James Jeans, *Physics and Philosophy* (New York: Cambridge University Press, 1958), p. 183.
3. Anghel N. Rugina, *Geldtypen und Geldordnungen, Fundamente für eine echte allgemeine Geld- und Wirtschaftstheorie* (Stuttgart: W. Kohlhammer Verlag, 1949).

4. Anghel N. Rugina, "Programme de Stabilisation Économique, Financierè et Sociale pour la France," *Revue d'Économie Politique*, Mars-Avril 1959, pp. 179-213.
5. Vilfredo Pareto, *Corso di Economia Politica*. Volume primo, 1953, Edizioni Scientiche Einaudi (Torino: Editore Boringhieri, 1967), p. 26.
6. Albert Einstein, *Out of My Later Years* (New York: The Wisdom Library, 1950), p. 100.
7. Pierre Teilhard de Chardin, *The Phenomenon of Man*, with an introduction by Sir Julian Huxley (New York: Harper & Row, Publishers, Inc., 1959).
8. See: *Webster's Dictionary of the English Language*, 1950, p. 1892.
9. Anghel Rugina, "Social Liberalism. The Integral Democracy of Tomorrow," *University of Portland Review*, May 1951.
10. See: The Role of Principles in Economics and Politics, a Presidential Address at the 63rd Annual Meeting of the American Economic Association, Chicago, December 28, 1950. Reprinted in: Frank H. Knight, *On the History and Method of Economics* (Chicago: The University of Chicago Press. Copyright 1956 by the University of Chicago Press. Second Impression, 1958), p. 277.

2. AMERICAN CAPITALISM: WHAT KIND OF AN ECONOMIC SYSTEM?

The Application of an Orientation Table for Sociology, Economics, Finance and Political Science*

Lesson from the American Experiment:
Economic freedom without an institutional framework based on "Numeraire" creates social injustice, and that in turn undermines the foundation of a free society.

1. *Introduction: Economic History Versus Economic Theory*

In 1955, in an article published in the international journal for social sciences *Kyklos*[1] (Switzerland), Professor Calvin B. Hoover of Duke University initiated a project of studying the economic systems of the major countries of the Western world. The emphasis was to be put not so much on matters of historical detail as on the framework and the structure of these Western economies. In more specific terms, the central issue of concern was the following basic question: With all the changes during this century and especially after the Great Depression of the 1930's and World War II, do we still have, in the Western world, national economies characterized by prevailing conditions of competition and "laissez-faire" as conceived in the classical tradition? In other words, has the modern capitalistic system during the past decades been transformed into a brand-new regime, or are we just facing new developments within the same old framework? As a guideline, Professor Hoover has recommended in the same article a number of specific questions, all related to the same central issue.

The main purpose of my contribution is to present the argument about the mixed nature of American capitalism and the proportion between competition and monopoly, an issue raised in the 1930's, hotly debated in the 1950's and not yet settled in the 1970's. Obviously we are faced here with a complicated subject: one part belonging to *Economic History* and another part being related to the *History of Economic Thought.* Indeed, to master the issue we need both factual information and analytical tools. In addition, we must always be on the alert not to fall into the trap of the nineteenth-century *Methodenstreit* in the German Economic School. Economic history and economic

*This paper was presented at the International Congress of Economic History and History of Economic Theories held in Piraeus, Greece, on March 10-14, 1975.

theory are both indispensable for a complete body of the science of economics, which of course has other parts.[2]

The major task, to be sure, is not to convey merely a historical or institutional picture of the American economy. That would not be sufficient in dealing with the principal issue raised in Hoover's project. A few methodological remarks are mandatory. The economic facts in their original form do not possess by themselves the power of expressing problems or indicating solutions to those problems. They may, however, acquire such a quality as soon as we associate them with certain adequate concepts or techniques of reasoning, developed through the independent process of abstract or theoretical thinking. Our subject, therefore, demands both an empirical and a theoretical treatment.

It is true that economic history and economic theory exist within a larger body where they touch and complement each other. But otherwise each has its own objectives in terms of knowledge, and the communication between them often is broken, out of order, or simply ignored. How important and delicate this communication is can be seen from the observation that identical economic realities aligned with diverse theoretical concepts or models lead to entirely different conclusions, meanings and judgments. Thus we should not be surprised to hear later how sharply American economists are divided on this very subject regarding the nature of the economic system of their own country.

The empirical documentation itself also poses many problems. We must recognize that the American economy is not "just another" national economy in the usual sense. It is rather a subcontinental economy with all the variety of national resources and branch of activities characteristic of such a vast geographical area. Yet it is not unique simply because of its magnitude. What the Americans did with these resources, under the framework of personal freedoms, private property and individual initiative combined with political stability, represents a unique version of modern civilization.

There is no other country in the world where modern industrial society has emerged in such unprecedented complexity and variety on a large scale. The American economy in this respect offers an immense mosaic of similar and diverse elements and combinations. Any group of scientists equipped with the necessary tools as well as patience, and free of any preconceived dogma, may, I am sure, uncover in the United States all possible kinds of markets and economic behavior. To reconstruct in miniature such a vast and intricate body as the American economy demands not only a highly qualified skill but also an entire laboratory of economic data and analytical tools, much of which are not available at the present time.

Returning to the main theme: What kind of economic system does the United States have? Is American capitalism passing through a radical transformation toward something new, or is what is going on nothing but a natural development within the same old framework? How should we evaluate the many events and reforms, especially since the 1930's? Do they represent a "change of system," or a "change within the system"? These are the kinds of questions with which we are faced.

2. *The Interpretation of Economic History: A Battle of Concepts in the American School of Economics*

Back in the early 1920's one could have defined American capitalism as a free enterprise system, or laissez-faire capitalism, without facing too much of an argument. Indeed, here is how Harvard Professor Sumner H. Slichter described it at that time: "It may seem a strange way of doing but we organize industry by, in effect, saying to each individual, 'Choose your own occupation. Produce what you like. What you do, to whom you sell, what or from whom you buy, the prices you get or give, are all your own concern. You are free, subject to a few restrictions, to produce whatever you wish regardless of whether or not it is needed, regardless of whether or not too much of it already exists. You are likewise free to refrain from engaging in any occupation no matter how acute may be the shortage of goods or how pressing the need for your help. You are free to buy from whoever is willing to sell and to sell to whoever is willing to buy. You are equally free to refuse to buy or sell whenever you please and for any reason or no reason.'

"This is what we mean by free private enterprise. Under it the government confines itself in the main to the suppression of fraud and violence and to the enforcement of contracts. It does not itself engage in or attempt to guide the course of industry. It pursues a 'let alone' or 'hands off' policy."[3]

Even though Slichter himself did not consider the modern, laissez-faire capitalism as ideal, I nevertheless think that he expressed fairly accurately the way in which the American economy was viewed in the 1920's. It was a decade when the basic ideas of Leon Walras, Alfred Marshall, J. B. Say, Adam Smith and other classical economists were still accepted in principle by the majority of professionals in the field.

The model for analysis used by most economists of that time consisted of a conceptual framework in which competition and monopoly were conceived as two primary elements representing two opposing economic forces. In addition, competition was considered as an all-decisive factor which, in a system of political democracy and economic freedoms, leads automatically toward stability from within. Monopoly was viewed as a disturbing element which cannot grow if the government does not support it.

To this analytical apparatus, a second characteristic should be added. Classical economists were not sufficiently aware of the fact that economic realities of their time were representing a mixed system where monopoly was almost as strong as competition, if not even stronger at times. Since Adam Smith classical economists have been dominated by the idea that, as long as the government was not interfering to create new monopolistic privileges or to support old ones, the market forces of competition from inside and outside would remain the decisive economic factor, pushing always toward stable equilibrium. This over-optimism supported the belief in natural laws in economics and gave the second characteristic, namely, that in the classical model competition was the rule and monopoly the exception.

Then came an Italian-born British economist, Piero Sraffa, who in an article published in 1926[4] tried to prove, or assumed, that the economic realities in the West viewed from the supply side were close to a model where monopoly was the rule and competition only the exception. With this article, Sraffa turned classical economics upside down in terms of application. Later the concept of imperfect competition as developed by Mrs. Joan Robinson (*The Economics of Imperfect Competition,* 1933) and that of monopolistic competition by Professor Edward H. Chamberlin (*The Theory of Monopolistic Competition,* 1933) reinforced Sraffa's departure from classical economics.

Finally, Lord Keynes, with his *Treatise on Money* (1930) and the *General Theory of Employment, Interest and Money* (1936), tipped the balance—even though from a different angle—in favor of an anticlassical economics. The Keynesian concept of the multiplier, full employment by government deficit spending, and managed currency without any backing certainly are alien to the classical analysis and way of thinking. Through Keynes' influence, the focus of study shifted from the classical theory of free competition to the investigation of other possible forms of market and economic behavior. On the European continent, moving in the same direction was the German economist Heinrich Freiherr von Stackelberg. In his *Marktform und Gleichgewicht* (Market Form and Equilibrium, 1934), Stackelberg advanced the analysis of oligipoly ahead of many other contemporary economists, although Augustin Cournot, with his classical work *Recherches sur les Principes Mathématiques de la Theorie des Richesses* (1838) remains the original pioneer.

While this anticlassical stream of ideas was growing, a number of well-known economists on both sides of the Atlantic, like Walter Eucken, Wilhelm Ropke, Luigi Einaudi, F. A. Hayek, Ludwig von Mises, Erik Lindahl, Gottfried Haberler, Frank H. Knight, Lloyd W. Mints, Henry Simons and others were trying to defend and save whatever could survive from the classical heritage. But the storm of the Great Depression and its consequences created unprecedented conditions which fostered the spread of the opposing stream. In conclusion, I think that without doubt the theoretical orientation in economics during the 1930's and up to the end of World War II, was in general, away from the classical approach.

Parallel with the new anticlassical trend in analysis there were also empirical studies whose results seemed—at least at the time—to match the situation in the theoretical field. In the United States, the pioneering work, *The Modern Corporation and Private Property* (1932) by Adolf A. Berle and Gardiner C. Means, was sending the warning that the American economy was under strong pressure from monopolistic concentration in business and industry. They went so far as to predict that "if the wealth of the large corporations and that of all corporations should each continue to increase . . . it would take only 30 years at the 1924-1929 rates for all corporate activity and practically all industrial activity to be absorbed by 200 giant companies."[5]

Arthur R. Burns, in his book *The Decline of Competition* (1936), reached similar conclusions: "The rise of the 'heavy industries,' changes in methods of selling, and the widening use of corporate forms of business organization are bringing, if they have not already brought, the era of competitive capitalism to a close." Burns thought at that time that American capitalism had "failed to preserve its competitive quality."[6]

These two pioneering studies fitted very well with the political spirit of the time, the New Deal era. Indeed, by 1935 U.S. Government circles were sharing the view of those economists who thought, as A. D. Kaplan put it later, that "big business policy was largely responsible for the depth and persistence of the depression of the 1930's."[7] This view was instrumental in determining the U.S. Government to launch in 1938 the "Temporary National Economic Committee" with the specific task of investigating the phenomenon of concentration of economic power in American economy. The political spirit is evident in President Roosevelt's message recommending the creation of this Committee. "Once it is realized," said the message, "that business monopoly in America paralyzes the system of free enterprise on which it is grafted, and is as fatal to those who manipulate it as to the people who suffer beneath its impositions, action by the government to eliminate these artificial restraints will be welcomed by industry throughout the nation. For idle factories and idle workers profit no man."[8] The report of this Committee was published in March 1941, but by then the international situation with war in Europe had shifted the interests of the New Deal administration from domestic to foreign affairs. The United States was already engaged in a full national defense mobilization.

At the beginning of the 1940's it seemed as if the doctrine of a structural transformation of the American economy was accepted as being true without too much opposition. Here is how the situation was reported at that time: "In recent years it has become fashionable in academic, and to a lesser extent, in business circles to assume that the competitive system is on its way out. With some persons this opinion springs from wishful thinking based upon their allegiance to alternative types of organization ranging all the way from unsupervised private cartelization of industry to a collectivist economy. Others come reluctantly to the belief that competition is passing and regard the decline of competition as the source of problems and dangers which they would gladly avoid."[9] Although reference was made to the "dominant American sentiment for continuance of the competition system," nevertheless, a widespread view of the time, as reported in the same place, was "that whether we like it or not, competition is doomed." The direct implication of such an interpretation was that government should step in and either stop the process of business concentration or develop an adequate machinery for direct control of big business. That would have meant, of course, a shift toward a government-directed economy. The history of both ideas and facts, however, did not follow these expectations of doom for competition as voiced by some prominent economists in the 1930's and early 1940's.

The first work which opened the road for a new vista in the battle of classical versus new anticlassical concepts and reasoning was an article by Professor John Maurice Clark, "Toward a Concept of Workable Competition" (1943). Professor Clark was not thoroughly satisfied with the existing theoretical equipment—the theory of imperfect competition (by Mrs. Robinson) and monopolistic competition (by E. H. Chamberlin)—especially when applied in the field of U.S. economic policy. Regarding perfect competition he went along with the spirit of the time, namely, that it "does not and cannot exist and has presumably never existed." He did not deny, however, that the model of perfect competition could be considered as an ideal standard to compare and judge "actual competition conditions." Yet he doubted its usefulness because, in his estimation, it was an "unreal" standard. Thus he wanted to find another concept which was "the closest available working approximation to that ideal, under actual conditions."[10] This was at that time a new concept of workable competition.

In my view, Professor Clark did not provide a clear-cut definition of the new concept. It is supposed to be between the model of pure oligopoly where imperfect competition is "too weak" (monopoly) and the marginal case of oligopoly where imperfect competition is "too strong" (cutthroat competition). Professor Clark thinks "that workable competition needs to avoid both extremes" (*op. cit.,* p. 243). In another place and following the same line of thought, he describes the phenomenon in this way: "It is something intermediate between pure oligopoly and the ruinously low prices likely to result from unlimited market chaos: more strongly competitive than the first, and more workable than the second" (*op. cit.,* p. 253).

The new concept of workable competition, according to its author, had application to both short-run and long-run conditions. In the short-run analysis the price under workable competition would be above the marginal cost, so that an extra profit differential would be falling into the hands of entrepreneurs. This result led to the conclusion that "some forms and degrees of discrimination have a place in a scheme of workable, as distinct from perfect, competition" (*op. cit.,* p. 250). To find a place for his concept in the long-run analysis, Professor Clark worked out a scheme of reasoning with the conclusion that "there is typically no definite 'optimum size' but rather a wide optimum range of size, within which most plants fall" (*op. cit.,* p. 249).

The concept of workable competition was not directly linked, by its author, to the classical model of "effective" competition where competition was supposed to prevail over monopoly to a large extent, even though I think it should be. Nevertheless, the appearance of this concept in the early 1940's signalled a new situation where the proposition that American capitalism was more monopolistic than competitive was still open to debate.

For a while after World War II it looked as if the Berle-Means-Burns doctrine of the 1930's was accepted as being representative of the average opinion among American economists. Professor J. K. Galbraith joined the old group. Using old and new material on the same side of the argument, he reached the conclusion that "oligopoly is the appropriate assumption in dealing with industrial markets in the United States."[11] In his opinion this point of view had already become an established "assumption in American economic thought." Further, Professor Galbraith raised his conclusion to a general statement: "Oligopoly, by all evidence [is] the ruling market form in the modern economy" (*op. cit.,* p. 127).

In another article at that time, Professor Joe S. Bain, reviewing both empirical and theoretical studies by American economists since the 1930's, reported similar results. In reference to general investigations about the American market structure, Professor Bain thought there was a general opinion that the dominant patterns were (1) concentration of output among few sellers; (2) reduction to a few buyers in producer goods markets; (3) product differentiation for almost all consumer goods and a number of producer goods; and (4) a potential oligopoly (or oligopsony) in many significant subvarieties of concentration and fewness. In one sentence, he took the same position as Professor Galbraith, namely, that "pure competition . . . and . . . monopoly are in practice rather special cases, and that oligopoly was the general case . . ."[12] and this would then be a major characteristic of the American economy.

In the late 1940's and early 1950's, however, a strong reaction against this view emerged, and a new orientation developed. A number of new economists questioned the validity of the more popular doctrine that the American economy during recent decades had changed its framework rapidly. In a few years a full battle of concepts was in progress. Empirical and analytical evidence was marshaled to the support of the new orientation. As previously mentioned, the launching of the concept of "workable competition" in the early 1940's by Professor J. M. Clark showed, in a way, a sign of dissatisfaction with the existing theoretical apparatus and a desire for new tools. Conditions of war, however, impaired a full discussion of the issue.

The reasons for the new orientation may be many. *First,* the removal of war regulations in the economy and the numerous labor strikes after the war probably contributed to a revival of the economists' interest in the study of competition and its application to the American economic scene. *Second,* a report of the Federal Trade Commission on changes in concentration in manufacturing, 1935-1947 and 1950 (U.S. Government Printing Office, 1954) did not confirm at all the results predicted by the earlier studies of Berle and Means. The report showed that between 1935 and 1950 the increased concentration in manufacturing for the 200 largest companies was relatively very small, rising only from 37.7 to 40.5,[13] measured by percentage of total value of product of all manufacturing industries. These results seem to be reasonable. They indicate that even though big business during the period 1935-1950 undoubtedly increased, nevertheless the economy, and with it the manufacturing industries as a whole, had grown to such a large extent that the degree of concentration actually changed very little.

Professor Clair Wilcox was, in all probability, the first new economist who directly challenged the thesis advanced by Professors Galbraith and Bain that the American economy practically was characterized by oligopoly and monopolistic competition. In a paper, "On the Alleged Ubiquity of Oligopoly," presented at the sixty-second annual meeting of the American Economic Association,[14] he called attention to the fact that the previous studies on concentration in the American economy were less conclusive than they seemed to be. For instance, referring to the Berle-Means investigation of the 200 largest concerns, which in 1929 allegedly controlled 49% of nonbanking corporate wealth, Wilcox found that in this magic number "200" were included 95 public utilities, 4 complete monopolies and 13 corporations engaged in such competitive business as retail distribution, lumber, shoes and textiles. Thus in reality among the 200 corporations only 89 were oligopolies. But that was not all. These 89 concerns appeared in only 23 or 24 of the 275 industry categories contained in the Census of Manufacturers. In other words, giant corporations were present in 23 or 24 industries, but they were absent in more than 250. In view of the fact that these statistics tell nothing about the real structure of the particular markets for various products of each industry, Wilcox came to the conclusion that such information gathered in the past "gives us no index of oligopoly" (*op. cit.,* p. 68). He further raised the point that all the studies about concentration were concerned only with manufacturing industries which accounted for "less than $2/5$ of the income produced by unregulated private non-financial enterprise" (*op. cit.,* p. 69). Therefore, according to Wilcox, they completely ignored the markets in agriculture, fisheries, forestry and mining, construction industries, wholesale and retail distribution and in the service trades, that is, a sector of the economy representing more than three-fifths of the income. Professor Wilcox did not deny that the list of consumer goods produced by oligopolies in the United States was fairly long, but his point was that "the part of the consumer's dollar that goes to pay for such goods is very small" (*op. cit.,* p. 72).

Finally, he asks this question: "What, then is the relative significance of oligopoly in the American economy?" This problem, Wilcox acknowledged, will remain unanswered until somebody first works out a classification of products that has some relation to "market realities" and then is able "to determine the 'spatial limits' of the market areas within which these products compete for sale" (*op. cit.,* p. 72). This, however, is not an easy task. Nevertheless, when all this was achieved, Wilcox pointed out that a correct analysis would reveal that our economy was moving toward more rather than less competition. This new conclusion represented just the antithesis of the previous views.

In another article, "Concentration of Power in American Economy,"[15] Wilcox gave more reasons for his optimism on this issue. In addition, he thought that competition sometimes could be more effective when there are a few large corporations rather than when there is a large number of small ones. He visualized also that great power among sellers might be diluted by changes in technology, new available substitutes, the rise of new competitors and possible shifts in demand.

Furthermore, he made the observation that no study of concentration of output could reveal in the long run the real degree of competition for "the markets of consumers' goods in the United States." The main reason lay in specific conditions of the American economy. The continuous progress and growth of American transportation and communication had the effect of making these markets more wide and more flexible; and open, flexible markets are competitive by definition. The industrial research which supplied so many substitutes is another force of competition enlarging the boundaries of products. Wilcox ended his presentation with an idea which from then on occupied the mind of other economists. "Whatever the concentration of power in the American economy," he concluded, "it should be noted that it has not prevented a repeated reformation of the patterns of production and distribution, a progressive development of technology, a steady flow of new products, or continuous cultivation of new tastes, a constant improvement of quality and an ever-widening provision of goods and services" (*op. cit.*, p. 218).

Professor George J. Stigler of the University of Chicago is another pioneer of the new orientation. In one of his five lectures delivered at the London School of Economics in 1949, he spoke on the subject "Competition in the United States." He pointed out as a first task the definition of a competitive industry because only in this way may we hope, as he put it, "to classify the endless variety of forms of industrialization to be encountered in the American economy."[16]

To fulfill this task he started with the classical model by assuming that competition in the long run will make price equal marginal cost. Taking this limiting, equilibrium position as a standard, theoretically it was not difficult to differentiate between competition and monopoly, because the strength of a monopolist may be measured—as Professor Stigler correctly observed—by "the difference between price and long-run marginal cost." The difficulties would arise in practice when we moved away from this equilibrium position. At any other time (but not too far from the limit) the economy would be in a dynamic stage, and we would have to accept the fact that the competitive price might recede from the long-run marginal cost, depending on the real conditions in the market. If so, reasoned Stigler, then the dividing line between competition and monopoly should also be made more flexible within a reasonable range. On this analytical background, he formulated the concept of a "competitive industry" as being oriented to two conditions: (1) a large number of independent firms, none dominant in size, and free entry for additional firms; and (2) a few firms, even of relatively large size, but whose behavior should not deviate too much from a competitive situation.

A close examination of the two conditions in Stigler's concept shows that we are dealing here with the classical view on competition enlarged to match more or less the features of a modern dynamic economy.

Professor Stigler used his analytical tools to assess the structure of American economy in 1939 and came to these overall estimates:

Competition	55.2 per cent
Compulsory cartels	2.5 per cent
Monopoly	24.4 per cent
Not allocable	17.9 per cent

Discarding the unallocable sector, the estimates become:

Competition	67.3 per cent
Compulsory cartels	3.1 per cent
Monopoly	29.7 per cent

He also took the corresponding allocation of the number of persons engaged in production in 1939, and the results were:

Competition	76.5 per cent
Compulsory cartels	3.8 per cent
Monopoly	19.7 per cent

To Stigler, for the whole American economy "it seems conservative to estimate that the competitive industries were producing seven-tenths of the national income in 1939, and utilizing more than four-fifths of the labor force."[17]

In the overall picture, his conclusions were that, in the United States in this century, competition had increased while concentration in general had decreased.

By the early 1950's two opposing doctrinal interpretations were competing in the market of ideas to explain the nature of the American economic system. In 1951 the International Economic Association with the support of UNESCO organized a roundtable conference at Talloires in France on the subject *Monopoly, Competition and Their Regulation.* A paper, "Monopoly and Competition in the United States of America,"[18] was presented by Professor R. B. Heflebower. The results of this paper can be easily envisioned from the way it starts: "*Competition* outweighs monopoly by a wide margin in the American economy today." This picture of the American economic system follows the same lines as those of Stigler and Wilcox. Heflebower's conclusion was: "Resources do adjust as pulled by shifts in final demand. Only in a few industries are there unusually high profits. Income has become more rather than less equitably distributed, particularly in the last two decades. In each of these respects the situation might be better, but the economy as a whole, as operating now, reflects the presumed benefits of a competitive market system" (*op., cit.,* pp. 110-111).

Another member of the American delegation, Professor J. M. Clark, in a different paper, "Competition and the Objectives of Government Policy,"[19] brought up the point that "Americans do believe that competition has an important place in the economic system." In the argument whether the American economy was more monopolistic than competitive or vice versa, Professor Clark did not take a clear-cut position. Nonetheless, in his conclusions one of the purposes of his paper was, in his own words, "a desire to counteract . . . the pessimistic view of competition" (*op. cit.,* p. 336).

From the reading of the papers and discussions held at this international roundtable conference, a sort of divergence, if not direct conflict, arose between American and European experts. American economists were rather optimistic about competition and its working, whereas, their European colleagues were more pessimistic on this issue. An American reviewer of these papers and discussions at the Talloires Conference, Professor Tibor Scitovski, later remarked that the opposition between European and American members cannot be explained "with the aid and within the framework of economic theory." Until a better theoretical apparatus is available, in his view we should be content with whatever empirical evidence is available. "For it seems obvious," wrote Professor Scitovski, "that the superior performance of the American economy must have something to do with its having these 'more and stronger elements of competition,' whose existence most American members of the Conference asserted, but whose nature and significance was not explained."[20]

The issue whether the mixed American capitalism was more competitive or more monopolistic continued to be debated hotly in the early 1950's. More economists joined both sides of the argument, so that by 1953 it was possible to have the sixty-sixth annual meeting of the American Economic Association devoted almost entirely to an assessment of "the fundamental nature of the American economy at the current point in time."[21]

About forty major papers, with an equal number of official discussants, were concentrated on the same central problem. Great credit should be given to Professor Calvin B. Hoover, who, as President of the American Economic Association that year, was instrumental in conceiving and putting forward such a unique program for an unusual annual convention. A synopsis of these papers and discussions is not possible here simply because a large number of economists participated and the printed material involved covers approximately seven hundred pages. For those interested in this subject, however, the volume with these papers is highly recommended for consultation.

The battle of concepts between the two opposing schools of thought was continued with even more intensity at this 1953 Conference. The presidential address delivered by Professor Hoover on that occasion[22] advanced the thesis that the American economy over the previous fifty years had suffered fundamental changes in many directions. He stressed the development of big corporations at the turn of the century, the growth of big labor unions in the 1930's and the extension of big government with social security and other controls over banks and the stock market. All these developments seemed to confirm the validity of the Hoover Thesis. Indeed, Professor Hoover strongly defended the view that in the 1950's the U.S. economy already incorporated a brand-new system, which he called "organizational economy," or "welfare capitalism." Following Hoover's line of thought we need new theoretical tools, different from the classical concept of competition and monopoly, if we want to understand the real nature and the true problems of American capitalism in the twentieth century. Professor Hoover pointed out in the same place that we already possess such new concepts as monopolistic competition, oligopoly, countervailing power and imperfect competition. If only the majority of economists could be convinced to discard the old tools and use the new ones to the full extent!

Looking through the multitude of papers presented at the 1953 special meeting of the A.E.A., the above interpretation no longer appears to be unquestioned or unanimously accepted. Instead of general agreement, we find a sharp division of opinion in the profession. One group, known in America as "liberals," loudly defended and expanded the same position as that expressed by Hoover, namely, that the mixed American capitalism of the 1950's was entirely different from the system assumed in classical economics.[23] The other group, formed mainly by "conservative" thinkers (in the American sense, but otherwise closer to the nineteenth-century type of European liberals), argued as strenuously as the first for the opposite thesis, namely, that, with all the changes of the last decades, the structure, the functioning and especially the performance of the American economy were still within the limits of the free enterprise system, and thus the classical theory on competition and monopoly were applicable to present-day conditions.[24]

The heart of the matter in the argument was not so much about the institutional changes, which were recognized by both sides, but rather about their significance in terms of applied theory. In effect we are faced here with a new version of an old issue—economic history versus economic theory.

3. *In Search of New Analytical Tools to Resolve Old and New Problems*

Economic science has no doubt made progress in this century through the development of new concepts and techniques of reasoning, and especially because of the application of mathematical tools. Unfortunately, the old basic problems in the field, i.e., the determination of rent, wages, interest, profit, taxes and foreign exchange, under different conditions are still unresolved, both in theory and practice. In this context Professor G. Warren Nutter made an interesting observation at the 1953 A.E.A. meeting: "Each little piece of theory has an appearance of order and even elegance, but the whole does not, boundaries interlace or fail to meet. Current theory contributes this: it sets forth with precision all the reasons why we cannot say anything precise about the behavior of prices."[25]

Following the thought of Professor Nutter, I think that the missing link between individual pieces of theory, usually associated with micro-analysis, and the whole theory which refers to macro-analysis, lies in the field of the methodology of science. Classical economics was mainly concerned with problems of stable equilibrium, and therefore the relationship between micro- and macro-analysis did not pose any problem for it. New, contemporary economics is concentrated mostly on disequilibrium conditions, and thus the relationship between the two approaches has raised new problems.

4. *The Method of Ex-Post Analysis or "Thinking in Reverse" Used by Keynes Has Produced a Revolution but Also Confusion in Economics*

Lord Keynes first observed in this century and raised a new problem of an open conflict between classical theory when used in micro-analysis and its integration into macro-analysis when applied to given economic conditions after World War I. Since in applied theory he could not uncover a bridge between micro- and macro-analysis, Keynes decided to reverse the sequence of events in the approach and method of reasoning. Instead of beginning with a micro-analysis study in a given problem as most, if not all, other economists did, he started with a macro-analysis. In addition he abandoned the traditional *ex-ante* approach of "forward thinking" (reasoning from primary cause to effect) in favor of the *ex-*

post analysis or the method of "thinking in reverse" (reasoning backward from effect to cause).

Keynes was right in observing a conflict between micro- and macro-analysis when tools of classical economics were used indiscriminately to make prognoses of problems faced by modern economies in a chronic disequilibrium, but he was wrong when he inverted the traditional method of reasoning by shifting from the *ex-ante* to the *ex-post* analysis without an explicit warning and a necessary explanation. The inverted method of reasoning, originating with Keynes in this century, created much confusion and resentment among the living classical and neo-classical economists. Now the confusion is spreading to a younger generation of economists who took for granted the Keynesian message of active government intervention to control public and private spending in order to achieve full employment and price stability. They now discover in the 1970's that this was more or less a myth, not a scientific solution.

Let us look at a few examples to see the difference between the two methods of analysis and, in this way, reveal the character of the new Keynesian revolution in economic thinking. If we consider the economic process through the *ex-ante* approach, i.e., thinking forward, then it becomes clear that the sequence of events is *first savings* (capital formation) and then new investment. If we change the approach, shifting to the *ex-post* analysis, i.e., thinking backward, then it appears as if *new investment is first* and savings after. Of course, in real life and with reference to modern capitalism, capital formation in the first case is based on free, voluntary savings and in the second on forced, involuntary savings (reduction of real income by the inflation effect) so that the models in terms of reality content are not the same. However, by the use of contemporary logic (of the Russell and Wittgenstein type), which is concerned mainly with the form of expression of a statement and not with its content, the two propositions appear similar, only differently formulated. Classical logic, on the other hand, included in its object of study both form of expression and content, and therefore could not accept such a conclusion.

The list of examples of this nature can be enlarged. The same conclusion can be reached by considering the relationship between "spending" and the phenomenon of depression or boom. By using the *ex-ante* analysis there *first* appears a *decline of economic activity* and therefore of income of a previously inflated boom, which induces a depression; thereafter naturally follows the effect of "less spending" and eventually "less saving" in the aggregate. Changing to the Keynesian *ex-post* analysis, or thinking in reverse, *first* comes *less spending* and after that a depression with all other consequences. A great argument could develop here on the very question: Which relationship is true—first output-income then spending, or first spending and then output-income? A good conservative would take the first relationship as being true, thus refuting the Keynesian thinking and favoring classical economics. A loyal liberal in America, on the other hand, would accept the second relationship and refute classical economics, preferring the Keynesian variety. Such attitudes do exist in America, and that is why the gap between liberals and conservatives in the 1970's appears to be as big and sharp as it was in the 1950's or the 1930's.

At stake is a fundamental problem in methodology, which cannot be resolved until a bridge is constructed first between classical and contemporary logic (where the roots of the argument are located), and, second, between classical and contemporary economics (not in the sense of uniting them immediately, since that is probably not possible, but rather to recognize them as different, independent entities until a final solution may be worked out). In any case, the sequence of events in the analysis of a problem is of paramount importance, because in the end the practical solution adopted will depend upon the approach used.

Using the classical *ex-ante* analysis the solution will be related to the primary causes of an event like depression, whereas in applying the Keynesian *ex-post* analysis the solution will be directed at some unpleasant effects like "less spending" or "less employment" during a depression, ignoring or pushing aside the question of the causes inducing those events. We can see how complicated the relationship between economic history and economic theory may become, because the same economic facts or history viewed through diverse analytical techniques may lead to entirely different conclusions.

The most notorious case is that of the "paradox of thrift," whereby savings analyzed through the classical approach appear as an active element providing capital formation for economic progress, and thus represent both an individual and a social virtue. If we shift to the new Keynesian approach, that is, looking backward after the economic process has been completed, then the same savings appear as a loophole in the aggregate demand, or a passive element impeding economic progress and thus emerging as a private and social evil producing harm to both society and the individual. It is enough in this respect to remember the famous bananas parable, with Keynes' description of how, on a happy island where people enjoyed life, the new idea of a thrift campaign brought economic disaster, forcing the entire population (*a*) to starve to death, (*b*) to call off the thrift campaign, or (*c*) to accept government intervention in stimulating new investments.[26]

If the bananas parable were true, one would be even more baffled by other questions which can inevitably be raised. For instance, should society, through its institutions, i.e., government, encourage or discourage free people to save? Suppose in a given country a liberal government rigorously followed the lesson from the bananas parable and tried to restrict (directly or indirectly) saving by the people. How, then could the necessary capital formation for economic progress in that community be provided? In that case there seems to be no choice but to use social coercion by government! On this road are we not facing an open contradiction between a free society and this particular economic order controlled by the government?

The same explanation can be given to the theory of the investment multiplier, in the sense that it is the product of the same method of thinking in reverse. The Keynesian observation of the existence of "involuntary unemployment" during a depression is absolutely correct. His position that, with the help of the classical doctrine (as developed up to the 1930's), we could not account for this phenomenon is also valid. What went wrong springs from the point at which Keynes, instead of searching for the causes leading to this phenomenon of involuntary unemployment and developing a badly needed theory of economic disequilibrium, reversed the process. By thinking backwards his genius forged the theory of the multiplier, which fitted his problem. Indeed, his famous assumption in his *General Theory*, where he equated

$$1 - \frac{1}{k}$$

to the marginal propensity to consume, does not have any rational explanation, except that this was a sort of lucky combination, in fact a mathematical trick invented by a genius, which worked to prove his theorem that $\triangle Y_w = k. \triangle I_w$.[27] Thus, from the point of view of contemporary, formal logic, the theorem is all right, but if we decide to use classical logic—that is, to introduce also the quest for reality content in that assumption—then we are in trouble with the same theorem, specifically in its application to real life. This is a case where a theorem is formally true but not valid in practice. This interpretation seems to be confirmed by the economic conditions in the United States and other democratic countries where Keynesian policies were applied on a large scale after World War II, but, instead of full employment and price stability in the 1970's, we are faced with large unemployment and high inflation, not to mention the troubles with the balance of payments. Where then is the miracle of the multiplier?

This critical evaluation should not be interpreted as an attempt to diminish the stature of Keynes, who for all his contributions still remains the greatest economist of this century. It would be a disservice to his memory, however, if those who have something to say for a better understanding of his work were to keep quiet just to avoid controversial positions or interpretations in regard to the master. If alive, Keynes, certainly would not like this kind of behavior. Among well-known Keynesian economists in America, John Kenneth Galbraith is one who defected from the old guard, and in recent years he has been loudly declaring that the fiscal and monetary policies recommended by Keynes did not and cannot work.[28] The rest of the Keynesian disciples are divided between "monetarists" like Milton Friedman and "fiscalists" like Paul Samuelson, both groups, however, sharing the same old allegiance to the master. Another strong dissenting voice against the continuation of the new economics policies and way of thinking came recently from Professor John Jewkes of Oxford, who wrote: "Within less than one generation British Governments have twice fallen victim to the hallucination that they possess the knowledge and power positively to determine the rate of economic growth through central economic planning, and twice, in the grip of these ideas, they have embarked upon massive figuring and the preparation of elaborate economic blue-prints which have quickly led to confusion and frustration. Twice is a lot."[29]

A clarification in point of research methodology used in classical economics versus Keynesian economics would be of great help also in understanding and, if possible, mediating between liberal and conservative economists in America. Personally I think that the liberal-conservative dilemma can be resolved, but not by pushing or inducing intellectuals or common people to accept blindly or to be amenable to the new method of "thinking in reverse," because this is not going to work, it being contrary to common sense and to the cultural heritage of our civilization, in addition to not being efficient in satisfactorily resolving the practical problems of the last four decades. A better way is to show that there is another model of thinking, specifically the system of stable equilibrium conditions, here called "Social Liberalism,"[30] in which it makes no difference whether the *ex-ante* or the *ex-post* analysis is used, because in a model of close to 100% consistency, both approaches will produce similar results. We are talking about that unique combination of a social, economic, financial and political order which has "stability from within" and satisfies all basic conditions for stable equilibrium.

Unfortunately, both liberal and conservative economists in America, embroiled in a long-standing argument without access to an open avenue, have so far missed seeing the target of this unique combination, which, in my view, could unite a disunited intellectual house. But in a free society nothing is impossible; the future therefore still remains open to change and innovations.

5. *Ten Unsettled Issues Awaiting a Solution*

The construction of a blueprint for a free and stable society and economy of tomorrow in America and elsewhere requires more theoretical work and the contribution of sociologists, economists, psychologists, political scientists and men of letters to align all the consistent parts of the new order of inner stability. In this extraordinary endeavor of many scientists in many fields, there are a number of issues which are not yet settled:

(1) We do not yet have the methodology for crossing all the different branches of the study of human societies and for scientifically identifying the organic relationship among various possible social, economic, financial and political systems. This article provides an orientation table further on for this purpose.

(2) We do not have a reliable instrument for measuring and locating at this moment in history the position of American capitalism or for that matter the position of any other national economy. We talk about mixed systems, but the proportions of combined elements and forces may vary from 0 to 100%.

(3) We do not have a comprehensive map of all possible systems, and therefore we are not able to judge the direction of so many changes which take place today. In other words, we do not know precisely where we go from here, and therefore we are pawns at the mercy of history.

(4) During a debate of four decades between liberal and conservative economists in America only two terms were used: competition and monopoly (oligopoly being conceived as a form of monopoly). But both competition and monopoly are economic forces which cannot act in a vacuum. Competition, for instance, in action has to be associated with an institutional framework which, depending upon the existing social, financial and political system, may allow it to function from zero (neutral stage) to 100% full intensity. The same is true for monopoly, including oligopoly.

(5) The whole argument about the nature and functioning of American capitalism started from the quest for stability versus instability. Yet the concept of stability from within (stable equilibrium) was never clearly differentiated from unstable equilibrium (or, as Keynes called it, "equilibrium with unemployment"), nor from stability from without (an artificial equilibrium imposed by social coercion).

(6) The term "dynamics" has been abundantly used in economics, but no clear distinction was made between a system with a normal rate of growth sustained from within (what may be called "dynamics of normal economics") and other possible systems with an abnormal rate of growth ("dynamics of abnormal economics"). We hear about normal and abnormal psychology, but no one has called attention to the existence of normal and abnormal economics!

(7) No system in the physical or social universe can have inner stability without a strong, positive parameter, with the major function of coordinating all other elements and forces. The economic system is no exception to this natural rule. Leon Walras was the first economist who observed that, in order to have stable equilibrium, competition is not enough; in addition he stated the requirement of "Numeraire" (100%-backed currency) and other conditions consistent with it. Numeraire in this case fulfills the function of a natural parameter. Yet, the function of Numeraire in a modern economy is ignored completely by those who call themselves "modern economists."

(8) There are forms of money like monetized debt or bank credit (called credit money), uncovered paper money (fiat money) or booty money, which in their nature are reciprocal to Numeraire and therefore must be called "anti-Numeraire." Since Numeraire is associated with stable equilibrium, anti-Numeraire by definition produces disequilibrium. Yet this organic relationship is completely ignored in the new, Keynesian economics actually dedicated to the study of disequilibrium conditions.

(9) "Disequilibrium" is another overused term, but we do not have a reliable instrument for precisely defining the area of a minor versus a major disequilibrium, which is of fundamental importance both for theoretical work and for matters of policy.

(10) Most contemporary economists would accept the fact that in the new, Keynesian economics, many if not all statements have a relative value. Yet the concept of relativity (dominant in the physical sciences) was never systematically introduced in economics. On the other hand, it is true that the position taken by Keynes in economics is similar to the position taken by Einstein in physics at the turn of the century.

6. *The Possibility Theorem and Other Tools Used in the Development of an Orientation Table for Sociology, Economics, Finance and Political Science*

From the point of view of methodology, we see that sociology, economics, finance and political science have reached the stage where so many models are used and so many views are expressed that we are faced with the danger of being flooded with contradictory information, and thus inevitably being exposed to a sort of repetition of the biblical Tower of Babel. And truly, an immense amount of research and publications are poured into the market of ideas every year; yet we still do not have nor can we agree on a reasonable solution to the basic problems in the various fields.

An orientation table is proposed next for the study of human societies, national economies, money and government. The purpose is to develop a scientific map of all possible systems, starting with stable equilibrium and ending with total disequilibrium, and in this way to have a reliable instrument for identifying the position at which the various theories are true and valid, or not valid at all. The table in each case was constructed on the basis of the application of a new Possibility Theorem.

The Possibility Theorem is a methodological device composed of three parts:

(1) The separation, in terms of concept, between a given primary element or force and the institutional framework in which this force may act, starting from inertia and accelerating to the maximum, according to the nature of the framework. The problem of "framework" thus becomes a fundamental issue, because possible fluctuations will actually depend not upon the force but upon the nature of the framework.

(2) The plausible hypothesis is made that the social, economic, financial and political world is of a dual nature, in the sense that it is composed of stable and unstable elements and forces, mixed in various proportions.

(3) In order to reach and maintain stable equilibrium, the framework of the system in question must have a natural, real parameter which serves to coordinate all the other elements or forces in the system. All major parts or variables in a stable system must, therefore, be consistent with the parameter.

Simply stated, the *Possibility Theorem* says: Once we have discovered or identified a force (like competition or monopoly) or an important element in human societies, which has been confirmed by repeated observation, the analytical task of a scientist is to make a thorough investigation and find out what could happen to this force or element in action, in all possible and conceivable frameworks.

A *framework* is a logical conception of a space-time entity or, in concrete terms, an institutional setup where the given force or element may be viewed in action or functioning, starting from inertia (static position) and moving to an accelerated maximum.

The same undertaking requires a theory of conceptual models, with the understanding that a model in science is always a logical framework where we search for a problem or a standard to which we refer our results, defined in terms of some assumptions of a qualitative or a quantitative nature. In addition, the concept of bipolar types in the sense of *Idealtypen* (Max Weber), as refined in Walter Eucken's work,[31] has been used. The rest is nothing but conclusions and consequences derived from the conceptual basis just outlined.

The following are orientation tables for sociology, economics, money, political science, equilibrium, uncertainty, risk and profit:

An Orientation Table for Sociology

Primary elements or forces:

a = free, voluntary action—the principle of social cohesion (Talcott Parsons)

w = forced, involuntary action—the principle of social coercion (Thomas Hobbes)

So. = social system (human societies organized according to certain principles)

MODEL No. 1 *So. a 100% and w 0%*—a free and stable society at its limit of perfection.

The area No. 1 of social harmony with minimum of conflicts.

MODEL No. 2 *So. 90% and w 10%*—a free and stable society with minor conflicts.

The area No. 2 of social harmony with minor conflicts, yet serious enough to constitute a problem.

MODEL No. 3 *So. a 60% and w 40%*—a free society with social problems.

The area No. 3 of social harmony contaminated with social conflicts of a permanent nature, yet still manageable by peaceful means, if the majority understands the situation and accepts the need to resolve the conflicts.

MODEL No. 4 *So. 50% and w 50%*—a mixed society split evenly between social cohesion and social coercion (a society with frozen patterns of social stratification).

The area No. 4 of continuous social turmoil where the revolt of the oppressed majority is open and in process of organization to overthrow the old system.

MODEL No 5. *So. a 40% and w 60%*—a mixed society where a minority has legal and institutional control upon a disadvantaged majority.

The area No. 5 of big changes in the structure of a society ridden by conflicts, dissent and open revolt.

From here a society may go through wise reforms toward a free and stable order as in Model No. 2, or it may plunge into a dictatorship of the right or the left or any other type.

MODEL No. 6 *So. a 10% and w 90%*—a society of dictatorship of any sort where the principle of social coercion becomes the rule in the hands of a despot, helped by the bureaucracy of a single political party.

The area No. 6 of tyrannical oppression of the many, where only a war or a bloody counterrevolution may change the situation.

MODEL No. 7 *So. a 0% and w 100%*—a society of dictatorship at its limit of absolute power.

An Orientation Table for Economics

Primary elements or forces:

a = free economic action—the principle of fair competition in an open market

w = imposed economic action—the principle of monopoly (including oligopoly and other forms of restricted markets)

Eco. = economic system (a national economy organized according to certain principles)

MODEL No. 1 *Eco. a 100% and w 0%*—a free and stable economy at its limit of perfection, or the system of pure and perfect competition.

The area No. 1 of stable equilibrium with full employment and minor fluctuations.

MODEL No. 2 *Eco. a 90% and w 10%*—a free and stable economy which can adjust by itself without great problems.

The area No. 2 of minor disequilibria which requires specific monetary or fiscal policies in order to reach equilibrium with full employment.

MODEL No. 3 *Eco. a 60% and w 40%*—a free economy of a mixed nature with competition still prevailing but with problems which may be solved by using specific policies skillfully.

The area No. 3 of intensified minor disequilibria, where the fluctuations are starting to become cumulative and make more difficult the application of specific policies to reach equilibrium with full employment.

MODEL No. 4 *Eco. a 50% and w 50%*—a mixed economy where competition and monopoly are of equal intensity (an organically static economy).

The area No. 4 of major disequilibria with permanent cumulative fluctuations, where the efficiency of the traditional monetary and fiscal policies is in doubt.

MODEL No. 5 *Eco. a 40% and w 60%*—a mixed economy where monopoly in diverse forms is prevailing.

The area No. 5 of major and disruptive disequilibria with open inflations or deflations, increasing chronic unemployment and cumulative difficulties in the balance of payments.

This is the time where major changes in the structure of such a mixed, troubled economy become inevitable. Such changes through wise reforms may lead to permanent stability of the type included in Model No. 1, but could also end with a government-controlled economy if the first road was missed or ignored.

MODEL No. 6 *Eco. a 10% and w 90%*—a government-planned and -controlled economy with or without collective ownership of the means of production.

MODEL No. 7 *Eco. a 0% and w 100%*—an absolute economic system of pure and perfect monopoly in the hands of the government.

An Orientation Table for the Study of Money

Primary elements:

a = Numeraire or 100%-backed, real currency—the principle of Numeraire

w = anti-Numeraire or not-covered, nominal currency—the principle of anti-Numeraire

Mon. = monetary system (national finance organized in accordance with certain principles)

MODEL No. 1 *Mon. a 100% and w 0%*—a 100% Numeraire-currency system.

The area No. 1 of monetary stability from within.

MODEL No. 2 *Mon. a 90% and w 10%*—a 90% Numeraire-currency system.

The area No. 2 of monetary stability with minor disequilibria which can be corrected by adequate policies.

MODEL No. 3 *Mon. a 60% and w 40%*—a 60% Numeraire-currency system.

The area No. 3 of monetary stability with often repeated and intensified monetary disequilibria, which with some special skill could be corrected by special monetary and fiscal policies.

MODEL No. 4 *Mon. a 50% and w 50%*—a 50% Numeraire-currency system (an organically static monetary system evenly composed of Numeraire and anti-Numeraire).

The area No. 4 of monetary instability characterized by major disequilibria where the working of the traditional monetary and fiscal policies is in doubt.

MODEL No. 5 *Mon. a 40% and w 60%*—a 60% anti-Numeraire currency system.

The area No. 5 of monetary instability with open inflations and deflations, where the cumulative fluctuations are moving in all directions and can no longer be controlled by the traditional policies.

This is the time where major changes in the structure of the monetary system are inevitable. These changes through wise reforms may go toward restoring monetary stability as in Model No. 2, but also may be directed in the opposite direction, toward a 100% anti-Numeraire currency system.

MODEL No. 6 *Mon. a 10% and w 90%*—a 90% anti-Numeraire currency system.

The area No. 6 where paper money and monetized bank credit are in the hands of the government.

MODEL No. 7 *Mon. a 0% and w 100%*—A 100% anti-Numeraire currency system.

An Orientation Table for Political Science

Primary elements:
a = government by consent—the principle of limited, delegated powers

w = government by coercion—the principle of absolute, inherent powers
Gov. = system of government, organized according to certain principles

MODEL No. 1 *Gov. a 100% and w 0%*—a 100% democratic government of limited powers at its limit of perfection.

The area No. 1 of political stability with little conflict.

MODEL No. 2 *Gov. a 90% and w 10%*—a 90% democratic government of limited powers conceived in realistic terms, i.e., which can be realized anywhere in the present-day world.

The area No. 2 of political stability with some minor social, economic and financial conflicts which require more power and means than usual to resolve them.

MODEL No. 3 *Gov. a 60% and w 40%*—a 60% democratic form of government which is forced to use 40% undemocratic methods because society and economy have problems that are not resolved in a "correct" manner.

The area No. 3 of political stability, contaminated with frequent and serious conflicts in the social, economic and financial order.

MODEL No. 4 *Gov. a 50% and w 50%*—a mixed form of government split evenly between democratic and oligarchical characteristics.

The area No. 4 of political instability because of continuous turmoil in the social, economic and financial order, so that the government is forced now to assume more and more powers in order to preserve the old system, even though this is not possible indefinitely.

MODEL No. 5 *Gov. a 40% and w 60%*—a 60% dictatorial form of government.

The area No. 5 of political instability with major and disruptive disequilibria in the social, economic and financial order.

This is the time of great changes in the political system. One possibility is to adopt correct reforms so that stable equilibrium be restored and thus government may go back to Model No. 2. The other possibility is to move toward a government-controlled society and economy, and consequently the absolute, inherent powers of the government have to be increased.

MODEL NO. 6 *Gov. a 10% and w 90%*—a 90% dictatorial form of government.

MODEL NO. 7 *Gov. a 0% and w 100%*—a 100% dictatorial form of government at its limit of absolute powers.

An Orientation Table for the Study of Equilibrium
Uncertainty, Risk and Profit

Primary elements or forces:
$a =$ stability from within (stable equilibrium)
$w =$ instability from within (disequilibrium) or artificial stability from without
Co = competition; *Mon* = monopoly; *Nu* = Numeraire; *Anti-Nu* = paper money and monetized bank credit
${}_vS$ = voluntary savings; ${}_fS$ = forced savings

MODEL NO. 1 *A System of 100% Stability from Within (Pure and Perfect Competition)*
Eco 100% *Co* + 100% *Nu* + *Fin* 100%${}_vS$

This is the Walrasian system extended to include finance.
At the limit: uncertainty is zero; no risk and no pure profits.

The area between Models No. 1 and 2 is of "*Normal Dynamics*" where the Hicksian model is located. The normal, equilibrium profits are the rule, and pure (extra, differential) profits the exception.

MODEL NO. 2 *A System of 90% Stability from Within*
Eco 90% *Co* + 10% *Mon* + 90% *Nu* + 10% *Anti-Nu* + *Fin* 90%${}_vS$ + 10%${}_fS$

The area between Models No. 2 and 3 belongs to "*Normal Dynamics*" too, but the degree of uncertainty is increasing; so do risk and pure profits.

The Hicksian model in its dynamic form is still valid in this area, because this is the territory of weak minor disequilibria.

MODEL NO. 3 *A System of 60% Stability from Within*
Eco 60% *Co* + 40% *Mon* + 60% *Nu* + 40% *Anti-Nu* + *Fin* 60%${}_vS$ + 40%${}_fS$

The area between Models No. 3 and 4 still could be included in "*Normal Dynamics,*" because in this mixed system stable elements prevail (60%). But the uncertainty has reached here a relatively high proportion (40%), and therefore risk and pure profits will have a tendency to rise to high levels too. This is the territory of strong minor disequilibria.

Here we can introduce the Knight's model of "unmeasurable uncertainty" on a rather large scale (40%). The Hicksian model, on the other hand, is on its way out, in terms of application.

MODEL No. 4 *A System of Only 50% Stability from Within*
Eco 50% *Co* + 50% *Mon* + 50% *Nu* + 50% *Anti-Nu* + *Fin* $50\%_v S$ + $50\%_f S$

This is the model of an organically static economy or of unstable equilibrium (Pareto) or "equilibrium with unemployment" (Keynes).

MODEL No. 5 *A System of 60% Instability from Within*
Eco 40% *Co* + 60% *Mon* + 40% *Nu* + 60% *Anti-Nu* + *Fin* $40\%_v S$ + $60\%_f S$

The area between Models No. 4 and 6 belongs to "*Abnormal Dynamics*" with a high degree of "unmeasurable uncertainty" (above 50%); therefore the existence of relatively high risks associated with high profits.

The theory of risk and profit by Frank Knight has full validity and application in this area.

This is the territory of major disequilibria and therefore exposed to radical changes toward Model No. 1 or toward Model No. 7

MODEL No. 6 *A System of 90% Artificial Stability Imposed by Government (Hidden Disequilibrium)*
This is the area of government-planned and -controlled economy and society.

MODEL No. 7 *A System of Pure and Perfect Monopoly Under Government Control*
Eco 0% *Co* + 100% *Mon* + 0% *Nu* + 100% *Anti-Nu* + *Fin* $100\%_f S$

7. *Preliminary Results and Further Studies*

The interest in problems of methodology in economics and other social fields has increased in recent years. The constitution of the History of Economics Society in America (1973) and the journal *History of Political Economy* confirm this trend. The organization of the first international Congress of Economic History and History of Economic Theories by the Graduate School of Industrial Studies in Piraeus, Greece, in March 1975, will further promote the interest and studies in the development of economics and other social studies. It is worthwhile to mention that the Greek school of economic thought, especially through the works of Professor Claude B. Bandaloukas[32] and Professor Lazaros T. Houmanidis[33] has advanced anew the thesis that there is a relationship between economic history and economic theory, but this is not to be confused with the famous Methodenstreit in the German economic school, where an antinomy between the two branches developed.

What can the orientation tables just outlined for sociology, economics, money and political science contribute to a better understanding of the liberal-conservative argument in the American school of thought? Can they provide some new help in furthering the work in methodology necessary to resolve the ten basic issues mentioned previously?

8. *The Organic Relationship Among the Social, Economic, Monetary and Political Systems*

Looking at the five tables, it is clear that a free and stable society requires in principle and in practice, a free and stable economy and a democratic form of government of limited, delegated powers. This relationship, in general terms, was shared by all liberal economists of the eighteenth and nineteenth centuries. In a somewhat fragmented form, the same relationship is recognized by conservative circles in America. The tables show further that, in the traditional thinking of the old liberal school (including today's conservatives in America), there was a missing link, specifically the requirement of a 100% Numeraire-currency system, as a natural parameter for the organization of the financial system of a free and stable economy. Exactly a century ago, Leon Walras, in his *Elements d'Économie Politique Pure* (1874), pointed out and proved theoretically that without exclusive use of Numeraire there was no chance to have stable equilibrium with full employment. Unfortunately, in terms of applied science, his voice was at that time and still is today not heard as much as it should be, especially in places where economic decisions at the highest level in government are made.

If in 1975 we look at what is happening in the United States and the rest of the free world under conditions of paper money and monetized bank credit (i.e., in a system of anti-Numeraire which cannot be controlled anymore than antimatter can in the physical universe), we can see the relevance and importance of the orientation tables in question, both with respect to theory and applied science. The tables show clearly and strongly that *the dream of a free, stable society and economy without fear of an oppressive form of government is impossible, by definition, without the natural parameter of Numeraire.* This explains the drama of the eighteenth and nineteenth centuries, when there was an almost unanimous consensus among intellectuals in all fields and common people that such a dream should become reality, and yet the liberal experiment failed. On the other hand, the same tables in the same strong language warn that the use of paper money and monetized bank credit on a large scale, i.e., a 100% anti-Numeraire currency system, is creating insurmountable economic and social difficulties, which in turn require the perpetuation of a dictatorial form of government of unlimited powers. In between, the tables show the existence of a large number of mixed systems of minor and major disequilibria leading toward one or the other order.

9. *The Subdivision of the Various Fields of Social Sciences*

In point of methodology, the five tables show why sociology, economics, the study of money and government actually should be divided into at least five independent parts as follows:

Sociology:

1. Sociology of a free and stable society;
2. Sociology of a free society with minor conflicts and disequilibria;
3. Sociology of a mixed society with frozen social stratification, or sociology of an organically static society;
4. Sociology of a mixed free society with major and open conflicts;
5. Sociology of a society dominated by a political dictatorship at its limits of absolute power.

Economics:

1. Economics of a free and stable society or of stable equilibrium;
2. Economics of imperfect competition with minor disequilibria;
3. Economics of an organically static economy with unemployment;

4. Economics of a mixed system dominated by monopolies (oligopolies) and major disequilibria;
5. Economics of a government-planned and -controlled economy.

Finance:

1. Finances for a free and stable economy based on 100% Numeraire;
2. Finances for a free economy with minor disequilibria;
3. Finances for an organically static economy;
4. Finances for a mixed economy dominated by monopolies (oligopolies);
5. Finances for a government-planned and -controlled economy based on a 100% anti-Numeraire currency system.

Political Science:

1. The study of a 100% democratic form of government;
2. The study of a democratic form of government with minor disequilibria;
3. The study of a mixed democratic form of government facing problems of a static society.
4. The study of a mixed democratic form of government facing problems of major disequilibria;
5. The study of a completely dictatorial form of government at its limits of absolute power.

One basic question could be raised: What is the justification of such a subdivision? If we look at the tables, all models on the upper part of the map, mathematically conceived, are reciprocal to all the models located on the lower part. Consequently, any problems researched in a model on the upper part must have, by definition, a solution which is exactly opposite to the solution of the same problem investigated in a model on the lower part.

10. Competition or Monopoly (Oligopoly Included) Alone Cannot Define the Nature and Functioning of an Economic System

All classical economists (with the exception of Walras), including those American economists who have so far taken part in the conservative-liberal argument about the real nature of American capitalism, have missed seeing the fact that competition and monopoly in any form are just economic forces which cannot be judged by themselves but must be examined in conjunction with a definite financial and economic framework where these forces may act to a certain degree or not at all. In addition, they overlooked the fundamental point that the financial framework depends upon the proportion between Numeraire and anti-Numeraire in the system.

The tables suggest, for instance, that competition or the law of supply and demand or Say's law of the markets in practice do not and cannot work efficiently to reach and maintain equilibrium prices unless the financial system is based in a large proportion on Numeraire. To wait for miracles, expecting that the law of supply and demand will somehow, regardless of the nature of the financial system, come through constitutes an illusion inherited from the time when the expression of "laissez-faire" was converted into a political instrument to defend vested interests in business. Competition is an economic force, but, as in the case of any other force in the physical or social universe, it cannot work to its maximum intensity unless it is acting in a most appropriate framework. The same is true for monopoly (oligopoly included).

11. Stable Versus Unstable Equilibrium, or Walras Versus Keynes

The tables help further to identify the area where the concept of stable equilibrium is true and valid as compared with conditions of unstable equilibrium. Unfortunately, the distinction between "stable" and "unstable" equilibrium is not yet clarified in the field, even though I think there is enough evidence to prove that Walras has used in his system of thought the first concept, whereas Keynes has used the second.

Stable equilibrium is the characteristic of that unique system which has a strong natural parameter and a consistent framework where all major variables in action have the natural tendency of converging toward one and the same point or position of stability from within. The problems in this system have a determinate solution with a high probability of prediction equal to 100% at the limit. Unstable equilibrium, on the contrary, is characterized by a mixed system or a combination of two diverging forces which are dominant and of equal intensity so that at the limit there is no fluctuation and the system appears in a static position. The problems in such a system do not have a determinate solution because the maximum probability of prediction to a solution at the limit is only 50%.

Walras saw clearly the distinction between stable and unstable equilibrium. He identified stable equilibrium as that system where there is only a unique solution at the point where the demand curve is crossing the supply curve and the prices are expressed in Numeraire. "Such an equilibrium," wrote Walras, "is exactly similar to that of a suspended body of which the center of gravity lies directly beneath the point of suspension, so that if this centre of gravity were displaced from the vertical line beneath the point of suspension, it automatically returns to its original position through the force of gravitation. This equilibrium is, therefore, stable."[34]

Walras recognized that, under conditions of unstable equilibrium, any changes of prices up or down will have a tendency to move "farther and farther away from the point of equilibrium." "This equilibrium," he continued, "is exactly similar to that of a suspended body of which the point of suspension lies directly beneath the centre of gravity, so that if this centre of gravity once leaves the vertical line above the point of suspension, it does not return automatically but keeps on moving farther and farther away until through the force of gravitation it reaches the position vertically beneath the point of suspension. Such an equilibrium is unstable."[35]

The above description seems to be consistent with Model No. 1 (*Eco a* 100% *Co* + 100% *Nu* + $100\%_v S$), or one close to it for *stable equilibrium,* and Model No. 4 (*Eco a* 50% *Co* + 50% *Mon* + 50% *Nu* + $50\%_v S$) for *unstable equilibrium* if we substitute the parameter of Numeraire for the point of suspension, competition for the force of gravitation and price changes for pendulum movements. There is no evidence, however, that Walras was aware of the long distance between the two systems viewed on a map of all possible systems.

The merit of Walras is that he was the first economist who explicitly pointed out and proved theoretically that the state of general equilibrium was not possible unless all prices and therefore all incomes were expressed in terms of a selected standard commodity he called "Numeraire." Given a system of open markets ruled by free competition alone, with all prices cried at an auction in terms of Numeraire, concluded Walras, "the condition of general equilibrium is fulfilled ipso facto."[35] This is the concept of the unique solution of equilibrium with full employment and price stability.

As a scientist, Walras, like all other classical economists, wanted to discover laws in economic life similar to the natural laws in the physical universe. "To this end," he wrote, "we shall suppose that the market is perfectly competitive, just as in pure mechanics we suppose, to start with, that machines are perfectly frictionless."[35] Without assuming a model of pure and perfect competition with 100% Numeraire, Walras could not have discovered and formulated mathematically the theorem of general equilibrium. His performance, without exaggeration, was the equivalent of a Newtonian law of gravity in economics. Newton in physics and Walras in economics represent two giant masters who used the classical method of thinking forward from cause to effect, in trying to discover the governing laws of a universe restricted in its content to a perfectly stable framework, even though both knew and mentioned that the real world in each case deviated from the ideal framework.

With the Walrasian model it is possible to prove that, in any system which in real terms is close enough to Model No. 1 (located in Area No. 1), the basic economic problems (rent, wages, interest, profit, taxation and foreign exchange) have a determinate solution expressed in terms of equilibrium price, marginal utility, marginal cost, marginal revenue and maximum utility to consumers, combined with maximum of return to producers. The tables show further that it is a mistake to think that the concept of marginal utility or marginal cost can be used in the same way and with the same results in other possible systems.

Let us use again the economic and monetary tables to recognize the territory where the concept of unstable equilibrium is true and valid, namely, in Model No. 4 ($Eco\ a$ 50% Co + 50% Mon + 50% Nu + $50\%_v S$). Immediately our attention is caught by the fact that the respective area is far away from the domain of stable equilibrium. It is possible that in this mixed system, too, the supply may equal demand since the system is static; yet, it cannot be at the same level as in a model of stable equilibrium, for obvious reasons. Looking more carefully at its composition, 50% competition and 50% monopoly, we can easily detect one major characteristic of this peculiar system, namely, that the available human and natural resources are not used to the optimum. This is the theoretical representation of a capitalistic economy in a depression, something similar to the "stationary state" as conceived by Ricardo. Without much debate this model can be considered as the territory of "unstable equilibrium" or perhaps better expressed "stable disequilibrium," or, as Lord Keynes called it, "equilibrium with unemployment."

Vilfredo Pareto also clearly delineated the line between stable and unstable equilibrium. He wrote: "An economic system is called in equilibrium when the change in one of the conditions of the system produces other changes which will initiate an exactly opposite counter-reaction. Such an equilibrium is *stable* when the change is of finite magnitude. It is *unstable* at the limit when the conditions of equilibrium do not hold except for changes infinitely small."[36] Again this definition is consistent with our economic table.

Alfred Marshall, who in so many other subjects is so clear, muddled the distinction between the two sorts of equilibrium. As far as the concept of stable equilibrium is concerned, he shared the same concept as Walras and Pareto.[37] In my view it is only with respect to unstable equilibrium that his position becomes debatable.

"Besides positions of stable equilibrium," Marshall wrote, "there are theoretically at least positions of unstable equilibrium: they are the dividing boundaries between two positions of stable equilibria, the watersheds, so to speak, dividing two river basins, and the price tends to flow away from them in either direction. When demand and supply are in unstable equilibrium, then, if the scale of production is disturbed ever so little from its equilibrium position, it will move rapidly away to one of its positions of stable equilibrium."[38]

On the same page, Marshall graphically envisioned the issue as shown in the diagram.

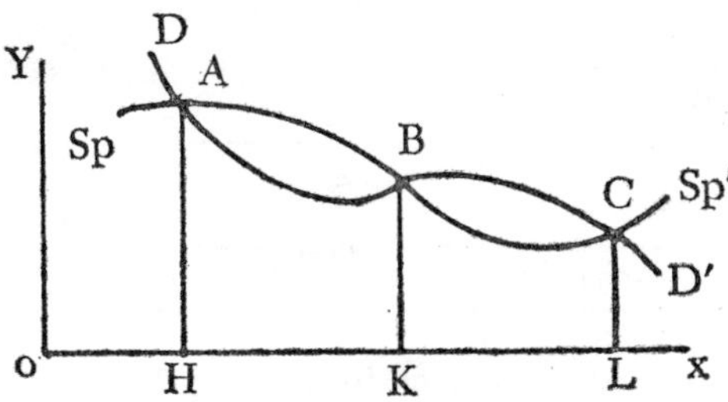

Points *A* and *C* represent two positions of stable equilibrium located in a territory of normal demand and supply curves. In between, Marshall interlocked point *B* at the crossing of an entirely different type of curves; I call them *inverted* or *abnormal* curves. Indeed, they represent an abnormal or inverted sort of behavior by both consumers and producers.

I think Marshall's presentation is debatable on methodological grounds. Point *B* with inverted curves cannot exist between points *A* and *C*, which are associated with normal curves. In order to have point *B* we must assume conditions of radical change in the behavior of both consumers and producers.

In a system of stable equilibrium with 100% Numeraire, money is stable, and therefore at higher prices consumers buy less and producers are inclined to offer more. This is normal behavior and explains why the demand curve has a negative slope and the supply curve a positive one. Points *A* and C satisfy this requirement.

To reach point *B*, the economic conditions must change so radically that at higher prices consumers buy more (the demand curve shifting to a positive slope), whereas producers offer less (the supply curve thus receiving a negative slope). This set of abnormal conditions can be envisioned only in a mixed economy at the limit with 50% Numeraire and 50% anti-Numeraire. Only then can the system be frozen at a certain degree of inflation or deflation and involuntary unemployment. Actually this is a structural disequilibrium locked in where the behavior of both consumers and producers turns topsy-turvy—a situation far from conditions of stable equilibrium.[39]

Point *B* (on Marshall's diagram) must therefore be presented in a separate sketch with explicit information about the change in the model. This is how we should view the distinction between regular, normal and inverted or abnormal demand and supply curves, respectively, between stable versus unstable equilibrium.

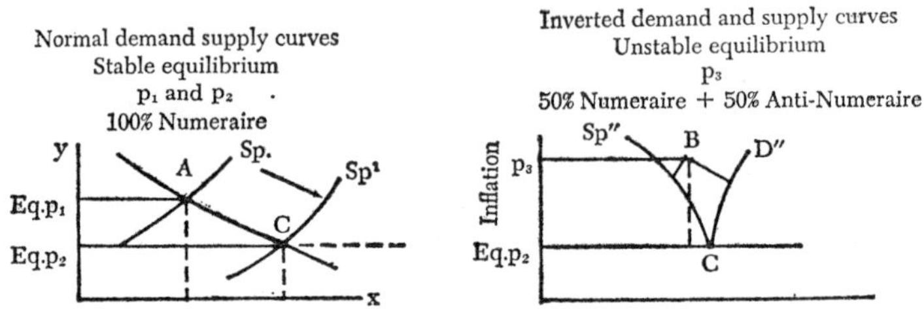

Lord Keynes undoubtedly was influenced to a certain extent by his venerated teacher, Marshall. In Chapter 11 of his *A Treatise on Money* (Volume 1),[40] Keynes uses the concept of stable equilibrium, without mentioning the basic requirement of Numeraire, just as Marshall had done. It is clear that neither Marshall nor Keynes was aware of the distance between stable and unstable equilibrium. Keynes correctly noted that, in the real life of his time, it was very difficult to find conditions where the volume of new investments was matched automatically by the amount of aggregate savings. But he failed to see that a disequilibrium between new investment and the rate of capital formation in the form of voluntary savings was not due to the free enterprise system as such, but rather to the large-scale use of the anti-Numeraire forces of monetized bank credit and paper money, which invalidated Say's law of the markets.

The greatness of Keynes, in point of methodology, consists in the fact that he freed himself both from classical economics and his teacher and raised to the rank of a major problem the issue of "involuntary unemployment" and the existence of "equilibrium with unemployment." Even though the expression "equilibrium with unemployment" does not have a full meaning except if equated with "unstable equilibrium," there is no definite text to prove that Keynes envisioned theoretically the long distance between stable equilibrium (with full employment) and unstable equilibrium (with unemployment). However, his practical observations and the bananas parable in Chapter 12 of the same *Treatise*[41] disclosed an economic world of stable disequilibrium far away from the classical model, a world that indeed can be matched with conditions of unstable equilibrium.

In his *General Theory,* Keynes made use again of both concepts of stable and unstable equilibrium, but this time, as might be expected, he concentrated mostly on the latter. His main interest was to discover and analyze unknown variables of the existing economic world of disequilibrium, so vividly revealed by the modern capitalistic system of his time. He was absolutely right in observing that "obviously, if the classical theory is only applicable to the case of full employment, it is fallacious to apply it to the problems of involuntary unemployment—if there is such a thing (and who will deny it?)."[42] But he was definitely wrong in the interpretation of Say's law of the markets. When Say stated his theorem "Supply creates its own demand," he did not mean that equilibrium, under a given set of conditions, will exist "for all levels of output and employment," as Keynes interpreted it.[43] Nor is it correct to say, as Keynes does, that, on the basis of Say's law, "Effective demand, instead of having a unique equilibrium value, is an infinite range of values all equally admissible."[44] This is, I think, a misrepresentation of Say's theorem. Classical economics relates to normal, Marshallian demand-and-supply curves that are crossing each other only at a single point. Therefore in the classical system of thought the effective demand and supply have only one, unique equilibrium value. If so, then the above criticism of Say by Keynes, even though brilliantly formulated as a piece of formal logic in the contemporary sense (Wittgenstein), has no foundation in point of correct methodology. And I am surprised that up to this moment, to my knowledge, no one has called attention to this unjustified misrepresentation of the classical doctrine. Keynes has butchered Say's law of the markets without due cause!

The only weakness in Say's theorem, as in all other classical laws, is that he did not point out explicitly the requirement of a financial system based exclusively on Numeraire and no monetization of bank credit, as Leon Walras later did. But once we introduce in a system of free markets the institutions of Numeraire and no monetized bank credit, then Say was correct during his famous argument with Malthus when he wrote to him: "From these premises I have drawn a conclusion which appears to me evident, but the consequences of which appear to have alarmed you. I had said—as no one can purchase the produce of another except with his own produce, as the amount for which we can buy is equal to that which we can produce, the more we can produce the more we can purchase. From whence proceeds this other conclusion, which you refuse to admit—That if certain commodities do not sell, it is because others are not produced, and that it is the raising produce alone which opens a market for the sale of a produce."[45] In this case, which represents stable equilibrium with Numeraire, the volume of real income in the economy over a period of time is equal to money income, and thus Say's reasoning becomes a masterpiece of *ex-ante* analysis and has no theoretical faults in its conclusions. In fact, Say in the same letter, just one paragraph before, stated that "to a proprietor of a mine, the silver money is a produce with which he buys what he has occasion for." The strong implication here is that Say, when he formulated his theorem, evidently had in the back of his mind the assumption of "silver money" as Numeraire, and therefore he was very sure that his reasoning was applicable to both the production of goods and services in general and the monetary sphere.

What Say did not observe was the fact that modern banks in his own time, through monetization and demonetization of credit in the form of anti-Numeraire, were creating conditions of disequilibrium where the working of his theorem would be broken in practice.[46] But all classical economists missed this point, which explains why their analysis appeared to be correct in theory but wrong in application. This gap between theory and practice has created, with the passing of time, a confusion which discredited the classical doctrine and with it the humanistic dream of a free and stable economy and society. This is a part of the drama of modern times, a new chapter in modern sociology, economics and political science which has not yet been written.

Keynes, like his predecessor Malthus, observed the gap between classical theory and existing economic conditions of unstable equilibrium and, by the application of the method of thinking in reverse, he attempted to provide more a practical solution for matters of policy (so badly needed in the 1930's) and an improvised explanation to back up his position, rather than a definitive explanation of what actually was wrong in the capitalist system of the twentieth century. His policies may be questioned in the 1970's—and in fact they are and on good grounds—but nobody can take away from Keynes the credit for being able to change the thinking of his time and to open new roads of scientific investigation. In this way others might have the incentive and the courage to proceed with new ideas in searching for better tools of reasoning and more efficient policies to carry out the torch of intellectual progress and a better life for coming generations. In this respect this writer, critical as he may be at times, considers himself a disciple of Keynes in the best traditional use of the term, that is, one who freed himself from the master's way of thinking in order to be able to enter unknown territories.

12. The Principle of Relativity and Uncertainty in Economics

Model No. 4 on the economic table (*Eco a* 50% + *w* 50%) is static in nature, and it stays in inertia as long as the two diverging forces remain of exactly the same intensity. As Pareto observed, this inertia or position of unstable equilibrium holds only for changes infinitely small. At the first significant disturbance, the system automatically goes into disequilibrium and cannot revert to its initial position by itself. Model No. 4 also divides the map into two different kinds of economic worlds. On the upper part are located all possible systems with minor disequilibria, including Model No. 1 of pure and perfect competition, or the realization at the maximum limit of price stability, full employment, maximum of social justice in the distribution of national income and the balance of payments in order.

It appears evident that the validity of the classical laws in theory and practice (assuming that we can fulfill all the required conditions) is absolute in the first Walrasian model and relative in all other models starting with Model No. 2 and ending with Model No. 6. This may be called the *Principle of Relativity in Economics.* More qualifications, however, are necessary. All models on the lower part of the map are, mathematically viewed, reciprocal to the models on the upper part. Thus any solution to a problem analyzed in a model on the lower part is reciprocal to the solution for the same problem located in a model on the upper part. Consequently, the principle of relativity cannot be the same all the way from Model No. 2 to Model No. 7. We have therefore to distinguish among three categories of relativity: (1) *Economics of Relativity I* for any model on the upper part (exception Model No. 1) characterized by minor disequilibria; (2) *Economics of Relativity II,* concerned with problems of a national economy and society in a stage of unstable equilibrium or frozen stagnation; and (3) *Economics of Relativity III,* related to any model on the lower part of the map characterized by major disequilibria.

The principle of uncertainty and risk, about which we hear so much, and which was introduced in economics by Frank H. Knight,[47] is also valid over the same area as the principle of relativity, to which it is related. As a point of methodology we should also distinguish among at least three principal categories of uncertainty and risk: (1) uncertainty and risk in a model of minor disequilibrium; (2) uncertainty and risk in a model of unstable equilibrium; and (3) uncertainty and risk in a model of a major disequilibrium. As far as the last limiting model of pure and perfect monopoly, or a 100% government-planned and -controlled economy and society, is concerned, the uncertainty and risk are veiled, beclouded. This model in its nature is of total disequilibrium (measured in terms of human nature and aspirations) but under full and rigorous government controls it can reach a certain degree of artificial stability from without.

13. The Impossibility Theorem

The ultimate dream of any scientist, in any field, is to get down to only one single primary element or force and thus be able to develop one single general theory to encompass both micro- and macro-analysis and to include all possible cases. In the economic field it was Lord Keynes who explicitly pointed out this extraordinary goal in the way he started Chapter 1 of his *General Theory,* where he wrote in 1935: "I have called this book *The General Theory of Employment, Interest and Money,* placing the emphasis of the prefix *general.*"[48] But is this goal possible at all?

In the physical sciences, Albert Einstein's ambition was the same, i.e., how to reduce all observations of the micro- and macro-cosmos to one variable and thus master one single, general theory, which he called the *Unified Field Theory.* He tried, like many other thinkers in philosophy before him, but in his confession in *Out of My Later Years,* the answer he gave in regard to this most ambitious and final project of his life was not in the affirmative. In Einstein's own words: "Thus the story goes until we have arrived at a system of the greatest conceivable unity, and of the greatest poverty of concepts of the logical foundations, which are still compatible with the observations made by our senses. We do not know whether or not this ambition will ever result in a definite system. If one is asked for his opinion, he is inclined to answer no."[49]

The truth is that this highest dream of a scientist in both the natural and the social fields is not possible, by definition, because the physical as well as the socioeconomic universe is of a dual nature, that is, composed of stable and unstable elements and forces. This is the essence of the Impossibility Theorem in terms of aspirations for a single, general theory to explain the whole domain in each field. The orientation table for economics helps to formulate and justify this theorem, in regard to the study of a national or international economy. Because all models on the lower part of the map, conceived mathematically, are reciprocal to all models on the upper part, there is no theory which can satisfy the logical conditions to be true and valid for the understanding of any possible model on both sides of the map. In reality any theory developed and applicable on the upper part will be negated in its counter-model on the lower part. That is what the Impossibility Theorem says.

In terms of applied science, the same theorem, with the help of the orientation tables, indicates that it is impossible to realize and maintain a free and stable economy and society with a government of limited powers without a financial system based on 100% Numeraire-currency which fulfills the function of a natural parameter; or to have a free and stable economy and society with a financial system based on 100% anti-Numeraire, for the obvious reason that such a combination is lacking a natural parameter. This is the second part of the Impossibility Theorem. Finally, as a third part, the same tables show that it is impossible to realize and prolong a government-planned and -controlled society and economy without a financial system based on 100% anti-Numeraire combined with absolute political powers, which in this case are necessitated by a system of total (hidden) disequilibrium.

14. Final Remarks: The Future of American Capitalism

The proper use of the orientation tables can help to resolve the conservative-liberal argument which in the 1970's is as sharp as in the 1950's. The Berle-Means-Galbraith-Hoover thesis is valid, but only when the dynamic American economy was represented by a model located on the lower part of the map, something which requires empirical evidence that the majority of all prices and incomes is determined by monopoly and oligopoly forces, specifically that they were above the equilibrium level calculated in Numeraire. This is a very difficult proof which has not yet been provided.

The Wilcox-Stigler-Nutter-Friedman thesis is also valid, but only for the time when American capitalism moves in the direction of more competition and more stability in prices and incomes, that is, toward a model on the upper part of the map. Again this requires empirical proof, which at present is far from being satisfactory.

As long as the mixed American economic system remains dynamic and is therefore moving up and down along the unstable equilibrium line marked on the map as *Eco a* 50% + *w* 50% (see the economic table), there is no chance to make reliable predictions about the future, because the maximum probability we can get is 50 per cent, and that is too low. The idea that the American economy at the turn of the century or before was close to a system of pure and perfect competition is false. In this respect the expression "laissez-faire capitalism" is misleading. The truth is that American capitalism was always represented by a mixed system, shifting up and down along the 50:50 line.

The basic problems in this century did not come from inadequate competition. Rather they all reflect the fact that the financial framework of the system was based only on a thin, fractional parameter of Numeraire in form of partially covered bank notes and bank deposits. Through the latest changes in the Federal Reserve Act in 1965 and 1968, when the rather thin requirement of 25% gold backing for official money was repealed, the whole financial system and economy were left without any concrete parameter for orientation and a reasonable calculation of prices and incomes. On August 15, 1971, by a decision of President Nixon, an additional blow was inflicted upon the American financial and economic order through the suspension of the convertibility of the U.S. dollar in international markets. Soon thereafter, this also brought on the international oil crisis, with a fourfold increase of oil prices in one year. The once powerful and convertible American dollar lost its reliability for objectively expressing prices at home or in international markets.

The future of American capitalism is hard to predict because the American economy is still stronger than any other economy in the world in terms of capacity of production. The U.S. government will never allow the Great Depression of the 1930's to be repeated. But the trouble is that the present crisis and that of the future are not going to be the same as that of the 1930's. At that time the U.S. government had only one problem: How to fight unemployment! The balance of payments did not pose any difficulties because the United States was a creditor country.

American capitalism in the 1970's is facing an unprecedented dilemma, in fact a paradox. When the U.S. government is fighting an inflation, then unemployment rises and this in turn forces the same government to abandon—at least temporarily—the goal of price stability. Then the government mobilizes its forces to fight unemployment, only to realize that inflation has meanwhile become more dangerous because the balance of payments has also been adversely affected. In this way the government has been forced to give up for a while the goal of full employment. There is a tedious merry-go-round, a sort of struggle between Scylla and Charybdis, with not a single chance to escape the worst—a government-controlled economy and society introduced by the back door!—unless there is a change in direction of government policies.

With the help of the orientation tables we can make a correct diagnosis of what is wrong in the existing conditions and in this way find the road to get us out of the present paradox, which prevails not only in America but in all democratic countries of the Western world. As to the diagnosis, the Impossibility Theorem mentioned earlier explains very clearly that a free economy and society with a government of limited powers cannot function normally with a financial system based on 100% anti-Numeraire in the form of paper money and monetized bank credit, such as the United States and other democratic countries have at this moment.

There is no doubt that the U.S. economic and financial system in 1974 was located in an area of a major disequilibrium, with cumulative fluctuations in all directions, so that the traditional (Keynesian) monetary and fiscal policies, including price and wage controls, are no longer workable to resolve the problems in question. What must be done refers *first* to the draining off of the existing internal and external inflation of U.S. dollars by the introduction of a new, heavier dollar, and *second,* to the reforming, at the same time, of the whole financial system (private and public), in order to be consistent with the natural parameter of Numeraire and other conditions of stable equilibrium, as this author has urged the U.S. government to do several times during the last decade.[50]

The actual issue is, therefore, not whether or not to aspire and undertake reasonable changes and reforms, as today's liberal-conservative argument seems to convey, but rather the quest for the kind of change and reforms we really need. And we can never solve this problem unless we first decide what direction we want to follow: toward the realization of a free, just and stable society and economy according to the Walrasian model, or toward a government-planned and -controlled society and economy according to the revolutionary version of the Marxian model. One additional comment is necessary. In Volume 1 of *Das Kapital* there is another version of the Marxian model neglected so far by economists, namely, one consistent with conditions of stable equilibrium and valid for peaceful times, after a revolution has been consummated.[51]

Scientists assuredly have the right and in a sense the moral obligation to work out the means and policies for attaining either one of the two directions. The ultimate decision of direction, however, in a free, democratic society remains with the voice of the majority of the people who are intelligently informed and consulted at the proper time. Thomas Jefferson's thoughts should be remembered here: "Educate and inform the mass of the people. Enable them to see that it is their interest to preserve peace and order and they will preserve them. Enlighten the people generally and tyranny and oppression of the body and mind will vanish like evil spirits at the dawn of the day."[52]

The shift in the debate from the status quo to a new order based on conditions of stable equilibrium could bring conservatives and liberals closer. Perhaps, too, even radicals of the new left and the new right in America and elsewhere could be brought together to avoid the unthinkable, that is, the prospect of modern capitalism sinking without the prospective of a better order to replace the old one.

The main lesson from the American experiment with capitalism and the welfare state is clear: economic freedom, which is vitally important for the preservation of the other human freedoms, without an adequate financial framework based on Numeraire-currency and other conditions for stable equilibrium creates social injustice and instability, which in turn undermine the foundation of a free society.

Boston, Massachusetts
January 1975

NOTES

1. Calvin B. Hoover, "The Relevance of the Competitive, Laissez-Faire Economic Model to Modern Capitalistic National Economies," *Kyklos,* Vol. VIII, 1955, pp. 40-55.
2. The complete body of economics is composed of five distinct parts: (1) economic history, (2) economic theory, (3) economic ethics, (4) economic policy, and (5) history of economic thought. Reference is made here to a paper, "A Composite Methodological Standard. The Possibility Theorem and an Orientation Table for Economics," presented by the author at the Conference of the (American) History of Economics Society held at the University of North Carolina, Chapel Hill, North Carolina, on May 29-June 1, 1974.
3. Sumner H. Slichter, *Modern Economic Society,* 1st ed., 1928 (New York: Henry Holt & Co., 1931), p. 36.
4. Piero Sraffa, "The Laws of Returns Under Competitive Conditions," Economic Journal, December 1926, reprinted in *Readings in Economic Analysis,* Vol. 2, *Prices and Production,* edited by Richard V. Clemence (Reading, Massachusetts: Addison-Wesley Press, Inc., 1950), pp. 54-69.
5. A. A. Berle and G. C. Means, *The Modern Corporation and Private Property* (New York: Macmillan Publishing Co., Inc., 1932. Copyright 1932 by Macmillan Publishing Co., Inc., renewed 1960), p. 40.
6. Arthur R. Burns, *The Decline of Competition* (New York: McGraw-Hill Book Co., 1936. Copyright 1936 by McGraw-Hill Book Company. With permission).
7. A. D. H. Kaplan, *Big Enterprise in a Competitive System* (Washington, D.C.: The Brookings Institution, 1954. Copyright 1954, revised 1964 by the Brookings Institution, Washington, D.C.), p. 29.
8. Kaplan, *op. cit.,* p. 30.
9. Corwin D. Edwards, "Can the Anti-trust Laws Preserve Competition?" in Papers and Proceedings of the 52nd Annual Meeting of the American Economic Association, *The American Economic Review,* Part 2, Supplement, March 1940, p. 164.
10. J. M. Clark, "Toward a Concept of Workable Competition," *The American Economic Review,* June 1940, p. 242.
11. John Kenneth Galbraith, "Monopoly and Concentration of Economic Power," *A Survey of Contemporary Economics,* edited by Howard B. Ellis, Vol. I, published by the American Economic Association (Homewood, Illinois: R. D. Irwin, Inc., 1948), 5th printing 1956, p. 107.

12. Joe S. Bain, "Price and Production Policies," *A Survey of Contemporary Economics, op. cit.*, p. 136.
13. *A Report of the Federal Trade Commission on Changes in Concentration in Manufacturing 1935-1950.* U.S. Government Printing Office, 1954, pp. 17-18.
14. Clair Wilcox, "On the Alleged Ubiquity of Oligopoly," *The American Economic Review*, May 1950, Papers and Proceedings, pp. 67-73.
15. Clair Wilcox, "Concentration of Power in American Economy," *Harvard Business Review*, November 1950, reprinted in *Outside Readings in Economics*, edited by Hess, Gallman, Rice and Stern (New York: T. Crowell Co., 1951), p. 210.
16. George J. Stigler, *Five Lectures on Economic Problems*, first American printing (New York: Macmillan Co., 1950), p. 47.
17. Stigler, *op. cit.*, p. 50.
18. Richard B. Heflebower, "Monopoly and Competition in the U.S.A.," *Monopoly and Competition and Their Regulation.* Papers and Proceedings of a Conference held by the International Economic Association, ed. by E. H. Chamberlin (Reprinted with permission from Macmillan London and Basingstoke, 1954), pp. 110-140.
19. *Monopoly and Competition and Their Regulation*, pp. 317-337.
20. Tibor Scitovski, "Monopoly and Competition in Europe and America," *Quarterly Journal of Economics*, November 1955, p. 611.
21. Foreword, Papers and Proceedings of the 66th Annual Meeting of the American Economic Association, Washington, D.C., December 28-30, 1953, *The American Economic Review*, May 1954.
22. Calvin B. Hoover, "Institutional and Theoretical Implications of Economic Change," *The American Economic Review*, March 1954.
23. A few papers representative of this view:
    John Kenneth Galbraith, "Countervailing Power";
    Arthur H. Cole, "Twentieth Century Entrepreneurship in the U.S. and Economic Growth";
    M. R. Benedict, "Attempts to Restrict Competition in Agriculture: The Government Programs";
    Joseph Shister, "Trade-Unionism, Collective Bargaining and Economic Growth";
    Edgar M. Hoover, "Some Institutional Factors in Business Investment Decisions."
24. A few papers representative of this view:
    George J. Stigler, "The Economist Plays with Blocs";
    G. Warren Nutter, "Competition: Direct and Devious";
    John Perry Miller, "Competition and Countervailing Power";
    Ross M. Robertson, "On the Changing Apparatus of Competition";

Richard B. Heflebower, "Toward a Theory of Industrial Markets and Prices."

25. G. Warren Nutter, "Competition: Direct and Devious," Papers and Proceedings, *The American Economic Review*, May 1954, p. 69.
26. John Maynard Keynes, *A Treatise on Money*, Vol. I, *The Pure Theory of Money* (London: Macmillan & Co., Ltd., 1958), pp. 176-178.
27. John Maynard Keynes, *The General Theory of Employment, Interest and Money*, Vol. VII, *The Collected Writings of John Maynard Keynes* (New York: Macmillan, St. Martin's Press, for the Royal Economic Society, London, 1973. With the permission of the original publisher, Harcourt, Brace, Jovanovich, New York), p. 115.
28. John Kenneth Galbraith, *The Affluent Society*, 2d ed., revised (Boston: Houghton Mifflin Co., 1969); *The New Industrial State* (Boston: Houghton Mifflin Co., 1967); *Economics and the Public Purpose*, (Boston: Houghton Mifflin, Co., 1973).
29. John Jewkes, *The New Ordeal by Planning* (Copyright 1968 John Jewkes. Reprinted with permission from Macmillan London and Basingstoke, 1968), p. ix.
30. Anghel N. Rugina, "Social Liberalism. The Integral Democracy of Tomorrow," *The University of Portland Review*, May 1951; "Capitalisme, Socialisme ou Liberalisme Social? Observations Critiques a l'occasion de la Conference Internationale des Sciences Économiques à Rome (1956), *Annales de Science Économiques Appliquées*, Tome XV, Nos. 1 and 4, 1957; "Un Plan de la Stabilisation Économique, Financière et Sociale de la France. Liberalisme Social," *Revue d'Économie Politique* (Paris), No. 2, 1959; "National Purpose: Social Liberalism, A 'New Society' of Tomorrow Based on Freedom, Social Justice and Stability," *Acta Scientiarum Socialium*, Tomus 3, Societas Academica Dacoromana, Roma-München, 1971.
31. Walter Eucken, *Grundlagen der Nationalokonomie. Vierte Auflage* (Jena, Verlag von Gustav Fischer, 1944), pp. 51 ff.
32. Claude B. Bandaloukas, "The First Manifestations of the Managerial Thought and Movement During the Greek Antiquity" (1969); "Epistemology of Management, Especially with Application to Business" (1970).
33. Lazaros T. Houmanidis, "Vers un Regime Économique Progressif. La Democratie Sociale." *Archives des Sciences Économiques et Sociales*, Vol. 46, Athenes, 1966; "Ein Dritter Weg. Fortschrittliche Wirtschaft in der Sozialen Demokratie" (1971).
34. Leon Walras, *Elements of Pure Economics or The Theory of Social Wealth* (1874), translated by William Jaffe. Published by the Ameri-

can Economic Association and The Royal Economic Society, R. D. Irwin, Homewood, Ill., 1954, p. 109.

35. Walras, *op. cit.*, pp. 112, 173, 84.
36. Vilfredo Pareto, *Corso di Economia Politica,* Volume primo, 1896 (Torino: Edizioni Scientifiche Einaudi, 1953; Editore Boringhieri, 1961), p. 26.
37. Alfred Marshall, *Principles of Economics,* 8th edition, 1890 (New York: The Macmillan Co., 1952), p. 346 and chapter V, p. 363 ff.
38. Marshall, *op cit.*, Appendix H, p. 806.
39. Anghel Rugina, "Memorandum on the Stabilization of the British Pound. A New Orientation for the 1970's" (1970), in manuscript.
40. Keynes, *Treatise,* Vol. 1, p. 151 ff.
41. Keynes, *The General Theory,* p. 176 ff.
42. *Ibid.*, p. 16.
43. *Ibid.*, p. 26.
44. *Ibid.*, p. 26.
45. Jean Baptiste Say, *Letters to Mr. Malthus on Various Subjects of Political Economy; Particularly on the Causes of the General Stagnation of Commerce* (Paris, 1820; London, 1821), p. 4.
46. Anghel N. Rugina, "Monetization of Public and Private Debt as the Principal Fountain of Modern Inflation," *Rivista Internazionale di Scienze Economiche e Commerciali,* Padova, 1971, Nr. 3.
47. Frank H. Knight, *Risk, Uncertainty and Profit* (1921). The London School of Economics and Political Science, 8th impression, 1957.
48. Keynes, *op. cit.*, p. 3.
49. Albert Einstein, *Out of My Later Years* (New York: The Philosophical Library, 1950), pp. 62-63.
50. Anghel Rugina, "The Problem of Inflation Has a Determinate Solution! A Blueprint for a U.S. Monetary, Financial and Economic Stabilization Act Based on Conditions of Stable Equilibrium" (1974).
51. Anghel Rugina, "A Monetary Dialogue with Karl Marx. Its Significance for Both Capitalist and Socialist Countries," *East European Quarterly,* Vol. VIII, Nrs. 3 and 4, 1974-5.
52. Saul K. Padover, *Thomas Jefferson on Democracy* (New York: Hawthorn Books, Inc., 1954), p. 23.

3. MONETIZATION OF PUBLIC AND PRIVATE DEBT AS THE PRINCIPAL FOUNTAIN OF MODERN INFLATION*

1. Monetization of Public Debt and the Problem of Inflation

Remembering the theory of a dual rate of interest by Wicksell, which by now is accepted by most contemporary economists, it follows logically from its content that there must also exist a theory of a dual concept of money and banking. Indeed, economic history confirms the existence of two bipolar types of money: (1) the original or natural type, which was 100% covered in a special commodity selected to serve as an *objective* standard of value, or what Walras called "Numeraire"; and (2) the secondary or nominal type of money, which was not covered and represented a sort of *artificial* standard of value.[1]

Usually in textbooks the first type of money is called *full-bodied* or simply *commodity money*,[2] and the second *"paper, credit or nominal money."*[3] If we assume a model of 100% commodity money or Numeraire with its adequate banking system, then this actually represents the set of conditions where we have a *natural* rate of interest, as defined by Wicksell in his original work.[4] If we change the model to a 100% paper, credit money and the adequate banking system, then that corresponds to another set of conditions where a *nominal* rate of interest—again as defined by Wicksell—is true and valid.

Introducing the famous Wicksellian gap between the two rates of interest, with the help of the theory of conceptual models of today we can visualize the logical necessity that the existence of a gap requires also another set of conditions where the two bipolar types of money, so to speak, coexist at the same time. This would be a mixed monetary standard with an adequate mixed banking system. It is interesting to note that Wicksell made his observation about a dual rate of interest and a gap between them under the conditions of his time, namely, the modern gold standard, but this standard in reality represented a mixed monetary system which at the domestic level was about 90% credit money and only 10% gold money.[5]

We may say that the theory of dual interest rates by Wicksell was well conceived and realistic and has application for a better understanding of monetary conditions and problems of the mixed modern gold standard era.

What Wicksell did not see clearly, including all other implications,

---

*Published in *Rivista Internazionale di Scienze Economiche e Commerciali,* Anno XVIII, 1971, n. 3, Padova, Italy.

is the organic relationship between the theory of a dual system of interest rates and, as we say today, its adequate monetary and banking model expressed in explicit terms. Nevertheless, Wicksell deserves full credit for being the first to have observed the gap in the interest structure of a modern economy with a mixed gold standard, and he also constructed a meaningful theory with full application for the time when he made his observations. Without the Wicksell theory of a dual interest rate we can never understand the true nature of the mixed modern gold standard, which indeed was dual and in the first place explains the whole phenomenon observed so masterfully by him.

The science of monetary economics of today cannot neglect the contribution of Wicksell, because we have great need for more work of a purely conceptual nature to build up a complete theory of gaps in regard not only to modern money and banking but also to incomes (wages, rents, profits and taxes), investment, and capital formation. The extension of the Wicksellian theory of gaps opens a new vista; in fact, it is instrumental for a more meaningful and plausible explanation of the business-cycle phenomenon, which in itself is the result and expression of multitudinous gaps.

The subject of monetization of debt is associated with the second type of money, which may appear as paper money (banknotes issued by the central bank or notes printed directly by the government), or as pure credit money (uncovered bank deposits created by private banks but also by the central bank). We shall investigate first the monetization of public debt as related to the problem of inflation.

It must be clear that not just any public debt is monetized. In fact, when government borrows money directly from the people or institutions other than modern banks, then the respective debt is based on covered credit, specifically on the amount of funds already existing in the economy and which now shifts from the private sector into the public sector. This kind of public debt does not change the supply of money in circulation; it is noninflationary by definition.

There are cases, however (in the United States very often) when the government borrows large amounts in billions of dollars, sums that would be difficult to get directly from the public on short notice. In such cases the government appeals to a so-called "pool" or a group of banks to take over the public debt, even though sometimes only temporarily, because meanwhile the banks can sell such titles of public debt to small or medium-size investors.

How a large portion of the public debt becomes monetized is the real problem. First of all the central bank (in the United States the Federal Reserve System) supports the market of government securities in order not to have wild fluctuations, which would be harmful to the public credit. There was a time during World War II and until 1951 when the Federal Reserve System provided 100% support to government securities, that is, this central bank was willing to buy government securities from private banks at any time and in unlimited quantities. Thus the price of government securities was close to parity, and there was absolutely no risk in trading with public securities. But the Federal Reserve System under such conditions soon could not conduct any effective monetary policy. The Accord of 1951 between the U.S. Treasury Department and the F.R.S. has restored some independence of the American central bank in the sense that the support for government securities after that was restricted more or less only to short-term securities.

Private banks agree to deal in government loans because they can use the respective securities as collateral to provide, when needed, additional reserves of official money from the Federal Reserve System. It must be remembered further that modern commercial banks in the United States, as elsewhere, conduct business in accordance with the fractional reserve principle. This means that private banks need only a fraction of official money, for instance, 1/5 or 1/10 (called required or legal reserves) from the total amount of lending. The differential of 4/5 or 9/10 is created by private banks during the process of lending activity; this is the occurrence of *monetization of debt.*

How does the monetization of public debt take place? Let us assume that the U.S. government borrowed from private banks $500 million in order to satisfy an additional demand for public funds, either for the case of a budgetary deficit or for paying a portion of the maturing national debt which could not be refunded. We assume further that the required legal reserves are 10%.

The pool of banks in question have to put together only 1/10, that is, $50 million, in excess reserves and take over the loan of $500 million. The rate of interest will be calculated for the entire amount, but we leave out the interest because the main problem is to explain the process of monetization of public debt. In the books of the pool of the banks in question, the situation will look like this:

(1) The Pool of Banks W & Cie

Assets		*Liabilities*	
Excess reserves	$ 50 million	Demand deposits for the account of the government	$500 million
Government securities	$500 million		

The monetary law requires that commercial bank members of the F.R.S. must hold a certain per cent, in this case 10%, of the outstanding liability in official money. In the above situation the American pool of banks satisfies this legal requirement with the existence of $50 million excess reserves.

We can see how the government loan of $500 million has been monetized in the private bank system through the fractional reserve principle. The U.S. government can draw checks upon this pool of banks up to the amount of $500 million, as if this sum of money had been deposited, but in fact it wasn't! This is the miracle of modern banking, when, on the basis of $50 million excess reserves in official money, another $450 million was created. That this monetized public debt is inflationary as soon as the U.S. government has signed checks up to that amount, there is no doubt. Obviously the supply of money has been increased by the same amount, and the production of goods and services at that moment is to be regarded as a constant.

The situation certainly may become more complicated. Some firms which received checks from the government may ask for cash or official money. Let us assume that this additional demand for cash is for $50 million. All the private banks need to do in such a case is to pass $50 million in government securities to the central bank, namely, the Federal Reserve System, and receive the equivalent amount in cash. Certain rules of the game exist, in the sense that private banks cannot at all times do this, but this is a part of regular business, so that we assume that in this particular case there was no hindrance.

Now the Federal Reserve System has monetized the $50 million public debt, and the economy has increased the supply of money in circulation by the same amount in official money. In the books of the Federal Reserve System, the operation will appear thus:

(2) The Federal Reserve System

Assets		*Liabilities*	
Government securities	$ 50 million	Notes or deposits for the account of private banks	$ 50 million

In this particular case what actually took place was a conversion of private bank credit money into central bank credit money. Meanwhile, the U.S. government has completely used its account with the respective pool of banks. The checks signed by the government have come into private hands, and we assume that they were deposited with the same pool of banks. The situation in the books of the pool finally will look as follows:

(3) The Pool of Banks W & Cie

Assets		*Liabilities*	
Required reserves	$ 45 million	Demand deposits for private accounts	$450 million
Excess reserves	$ 5 million		
Government securities	$450 million		

The monetized public debt of $500 million is now in private hands and will continue to circulate in the economy.

If the liquidity of the economy is not satisfactory, which is usually the case during an inflationary period, then the rest of the $450 million in government securities may reach the Federal Reserve System entirely. Private persons cannot push government securities into the Federal Reserve System because they do not work directly with the central bank, so that the process has to go through the private banking system. Ultimately the private banks will receive from the central bank an additional amount of reserves of $450 million in notes or deposits with the Federal Reserve System.

Now, for the total amount of current liabilities in the form of demand deposits ($450 million), the pool of banks in question needs to hold only 10%, or $45 million. We see how the private banks have appropriated a new fountain of excess reserves. The process of monetization of more public or private debt is now open for repetition on a much larger scale, but it requires time.

How important this problem of monetization of public debt is, and what other implications and issues are involved, can be seen from the following table with reference to the United States.

Gross National Product (G.N.P.) (in billions)		*National Debt (in billions)*		*Federal Government Expenditures (in billions)*	
1929	$103.8	(1930)	$ 16	(1929)	$ 2.6
1939	$ 91.3		$ 48	(1940)	$ 10.1
1946	$211.1		$259		$ 74.1
1951	$328.2		$259		$ 56.3
1960	$600.0		$324		$100.0
1969	$930.1		$370		$192.0

Source: Survey of Current Business by the U.S. Department of Commerce and Federal Reserve Bulletin.

In 1946, one year after the termination of World War II, the national debt in the U.S. stood at $259 billion. During the same generation this debt has increased to $370 billion in 1969, and this happened in a time of prosperity when the American people enjoyed the longest boom in American economic history. If a government in a capitalist country cannot repay its debts during a period of prosperity, then something is wrong with that country, and scientists should begin to search for the causes of the deficiency! In such a case, it is important to look for a diagnosis and find out whether this is a problem within the system or a problem of the framework of the system.

The table given above shows very strongly that in all probability the United States has a financial problem related to the financial framework of the system. Since 1929 the U.S. Gross National Product increased by 9 times, whereas the national debt jumped by 23 times. Because we know by now that a large part of this national debt has been monetized, we can see clearly where one principal source of today's insidious inflation is located. The cost of the U.S. national government over the same period of time increased by 74 times. This growth in the national debt and the cost of government cannot be considered normal and sustainable in the long run.

The danger is that, if this situation continues at the same tempo it has since 1929 and is not efficiently checked, then one day the U.S. government will not be able to repay any part of the national debt, not even the interest! Because a modern government cannot be declared bankrupt, there would be no alternative under those emergncy conditions but to nationalize banks, including the people's savings, and/or other industries.

There is not sufficient space here to argue further why the unchecked accumulation of national debt is a social evil and represents a great danger for the future of any free society.[6]

Proof that political leaders do not see the danger involved in this issue is at hand. The new Nixon Administration asked the U.S. Congress during its first month in office, in January 1969, to raise the ceiling of the national debt by $12 billion, that is, from $365 billion to $377 billion, and Congress easily agreed with very little debate. As if this were not enough, the same Administration, approaching June 30, 1970, asked Congress for another jump of $18 billion, bringing the U.S. national debt to the limit of $395 billion. The U.S. Congress again has agreed with the request without raising any serious questions about the procedure, which in fact represents a disguised form of budgetary deficit. How could the American inflation, about which everybody talks but nobody does anything constructive, ever be stopped, not to say cured, when we remember that a rise in national debt in a capitalist country is associated with monetization of debt?

In the future, the situation may become even worse. Here in the U.S.A. we have already reached the point at which about $115 billion of the national debt is maturing each year. Because the U.S. Treasury is not in the position to repay any significant portion of this annually maturing debt, with the help of private banks and the support of the Federal Reserve System, this $115 billion matured debt is refunded or postponed. The cost of interest for performing this annual refunding has now reached the staggering sum of $15 billion, without repaying a cent from the capital involved in the national debt. In the overall budget of the United States, the cost to service the national debt has become the biggest spending item after national defense. And this is not quite the complete picture of the situation. In the 1970's we are approaching conditions when bigger and bigger chunks of the national debt will mature, which in turn will exercise more and more pressure upon the U.S. money market. Thus the rates of interest will be pushed to rise or stay at a higher level and the cost of servicing national debt will mount.

In the 1970's we should also take into account an ever-increasing national debt in foreign hands, as for two decades now the United States has had a continuous chronic deficit in the balance of international payments. At the 1970 annual meeting of the International Monetary Fund in Copenhagen in September the Managing Director, Mr. Pierre-Paul Schweitzer, warned, according to a reporter in the *New York Times,* that "from now on the United States should settle a good part of its balance of payments deficits by paying out gold and other monetary reserves rather than by having other countries pile up dollars."[7]

This is a very serious affair which should be brought to the attention of the U.S. government. If the other creditor countries would really press to get gold or other in-gold-convertible currencies, then both the creditors and the United States would face a dilemma with unpleasant consequences. The U.S. gold stock reserves are at about $11 billion, whereas foreign claims upon the U.S. Treasury are estimated between $35 and $40 billion (1969). The creditors cannot get what they want even if the U.S. government were willing to lose the entire gold stock. How about the international monetary system, which is based on the practical requirement of a U.S. dollar convertible in gold? This shows that American capitalism is somehow cornered or in danger of being cornered if a reasonable and efficient monetary and banking reform is not conducted before more difficulties arise.[8]

In conclusion, I think that, if the U.S. government really wants to stop and cure the present inflation with which we are struggling so desperately, it must introduce a project of law requesting the U.S. Congress to prohibit any further monetization of public debt and to accept a plan for a gradual amortization of the existing debt over a period of time, e.g., 25 years, as a part of the annual budget. That would mean a significant release in today's pressures on the U.S. money market, and the rates of interest inevitably will go down in a natural way. Such a reform would open a new era of normal conditions in the financial sector of the public economy, i.e., in government affairs.

Perhaps a word is necessary to call the attention of the reader to the fact that the dangers involved in the monetization of public debt are not specifically limited to capitalist countries, even though herein lies a potential force of destruction for the Western world. Lord Keynes saw the danger long before this writer when he wrote: "Lenin is said to have declared that the best way to destroy the Capitalist System was to debauch the currency. By a continuing process of inflation, governments can confiscate, secretly and unobserved, an important part of the wealth of their citizens." And after making a few more remarks about this arbitrary kind of confiscation, Keynes concluded: "Lenin was certainly right. There is no subtler, no surer means of overturning the existing basis of society than to debauch the currency. The process engages all the hidden forces of economic law on the side of destruction, and does it in a manner which not one man in a million is able to diagnose."[9] Additional comments on the danger involved for the future of the capitalist countries would be superfluous at this point. The genius of Lord Keynes has spoken most forcefully and with rare clarity.

The danger of instability and the perpetuation of social injustice through the monetization of public debt touches, perhaps with even more intensity, the rival system of modern capitalism. The socialist-Marxist countries are using the same technique of monetization of public debt on a much larger scale than in the capitalist countries. The only technical difference is that under modern capitalism the process of monetization of debt is accomplished with the help of private banks in cooperation with the central bank, whereas in the socialist-Marxist countries the process goes directly through the state central bank and, of course, at the command of the government. For those countries there is no other practical way, because they do not have a market for government securities. But in the books of the state central bank in a socialist country the situation looks very similar to the one exposed earlier:

(4) State Bank of a Socialist Country R

Assets		*Liabilities*	
Government plan (loans to various state agencies)	500 million R.	Printed money (notes) and/or free balances or equivalent to bank deposits for the account of the government	500 million R.

The socialist countries, it is true, do not need to worry about excess or additional reserves, because by the nature of the political system such reserves (in paper money) can be created, with one restriction—for international purposes—virtually in unlimited quantities. This fact, however, does not change one iota the problem created by monetization of the public debt even in a socialist country, that is, an automatic inflation with myriad distortions, misrepresentations, misjudgments and maldecisions in planning for the whole country; investments, production, capital formation, distribution and consumption and foreign trade are distorted. It is true further that inflations in the socialist countries are not of the open type (as under capitalism) but are hidden because of the freezing of prices by the government. Yet, for the problems of financial stability and social justice in the distribution of income, it makes no difference whether the inflation is open or hidden—the end results are the same: the real income of the masses is reduced. Nowhere in those countries is the instability due to monetization of debt more evident than in the sphere of the balance of international payments, where all are suffering from a chronic deficit or a lack of full participation in the international movements of capital, merchandise and services.

Being realistic, one cannot be wrong in saying that modern capitalism up to this moment, with all its imperfections, has attained a relatively good performance as compared with rival systems. One of the main reasons for the relative success under capitalism and in view of the light of this work seems to be the fact that under conditions of the modern gold standard (still retained at the international level) the monetization of public debt and the ill effects of the inflationary effect were somewhat restricted, even though far from being completely annihilated.

2. *Monetization of Private Debt and the Problem of Inflation*

Very often we find in leading financial newspapers or in talks given by bankers or business executives the opinion that our Federal Government is the sole culprit in producing the present-day inflation, specifically by allowing deficits in the budget. If this reasoning were correct, the problem of inflation could and should be solved simply by balancing the government budget. But we know that simply balancing the public budget is not sufficient to solve the problem of inflation. It is certain that the Federal Government shares a responsibility for the present inflation, but is not the lone guilty party.

The other bigger source of the existing inflation lies in the monetization of debt for private purposes. When this is done to increase production, there appear some good reasons mitigating the social harm, but when it is used to finance pure speculations in the securities market, there is only more harm and the benefit of additional profits to a minority of speculators and other vested interests in the banking system.

I want to make it clear that there is no question here of attacking the American banking system, as do some radical thinkers in accusing bankers of being a part of a conspiracy in Wall Street or the Establishment which controls and manipulates our society and economy. Having worked in a bank myself, I know how indispensable the services of banks are in a modern, civilized society. In point of administration and servicing customers, American banks are without equal in the world.

My argument is that I question the wisdom at the foundation of our banking laws structure—namely, in regard to both private banks and the Federal Reserve System, which are based on the fractional reserve principle of banking. I think both are very weak since they have been creating problems for a long time for our society and economy (the existing inflation with all the social and economic troubles at home and difficulties in the balance of payments) without being able to solve those problems correctly and in an equitable manner. I do not recommend diminishing in any way the independence of the American central bank system. But of what use is that independence if the F.R.S.—under present-day conditions—cannot control the supply of bank credit money in such a way as to have a stable equilibrium supply of money with no inflation and no deflation? If they had the formula or the technique, the F.R.S. would have applied it, at least during the last five years.

As a former central banker, I suspect, or more truthfully, I *know* that they have no formula for calculating the stable equilibrium supply of money; therefore, their efforts to conduct monetary policies in order to stop inflation are futile, not to say meaningless. If the central bank were challenged in the courts on how it justifies the prerogatives with which they are entrusted by law (to defend the stability of the dollar), I am afraid the central bank would lose the case.

Further, I do not condone in any way the idea that the big banks have to be nationalized or that we have to apply more controls on banks than we already have. None of our problems of today would be solved by nationalization; rather, in addition, more grievances would be created. All I want to stress is that our private banking system ought to enjoy only that degree of independence which is consistent with the general requirement of social justice in not producing any harm to the economy as a whole or its parts or to society. What I have in mind is to create that financial structure which helps the economy to reach conditions of stable equilibrium and full employment in the short run as well as in the long run. This in practice would mean fewer banking controls and regulations than exist today.

The private American banks of today, with the help of the F.R.S., are actually "issuance banks" to an extent of 85 to 90%, that is, private financial institutions which create money in the form of "pure bank deposits" to do lending business in competition with other banks and for the purpose of making a profit. These pure bank credits are covered only by a small fraction of official money, one might say covered by "nothing," because new "official money" after 1968 is represented by empty figures in the books of the Federal Reserve System. No other institution in the country, not even the Federal Government, may conclude a contract of business having only a small fraction of the necessary funds (averaging 10 to 15%) and creating the missing difference of 85 to 90% through the mechanism of monetization of private debt.

How does the process of monetization of private debt appear in the books of a commercial bank which we assume is a member of the F.R.S., i.e., it has access for renewing its reserves whenever in need, of course observing certain rules of the game?

Here we have a giant corporation like Ford Motor Company or General Motors which wants $150 million to construct a new plant. A credit application is introduced for the same amount with a large commercial bank in New York City or Chicago. We assume that the application has been accepted and the credit granted after the whole project was evaluated and found reasonable and profitable. Our commercial bank belongs to the category of 10% reserves requirement.

It is unnecessary to stress further that the credit in question is not paid in cash, for in that case there is no monetization of debt. As usual a loan of this size grants the big corporation the privilege of drawing checks upon the respective bank up to the amount approved. The corporation makes use of this credit by signing checks in the course of routine business. The holders of these checks, A, B, C, D, happen to be located in the same area, and they deposit these checks in the same large bank, which might also happen to have several branches spread over a large area; the case is therefore plausible.

In the books of our bank this operation looks as follows:

(5) Big Bank No. 1

Assets		*Liabilities*	
Excess reserves	$ 15 million	Demand deposits	
Loans to		for the account of	
Corporation F	$150 million	A, B, C, D	$150 million

The calculation of the rate of interest was omitted as being irrelevant to the issue discussed.

It is clear from the books of this bank that the debt of Corporation F has been monetized and is now in circulation as an additional amount of abstract purchasing power over and above the existing supply of money; in one word, it is inflationary. Our big bank withheld from circulation $15 million as required reserves and created instead $150 million. The differential of $135 million is nothing but abstract purchasing power, or pure bank credit money.

From the above example of this operation in the books of a commercial bank we can identify what may be called the *first* rule or principle of the creation of bank credit money recognized by all contemporary economists: *Whenever in the books of a commercial bank a debtor and a creditor appear at the same time and an economic transaction of the same value has been accomplished, monetization of debt has taken place.*

There are, however, other forms of bank credit money, not yet recognized by contemporary economists. For instance, it is possible that the same bank may later grant a credit of $200 million to another Corporation G which buys the plant that Corporation F has just finished, and for some reason wants to dispose of it. Corporation F uses the check of $200 million to liquidate its previous debt of $150 million and deposits the remainder of $50 million with the same bank.

How does this new situation appear in the books of our bank?

(6) Big Bank No. 1

Assets		*Liabilities*	
Previous reserves	$ 15 million	Demand Deposits	
Additional reserves	$ 5 million	A, B, C, D, F	$200 million
Loans to			
Corporation G	F$200 million		

Because of the additional increase in the amount of outstanding liabilities and the legal requirements to hold at least 10% reserves, our bank needs an additional amount of $5 million cash or official money.

This problem is easy to solve because our bank can deposit government securities as collateral and borrow the necessary funds at the official discount. The bank could also use private channels by simply borrowing on short notice so-called Federal Funds, which are excess reserves of other banks not in use for the time being. The U.S. money market is very well equipped to deal with this kind of problem.

The question which now arises is just how much more bank credit money has been added to the existing supply? Contemporary economists are using the aggregate amount of demand deposits of all commercial banks as the standard measure to identify the total volume of bank credit money. If we use this traditional standard, the answer is $50 million; by looking at the balance sheet of our bank, demand deposits increased from $150 to $200 million.

The traditional procedure, however, is questionable in this particular case. In our case, the new monetization of debt took place *not* on the right side but on the left side of the balance sheet. Indeed, I think this is another form of credit money which follows what I would like to call the *second* rule of the creation of bank credit money. This rule says that *whenever there is a change in the identity of debtors in the books of a commercial bank and a transaction of the same value has been accomplished, monetization of debt took place for the same amount.* Thus in the above case not $50 million but $200 million additional bank credit money was created. If the amount of new debt just matches the old debt, there is absolutely no change visible in the balance sheet of a bank, yet the aggregate supply of credit money has been multiplied.

Finally, it is possible—as a matter of fact this will happen!—that the original holders of the bank deposits may decide at any time to use their bank balances by signing checks to make purchases or settle other kinds of obligations. We assume that these checks may be deposited with the same bank. If the aggregate amount of bank deposits remains the same $200 million, there would be absolutely no change visible in the balance sheet of this bank. The only change that could be discovered would be only if someone were allowed to investigate the books of the bank where A, B, C, D and F have disappeared and instead new names like L, M, N, O and P are the deposit holders.

The new situation appears as follows:

(7) Big Bank No. 1

Assets		*Liabilities*	
Reserves	$ 20 million	Demand deposits	
Loans to		L, M, N, O, P	$200 million
Corporation G	$200 million		

Following the traditional procedure in computing the aggregate amount of bank credit money as the total sum of demand deposits, by looking at the balance sheet we would conclude that there was no change in the supply of credit money. Yet new transactions of $200 million between A, B, C, D and F and L, M, N, O and P have been completed through the mechanism of modern banking.

It is possible now to formulate a *third* rule of the creation of credit money: *Whenever there is a change in the identity of the deposit holders of a commercial bank and a transaction of the same value has been accomplished, then monetization of debt has taken place, on the right side of the balance sheet alone.*[10]

This is the technical side of the problem of monetization of public and private debt. Obviously the private banks through this mechanism realize an additional profit of a large magnitude and exercise an extra financial power upon the economy. The two things seem *not to be justified* either by necessary functions or performance. Our commercial banks could be as good—as a matter of fact, much better—if they would forego use of monetization of debt. Eventually, for making modern capitalism more stable and more just in the interest of the whole nation, it would be better for enlightened bankers to study this problem and cooperate in finding a solution fair to all concerned.

3. *Conclusion: The Ultimate Cure for Modern Inflation*

If we really want to stop inflation and restore stable equilibrium for both domestic economy and the balance of international payments, then, among other things, the U.S. Congress should be prepared to pass a "law for social and economic justice" prohibiting monetization of public debt as well as private debt. This is the only equitable solution I can see to the conflict of interest between the banking practice of "monetizing debt" and the social harm inflicted upon society through the ill effects of inflation.

This, by the way, would not be the first time in modern history that this issue has become a subject of legislation. During the eighteenth century private banks printed their own money in the form of banknotes which were put into circulation through lending business exactly as is done today with bank deposits. The British economist David Ricardo first observed that, when private banks issued banknotes in competition with other banks, they automatically created conditions of a recurring inflation, with difficulties not only for the domestic economy but also for the balance of international payments. During the Napoleonic wars, because of a heavy loss of gold, Great Britain was forced to suspend the convertibility of the pound through the Bank Restriction Act of 1797. There was much discussion then of how to stop the loss of gold, and many were proposing to introduce controls of foreign trade and impose a gold embargo. Finally Ricardo came up with the explanation that the loss of gold was due to the internal inflation produced by private banks which were free to issue notes in competition. Ricardo should get the credit for first observing a "social evil" in the freedom of private banks to print their own money.

After a heated and prolonged argument on this subject between the followers of Ricardo (called the "Currency Principle") and the opposing view (called the "Banking School") during the first half of the nineteenth century, the British Parliament finally was convinced to pass the Robert Peel Act of 1844, which prohibited private banks from issuing notes. The European countries followed the British solution.

In the United States we had the same problem with private banks printing their own banknotes. The U.S. National Banking Act of 1863-65 tried to solve this problem by introducing a special tax of 10% on any private bank which wanted to continue the issuance of banknotes, with the exception of U.S. National Banks, which were put under government control in respect to capital and the privilege of issuing notes. Since this 10% tax was higher than the prevailing rates of interest in the market at the time, the provision of this law meant in reality a prohibition of private banks from issuing notes.

The theory of credit money, however, was not yet well enough developed to establish that banknotes were just one form of "monetization of debt" and that other forms might be possible, to which the private banks might shift as soon as the first form was prohibited. This is exactly what happened. Private banks in England, Europe and the United States bowed before the new legislation, but at the same time they gradually shifted to the issuance of bank deposits by making popular the use of checks in the course of the same lending business as before. How important is theory and science for the correct solution to problems in real life can be seen in this case! The concept of credit money was incomplete at the time. Consequently, the good purposes of the banking laws of the nineteenth century prohibiting private banks from issuing their own money never materialized, because private banks continued to do the same thing under a different cloak. We are now suffering again from the ills of the same inevitable inflation produced through this old practice by private banks: "monetization of debt," regardless of by what technique it is done. But this practice must terminate, according to the requirements of social and economic justice, which no longer can be ignored in the twentieth century.

The reform in question should not be viewed as disbanding or neglect of banking business, but merely the end of a malpractice by banks in creating their own money. In any case, the function of issuing money belongs by definition to the central bank, in our country to the Federal Reserve System, and should not be appropriated by any other institution, private or public. Such a reform would actually restore the Federal Reserve System to its proper functions.

Enough business is left for private banks in a modern, civilized society. Private banks could continue to administer a system of private credit granted specifically by private business but not to monetize it as they do today. If a given firm wants to grant credit up to a certain amount, this information could be channeled to a bank, and the bank could be entrusted to select the customers who merit such credit. The point is that in this new order the banks would not create "bank credit" but would be merely intermediaries between business and customers. The difference is enormous between the practice of today and the new method. Under the new method, "credit" granted by business (directly or through the banks) would not change the supply of official money in circulation, and therefore we would not have the occurrence of inflation. Today such credit goes into the banking system, and it is immediately monetized in form of additional bank deposits, which automatically fuel the machine of inflation. The "credit card" business belongs here too.

The drawing of checks in official money would be restricted only to persons who actually have a deposit in a bank, and the respective bank would be required by the new banking law to hold such deposits 100% covered in official money at all times. Indeed, when a customer puts his money in a checking account in a bank, he does so because he knows that he has bills to be paid, and checks will be used to the same amount until he renews his income to replenish his balance. When the bank will hold his account 100% covered as in the new order, the supply of money in circulation will not be decreased because his checks put into circulation by paying current bills will exactly match that amount. In addition, this new rule would render impossible the incidence of a "run on the banks," which, during crises of confidence, creates great financial calamities in a capitalist country.

Under this new system of banking, the money market finally would be separated from the capital market, and this is another problem of today's financial setup. Once the money market has been separated from the capital market, we enter into the territory of true financial stability. This is a natural phenomenon, because the money market has the function of immediately supplying available funds for liquidity (financial stability), whereas the capital market is supposed to supply medium- and long-term funds for investment purposes (economic growth and full employment).

NOTES

1. For a historical and theoretical review of the two bipolar types of money, see Anghel N. Rugina, *Geldtypen und Geldordnungen, Fundamente für eine echte allgemeine Geld- und Wirtschaftstheorie* (Stuttgart: W. Kohlhammer, Verlag, 1949).
2. For an explicit theory of commodity money, we owe very much to Carl Menger, the founder of the Modern Economic School of Vienna and also to the monetary architects of the Robert Peel Act of 1844 in England known as the Currency-Principle School.
3. The modern theory of nominal-, credit-paper, or state-money was first developed by a German, Friedrich Knapp, with his *Staatliche Theorie des Geldes* (1906), even though the well-known John Law experiment and failure with the issue of uncovered banknotes goes back to the early eighteenth century.

   Lord Keynes should receive the credit for giving this nominalist theory of money (conceived in crude economic terms by Knapp) a more attractive and generalized formulation, calling it the theory of "managed currency" or "accounting unit." See John Maynard Keynes, *A Treatise on Money,* Vol. 1, *The Pure Theory of Money* (London: Macmillan, 1930).
4. K. Wicksell, *Interest and Prices,* translated by R. F. Kahn and with an introduction by Bertil Ohlin (1898), Reprints of Economic Classics (New York: August Kelly, 1962); also, by the same author, *Lectures on Political Economy,* Vol. 2 *Money,* edited with an introduction by Lionel Robbins (London: Routledge & Kegan, 1935, fourth impression, 1956).
5. Rugina, *op. cit.,* pp. 281-293.
6. Here in the United States we have not yet had a serious debate on the consequences of an ever-rising national debt. A single known economist, Professor James M. Buchanan, in his book *Public Principles of Public Debt* (1958), has questioned the Keynesian doctrine according to which there was no danger in the accumulation of public debt as long as it was owned by the nationals of the same country. From the explanation given in this book, it appears evident that there is a serious problem in the ever-rising national debt. But Buchanan's book has received little attention from other professional economists and no attention whatsoever on the part of political leaders. He also acknowledged the influence of the Italian Economic School, mentioning in particular the valuable contributions of Pantaleoni, De Viti De Marco, Griziotti and Einaudi.

7. Edwin F. Dale, Jr., "Dollars Abroad Cause A Problem. Director of Monetary Fund Bids U.S. Settle Balance of Payments with Gold," *New York Times,* September 22, 1970.
8. In good faith one cannot share the unrestrained optimism of those economists who thought and still think that the use of Special Drawing Rights is the correct solution for present and future problems of the international monetary system. The SDRs are nothing but a new form of monetization of debt in international markets, which, if my observations are correct, would not and cannot bring the stability that we want but would encourage and in a way even impel a more stringent worldwide inflationary pressure, which already constitutes a problem. For more detail on this dilemma, see my article "An End to the Agony of the American Dollar?," *Rivista Internazionale di Scienze Economiche,* January 1970, No. 1.
9. John Maynard Keynes, *The Economic Consequences of the Peace* (New York: Harcourt, Brace, 1920), pp. 235-236.
10. An argument could develop on this last form of credit money. One may question whether the $200 million new L, M, N, O and P deposit holders represent a new form or are the velocity of circulation of the old form (A, B, C, D, F) of bank credit money. For more detail about the three rules governing the creation of modern bank credit money, see Rugina, *Geldtypen und Geldordnungen,* quoted earlier.

4. A 1959 MEMORANDUM ON REFORMS FOR AN EQUILIBRIUM SYSTEM OF BUDGET AND TAXATION*

In this brief analysis of the U.S. taxation and budget system, the major issue is not alone the fact that the U.S. Congress has, over the years, introduced a number of preferential tax provisions which now produce a substantial loss of public income. Such loopholes could be eventually patched by a comprehensive amendment to the existing tax laws. Unfortunately, in reality, it is certain that such patchwork could not correct the basic deficiencies of the American fiscal and budgetary system, because those deficiencies are "of the framework of the system" and *not* "within the system." We really need more far-reaching reforms, first in the method of thinking about this subject and then with respect to practical questions of techniques and means conducive to the realization of certain sound principles in the field of public finance.

Let us state the argument so far as it can be done within the limits of this short report. Six basic rules of sound administration of public finances could be sufficient to show the direction and the reforms for an equilibrium system of budget and taxation in the United States.

Rule No. 1. The budget for the Federal Government, containing the amount of public expenditures, arranged in groups of major items, should be presented first for approval by the people through a referendum conducted at the same time as the general elections every four years.

In a free society it is necessary to apply the democratic principle of separation of powers also to public finance. In other words there must be complete separation between decisions concerned with the volume of public expenditures and those concerning the power to tax.

Over the last decades we have accumulated sufficient evidence to conclude that the *United States lacks precise legal machinery to keep the total amount of public expenditures in equilibrium with the available public income.* We must therefore find a way to separate decisions regarding public expenditure from those concerning the power to collect public income (taxes). To have them both concentrated in one place, as we have now in the hands of our representatives in Congress, means monopolistic power, which is not only undemocratic but does not work in practice.

*This Memorandum was submitted to the Chairman of the Ways and Means Committee (Hon. Wilbur D. Mills), U.S. House of Representatives, Washington, D.C., on November 30, 1959.

Until this problem of a clear separation between the power to tax and the power to decide upon the volume of public expenditures is resolved correctly, there is no chance of attaining a stable financial system in the United States. The reason is simple: Public needs, like private needs, are unlimited and therefore no amount of public income would ever suffice to cover all of them. Restriction of public expenditures is therefore mandatory. The question is how to do it without creating other problems.

In the *private sector* this issue is solved by the basic principle of sound finance, which says that the *available income determines the volume of private expenditures.* Unfortunately, in the public sector, that is, in the study of public finance in recent times, a neomercantilist rule prevails, namely, the principles that *in government the expenditures determine the volume of income.* Evidently we are faced with an *inverted rule of finance,* which leads to disequilibrium. This is the true reason why the Federal Government cannot balance its budget, in addition to the fact that the U.S. dollar is not stable.

That the inverted rule of finance in the public sector leads to disequilibrium conditions in the economy can be seen from the following data:

Gross National Product GNP		*Federal Government Expenditures (in billions of dollars)*	*National Debt*
1929	104.0	3.0	16.0 (1930)
1958	400.0	80.0	280.0

The facts clearly and strongly speak for themselves. The GNP in three decades increased 4 times, while the Federal Government expenditures and the national debt increased about 20 times. There is no doubt that under these circumstances large masses of the American people were, through inflation and overtaxation, dispossessed of a significant share of their real income in order to make up for a disproportionate spending in the public sector of the economy.

What is the solution to this problem? *First,* we need a change in thinking about matters of public finance, specifically in repudiating the inverted rule of finance which creates disequilibrium and therefore is against the public interest. *Second,* we need to apply rigorously Rule No. 1 of sound finance, which was mentioned earlier. Accordingly, in a democratic country like the United States, the budget should be first presented directly to the nation for its approval at each general elections, with at least one alternative budget from the opposition party. Thus the American people, who pay the bill in the end, would finally have the power to decide the volume of public expenditures.

What, then, is the function of our representatives in budgetary terms?

Rule No. 2. Congress should have power only to collect (by tax) an amount of public revenue necessary to cover the expenditures approved directly by the people under Rule No. 1.

The wisdom of the representatives in Congress would then be to ponder on the best way how to raise public revenue, but no pork barrel legislation would be possible. On the other hand, the ordinary budget would be approved for a legislative period of four years and in this way the Federal Government would have an opportunity to program and conduct a flexible budgetary policy for a period of four years.

Should any extraordinary public expense arise which could not have been foreseen in the ordinary budget, then the same procedure of a direct submission to the people should be followed. And this is not an impossible thing. In Switzerland they do it for a long time, and the method works.

Rule No. 3. The smaller the number of taxes, the easier it is for people in a democratic society to evaluate properly the manner in which the total taxpayers' money was used for public services. In other words, a single tax system, whenever possible, is preferable to a multiple system of taxation, according to the experience we have from modern times.

In order to establish a simplified and unified system of taxation in the United States it is necessary to abolish the multitude of present taxes (federal, state and local) and replace them by three major taxes:

(1) A universal tax of 10% or 15% upon the annual GNP, that is, the annual volume of expenditures necessary to produce the national income. This general tax would represent a cost element of public services which will be added regularly to the other cost elements (wages, interest, rent and the normal profit as a return to management) which constitute the basis for the calculation of prices for goods and services.

The majority of the American people, if informed properly, would accept such a general tax *if* all other taxes upon income and sales were eliminated. The administration of this general tax would be very inexpensive compared to the present multiple tax system. The present income tax system, which has become inequitable and regressive, would come to an end. Business firms and producers of any articles or products would be required by law to compute the general tax in the same way as the other costs paid or imputed. At the end of every week they would send to the Federal Government the check for the amount of the tax added to each item (goods and services) sold during that week. Severe penalties should be provided for those who break the taxation law.

(2) Because of the need to repay a huge national debt (federal, state and local), and also for reasons of social justice, a supplementary tax on real property of any sort, including transactions in securities representing assets of any nature, is recommended. From this supplementary tax an exemption should be provided, namely, residential property reserved for personal use of a family but not exceeding a certain amount in value.

(3) For the same reasons mentioned under (2) a supplementary tax on inheritances of any sort [net assets] is also recommended.

This rather simple but unified system of three basic taxes seems to be better suited to the needs of a free, democratic society than the system we now have. The present multiple system of taxation has reached the oppressive stage. It is not surprising to find citizens' organizations (so-called "taxpayers associations") established in many places for the purpose of fighting new taxes or protesting against too high a level of taxation. The existing system is composed of so many different levies (at the three levels of government) that the U.S. tax structure appears to be a giant octopus in which it is impossible to determine the location of the head and the arms.

From the administrative point of view, the present-day multiple system of taxation in America is very expensive, less productive and uneconomical. Indeed, a huge bureaucratic apparatus (the mentioned giant octopus) constantly consumes, to a large extent unnecessarily, a substantial part of public income long before it is collected.

The time is ripe for shifting to a simplified and unified system of taxation so that the American people may have a chance to evaluate the performance of government agencies properly.

Rule No. 4. The public sector of the economy should be clearly separated from the private sector. This is the only effective method that would permit an attainment of equilibrium in government business and its finances.

Of course, living in an organized society, we need government at all levels, and, consequently, we cannot escape the duty of paying taxes. The real issue in a democratic society is *not* whether we are for or against taxation, but rather how we distinguish between "necessary" (legitimate) and "unnecessary (illegitimate) public expenditures and taxes. There is no objection to necessary public expenditures and the taxes adequate to cover them. It is only the unnecessary expenditures which automatically produce social inequities through overtaxation. And that is what aggravates the people and makes them protest against new or old taxes.

The crux of the matter is: *Who is to decide what is necessary and what is unnecessary in terms of public expenditures?* In a truly democratic society there is only one correct answer—namely, that those who must ultimately pay the bill (the citizens) should also have the legitimate power to make such decisions.

It is unfortunate that many economists believe that common people in this matter are "stupid" and consequently cannot be entrusted to make such decisions. This is not true at all! The American people, and for that matter any people in the world, are not "stupid" on the subject of taxation and government business. If a major political party wants to govern the country, then it must present to the people a budget where the public expenditures are divided in very definite and consistent groups of items, a budget which must reflect the needs of the nation. The voters should have an opportunity to examine that budget and, according to their conscience, to eliminate from it whatever the majority considers to be unnecessary expenditures.

For this reason, it was recommended under Rule No. 1 that the public budget (federal, state and local) be first presented to the people for approval. Whatever the majority approves becomes the legitimate and legal budget for a four-year period.

The privilege of deciding the volume of public expenditures must therefore be returned where it belongs, to the people, by a Constitutional amendment. *The privilege of controlling the public purse in a free society should not be delegated to any one person or political party or institution because there is where the evil of budget deficits and huge public debts starts!* Besides, in the name of what valid principle can we take away from the people this sacred right of deciding how much of their money should be used for public services?

When the power of determining the necessity of public expenditures returns to the people, we shall have an opportunity of ensuring that the marginal utility, i.e., the value of $1 paid in taxes, will be very close to the marginal utility of $1 used in the purchase of goods and services in the private sector. Only then will the *real* value of public services be equal to what people paid and what people really wanted. This is the fundamental condition of stable equilibrium in government business and finances.

The amount of taxes paid according to this new system of equilibrium in public finances would be equal to the least cost of wanted public services. This is also what may be called the "normal" level of taxation, based on the free consent of the majority. Any really democratic society should strive toward this ideal of a freely accepted, voluntary system of taxation, because this is a solid rock of survival in the present-day confrontation between democracy and dictatorship.

Rule No. 5. In a federal system of government, each level must enjoy a certain degree of financial independence from the central government.

Another basic problem closely related to that of simplification and unification of the taxation system is the question of determining an equitable distribution of the total public income between federal, state and local governments. It is a very delicate and difficult issue which must be solved first as a matter of principle. The idea of having the Federal Government take over the entire public income and thereafter give grants to the state and local governments (as the traditional method does) has to be rejected in principle because it creates a "*dependence effect*" within the concept of federal government.

In a free democratic society, the state and local governments should have a certain degree of financial independence from the national government. There is no independence in this respect if they do not have their own income, completely separated from the central government and in an adequate amount corresponding to the specific tasks entrusted to them. In other words Rule No. 5 reads: "Federal, state and local governments in a free society should be independent financially of each other." This is the true spirit of a federal republic.

Rule No. 6. The unified and integrated public income should be divided automatically at its source and in a certain proportion among federal, state and local governments.

From the practical point of view, a suitable solution to the above problem is to have a provision in the tax law that would require any public income to be divided automatically in three parts at its source. Following is a possible scale of distribution:

(1) 50% federal government,
(2) 25% state government and
(3) 25% local governments.

The first 50% would go directly to the account of the Federal Government; 25% would go directly to the account of each state where the income was created; and finally 25% would be distributed among the various local governments within that particular state.

Of course, the scale above is just an example to illustrate the implementation of Rule No. 6. After more study of the issues involved it could be changed to be more suitable to all parties interested. The purpose here is only to demonstrate how the principle of democratization in a federal republic should be applied not only for political but also for financial matters.

* * *

This is only a sketch of the reforms which are necessary to be fulfilled if we want to have in the United States an equilibrium system of budget and taxation. It would be an illusion, however, to think that the recommendations in this Memorandum are enough or could be successful if the stabilization of the U.S. dollar, banking system and securities market were not undertaken simultaneously.

Boston, Massachusetts
November 30, 1959

* * *

5. *FINAL REMARKS: A NEW WIND BLOWING IN THE U.S. CONGRESS, THE ADMINISTRATION AND THE WHOLE COUNTRY*

The above Memorandum, sent to the Chairman of the Ways and Means Committee of the House of Representatives, did not have much effect at the time, but 16 years later it seems that a new wind is blowing in Washington, and some new thinking is being done by legislators.

On the editorial page of the *New York Times* of December 3, 1975 a long letter entitled "Toward a Balanced Federal Budget" was published. The letter was signed by the Honorable Carl T. Curtis, U.S. Senator from Nebraska. "If the voters," said the letter, "could pick and choose the programs the Federal Government enacts in a fashion similar to bond issues, I have no doubt that the post-World War II never-ending spending spree would have ended long ago." The Senator is absolutely correct. But the interesting thing is that this proposition represents the application of Rule No. 1 of my 1959 Memorandum.

The Hon. Senator Curtis and the Hon. Representative Floyd Spence in the House have introduced a constitutional amendment requiring that the President and Congress live within the budget established each year. The entire letter deserves to be read with great attention and is reprinted by permission from the *New York Times:*

New York Times, December 3, 1975:
Toward a Balanced Federal Budget
To the Editor:

I note with great interest that the voters of New York have rejected the bond proposition before them Nov. 4.

Undoubtedly this is in part due to concern over the state of the economy. A good share of the negative vote, however, may have been due to a reaction by the voters to the ever-increasing burden of government brought about by profligate spending. Bond issues are about the only occasion when voters can express themselves directly on government spending, and the reasons for their decision may well not be limited to the merits of the particular bond issue.

Interestingly, a bond issue was *approved* in Baltimore, Md., where the city continues to enjoy a large surplus in the treasury. The people are smart enough to know when borrowing is safe and when it is not.

That brings me to the point of this letter. If the voters could pick and choose the programs the Federal Government enacts in a fashion similar to bond issues, I have no doubt that the post-World War II never-ending spending spree would have ended long ago.

However, the voters have no such opportunity. Instead they elect many politicians who vote for every irresponsible scheme in the book but who do not raise taxes in doing so, thus avoiding the political consequences of their actions. To remedy this situation, I introduced a constitutional amendment which would compel the President and the Congress to require the Federal Government to live within the budget which they establish each year. Failure to do so would automatically raise taxes. Only in cases of a national emergency, when three-fourths of the Congress vote to suspend the requirement, could deficits be incurred. Otherwise, the budget would either be balanced by the President and/or the Congress or the people would see the direct relationship between the spending programs and the new higher taxes. They would decide at the next election how well they like the arrangement. Chances are, however, that the budget would be balanced because politicians do not like to raise taxes when they have to face the voters.

I hope that the citizens of New York who saw fit to reject the bond proposition will contact their Senators and members of the House in support of my amendment. (An identical resolution has been introduced in the House by Representative Floyd Spence.)

Only when the people begin to stir will the President and the Congress take notice. The people have spoken locally in the last election. I hope they will extend the message to Washington. CARL T. CURTIS

United States Senator from Nebraska

Washington, Nov. 25, 1975

It is necessary to stress that the amendment in question alone would not suffice to reach and preserve an equilibrium system of budgets and public finances (as shown in the Memorandum), but nevertheless it represents sound new financial thinking in the right direction.

In the *Wall Street Journal* of December 4, 1975, it was reported that the Honorable William Simon, Secretary of the Treasury, in a speech before a conference of the Tax Foundation, made a suggestion that the Federal Government should consider a simplification of the individual income tax. His idea was to scrap the present system of exemptions, deductions and tax credits and replace it by a single, progressive tax. He thought that this would be simpler and more equitable to all taxpayers. He recognized further that the present tax structure is "threatening to erode the basic faith in the fairness of the system" and that many people believe "taxes are being imposed upon them without their consent, that too many of their fellow taxpayers are escaping their responsibilities through dozens of loopholes and that the code itself has become a labyrinth of legal double-talk."

Secretary Simon is correct in his observations and his suggestion in principle follows Rule No. 3 in my 1959 Memorandum, even though his attention was focused upon income, and not upon expenditure, as the basis for taxation. It is also fair to say that his observations refer only to the vagaries of the individual income tax system, whereas my Memorandum was concerned with the simplification and democratization of the entire U.S. tax system.

These two recent views, one from Congress and the other from the Administration, confirm the relevance of the material and recommendations included in the 1959 Memorandum. Some of those truths stated in 1959 have started to come to light through other channels in 1975. And probably we shall hear more of these in 1976 and thereafter.

The governors in various states have expressed, at the beginning of 1976, anguish and frustration that they cannot properly manage the budget under conditions created by the existing inflation and the national welfare system. A most impressive appeal to new thinking came from Governor Hugh L. Carey of New York State, who, in his Annual Message to the Legislature, stated: "We have learned that government and the people it serves cannot afford to solve all the problems of society. So we enter a new age in which our goals are less government, less spending, fewer government employees, less interference in the lives of our citizens and businessmen and a new spirit of cooperation by all individuals in government."

There is a new wind blowing in the whole country and literally crying for new thinking, new solutions, and better leadership. This book appears at a propitious moment. It states explicitly that in America and elsewhere there is need to reset the clock of history in the right direction. How to accomplish this change in thinking and in the direction of our policies constitutes the real contribution of this book.

At the center of any substantial improvement of modern capitalism lies first a long overdue monetary, banking and financial reform in accordance with conditions of stable general equilibrium. The greatest enemy in both prevailing systems (capitalism and socialism) is the large-scale use of paper money and monetized debt or credit. This is anti-Numeraire or a disequilibrium type of currency which creates instability (open or hidden), unemployment, and social inequities besides the need for curtailment of human freedoms in both systems.

Paper- and credit-money deceives political leaders, economic experts and the people in general. While on the surface it appears relatively cheap and easy to manipulate, nevertheless by its nature and function it inflicts incredible harm on human societies because there is no reliable method to control it properly.

Despite the problems and frustrations encompassing us, the author remain firmly convinced that an "ECONOMIC MIRACLE" in America it still possible—if our leaders in Congress and the Administration would undertake the necessary and adequate reforms before we reach the point of no return.

In concluding, the best challenge to the reader, regarding the future of human liberties, social equity and stability in America and elsewhere, is to remember the warning of the British philosopher Edmund Burke: "The only thing necessary for the triumph of evil is that good men do nothing."

Index of Authors

Index of Subjects